Creativity

in Art

and Science,

1860–1960

The

Cleveland

Museum

of Art

September 16–

November 8, 1987

An exhibition on

the occasion of the

Michelson-Morley

Centennial

Celebration,

Cleveland, Ohio,

1987

Creativity

in Art

and Science,

1860–1960

Edward B. Henning

Published by

The Cleveland

Museum of Art

in cooperation

with Indiana

University Press

Cover: Pablo Piccaso, *Fan, Salt Box, Melon,* 1909 (cat. no. 20).

Copyright 1987 by The Cleveland Museum of Art. All rights reserved
Editing by Sally W. Goodfellow
Design by Laurence Channing, assisted by Rich Sarian
Typesetting by The Cleveland Museum of Art Printing Department
Monochrome printing by The Emerson Press, Inc., Cleveland, Ohio 44114
Color printing by Great Lakes Lithograph Co., Cleveland, Ohio 44109
Distributed by Indiana University Press, Bloomington, Indiana 47405

Library of Congress Cataloging in Publication Data is on page 143

The exhibition is assisted by a grant from the Ohio Arts Council.

Contents

Lenders to the Exhibition

The Art Institute of Chicago

The Fort Worth Art Museum, Texas

The J. B. Speed Art Museum, Louisville, Kentucky

Solomon R. Guggenheim Museum, New York

Munson-Williams-Proctor Institute, Museum of Art, Utica, New York

A Private Collection

Foreword

So often the subsequent impact of a pivotal action becomes even more important than the action itself. Such was the case with experiments carried out in 1887 by Albert Abraham Michelson of the Case School of Applied Science working closely with Edward Williams Morley in his laboratories at Western Reserve University, a neighboring institution in University Circle in Cleveland. Recently Professor Philip L. Taylor of Case Western Reserve University, initiator of the current Michelson-Morley Centennial Celebration, has written that the epoch-making measurements of these two distinguished scientists "were not merely attempts to quantify the effect on the speed of light of the earth's motion in its orbit: they were a signpost leading us to a new and revolutionary concept of space and time itself."

Reflecting that same spirit of cooperation that made possible the experiment 100 years ago, Cleveland's various cultural institutions have appropriately joined Case Western Reserve University—the union of the two earlier institutions—in celebrating this proud moment of accomplishment in the city's history. Perhaps the key to the Museum's primary contribution to the celebrations may be found in Michelson's own words. When confronted late in life by an admirer of his considerable skills as a painter, who lamented that the scientist had abandoned his art for science, Michelson observed, "I did not have to choose, because for me they are inseparable."

It is fitting, therefore, that the Museum create an exhibition concentrating upon that which has been most innovative in the visual arts during a 100-year span close in time to the Michelson-Morley centennial. And in the spirit of the celebrations, we developed the idea of drawing upon the not inconsiderable holdings of this Museum. Certain works have also been borrowed to contribute to the realization of the thesis even as, sadly, it was recognized from the beginning that some ground-breaking works could never be lent by their respective institutions for a variety of practical reasons. Thus, the most important element in this undertaking is Edward Henning's challenging essay published here. It reflects a thoughtful synthesis of his studies as he worked with the Museum's collection of modern art during the past twenty-five years as Curator of Modern Art; not only has he worked with the collection, he has indeed created it.

Evan H. Turner, *Director*

This exhibition was planned as part of the centennial celebration of a crucial experiment by Albert A. Michelson and Edward W. Morley at Case School of Applied Science (now Case Western Reserve University) in 1887. These two eminent scientists attempted to measure the earth's velocity through space in relation to the luminiferous ether that, it was generally accepted, filled the universe and was therefore a constant factor against which such movement could be gauged. Although the experiment failed, Albert Einstein's special theory of relativity, eighteen years later, explained its failure on the basis that the ether does not exist. Since refutations of wrong hypotheses are essential for science to progress, the Michelson-Morley experiment stands as one of the most significant events in the history of science.

I decided to do an exhibition touching on analogies between the arts and sciences because the Michelson-Morley experiment occurred during one of the most creative periods in the history of both fields. Analogies between activities and products in the two areas appeared to be frequent and obvious. It soon became clear, however, that most parallels occurred on the outer fringes of the two disciplines, where creative individuals attempted to articulate previously unformulated experience. Artists and scientists invented forms to function as analogs for such experience—the scientists constructing their forms in mathematical terms and the artists developing theirs in terms of color, shape, line, mass, space, and other components.

My initial plan for the exhibition verged on fantasy: its focus would be crucial works by those artists who created highly personal styles that became paradigms for mainstream traditions in art—works that represent the first flush of innovation rather than mature styles and techniques. Unfortunately, key paintings such as Monet's *Terrace at Sainte-Adresse*, Cézanne's *House of the Hanged Man*, *The Bathers* by Seurat, and *Les Demoiselles d'Avignon* by Picasso would certainly not have been available as loans from their respective museums, and insurance costs for other, less famous works were still too high—so fantasy gave way to practicality.

The selection of artists was mine alone, and I expect much disagreement, particularly with the omissions—Edouard Manet, Auguste Renoir, Henri Matisse, and Willem de Kooning, among others. I even vacillated before including Vincent van Gogh, Paul Gauguin, and Georges Braque. Let me hasten to add that I consider all of these artists to be of major stature; indeed, I believe that Renoir's best paintings equal anything that Monet did, that Manet is one of the most beautiful painters of the nineteenth century, and that Matisse is the finest pure painter of the twentieth century. My objective, however, was to select only those artists who had developed a new view of the world that subsequently became part of the mainstream of Western art. It seems to me that Monet, Cézanne, and Picasso meet that criterion better than do Manet, Renoir, and Matisse.

The same questions will probably be raised about the styles that I selected as being the major tributaries of the mainstream tradition of Western art. Fauvism, Futurism, and Purism were among the movements omitted as being peripheral to the central developments. Expressionism—except for the American movement called Abstract Expressionism—seems to be a twentieth-century variation on an ancient tendency in art. The American movement was a synthesis of Abstraction and Surrealism and has little to do with deliberate violations of natural appearances to consciously express emotions. In any case, whatever blame ensues from these judgments is mine alone.

I could not possibly list all of the people who helped me with the preparation of this exhibition and book. Above all, of course, I am grateful to those who lent works of major importance to the exhibition. These include the Solomon R. Guggenheim Museum in New York; The J. B. Speed Art Museum in Louisville, Kentucky; The Fort Worth Art Museum in Texas; Munson-Williams-Proctor Institute, Museum of Art in Utica, New York; The Art Institute of Chicago; and of course, the familiar Anonymous Lender.

Turning to individuals, I should first like to thank the Director of the Cleveland Museum, Evan H. Turner, for giving me the opportunity to do an exhibition with such an interesting theme and for supporting my selections and ideas, even when they must have seemed a little strange. I also thank the Trustees for their encouragement.

When a museum organizes an exhibition, the entire staff is involved. The Registrar and his staff arranges the packing, shipping, insurance, and other details that go on long before and after the exhibition itself. The Utility Crew installs and dismantles the exhibition. The Photography Studio; the Print Shop; the departments of Development, Conservation, and Public Information play important roles in the ongoing process of putting together the exhibition and informing the public. The Department of Education plans lectures, slide-tapes, and other supporting events. The offices of the Assistant Directors, for Administration and for Finance, are involved. The Museum Designer installs the show, and the Administrator of Public Programs oversees all wall labels.

Writing the catalogue was difficult, yet interesting: many of the notions about analogies between art and science had to be developed there. I am grateful to Geraldine Kiefer, Susan Davis, and William Robinson for writing many of the catalogue entries about the works in the exhibition. William Robinson deserves special thanks for his additional help with many details and for keeping the records straight. In particular, the Head of Publications, Laurence Channing, who designed the catalogue and oversaw its production, has my thanks, as does Sally W. Goodfellow, who carried out an especially difficult and tedious job of editing with good humor. Judith DeVere and Cathy D'Addario provided invaluable help with necessary word-processing and typesetting procedures.

The Secretary of the Department of Modern Art, Patricia Krohn, was patient beyond belief in typing and retyping my many drafts of the text, and she has my special gratitude. I am also grateful to Tom Hinson, Curator of Contemporary Art, for generously allowing me so much of Mrs. Krohn's time.

I am very much indebted to Mihajlo Mesarović of Case Western Reserve University for reading the first three chapters of my manuscript and assuring me that my observations on science were not completely absurd. Of course, he is not responsible for the lesser degrees of absurdity of which I am probably guilty.

Finally, my heartfelt thanks to my wife, Margaret, who took time from her own busy schedule to read the text and make valuable suggestions.

Introduction

Surely there was a time when art and science did not exist, even as concepts. The activities now ascribed to these two disciplines must have been one and the same. When prehistoric man painted pictures of bison and antelope on the walls of his cave, it seems certain that he was creating sympathetic magic in an effort to understand and control his environment. In doing so, he created images that, we now recognize, have aesthetic value. He was both proto-artist and proto-scientist. Over the millennia separating this early creator from the ancient Greek world, where the concepts *artist* and *scientist* were born, these two tendencies disentangled themselves from one another and developed their own, specialized means of expression. By the middle of the twentieth century it was believed by many people that the arts and sciences had become two separate cultures.[1] It is true that they speak very different languages; yet, in certain fundamental ways, they remain alike.

It will be suggested here that creative artists and scientists both develop forms (theories, models, and works of art) to articulate their inner experiences in response to their observations of the world—or to certain ideas about the world. Both seek beauty in the forms that they create as analogues for their experiences of the world. Fundamental physicists have declared: ''Let us worry about beauty first, and truth will take care of itself.''[2] However, the scientist must finally submit his theory to strictly controlled testing in order to verify its truth, whereas the artist depends upon the response of his audience, especially of future audiences. There is no apparent reason why a scientific theory must be beautiful to be true, yet it is a fact that all true theories are beautiful. For both the artist and the scientist, beauty indicates formal symmetry or, at least, asymmetrical balance.

Although the forms developed by artists and scientists result from their efforts to articulate their experience in response to the world, that experience is, in turn, conditioned by the means of articulation used. The scientist constructs his forms in the abstract ''language'' of mathematics, while the painter develops his forms in terms of color, shape, line, texture, and other such components. (The sculptor depends primarily on mass and space.) This means that the structure of each form is determined by the ''language'' used and, therefore, analogy is the only possible means of comparison.

Parallels in the forms produced by artists and scientists within the same culture derive from a general, prevailing system sometimes referred to as the ''culture pattern,'' or, in a slightly different sense, as the ''Zeitgeist.'' This is a concept of a broad, general, and open system that allows for variations and conflicts within its over-all configuration. It is conceived here as being both determined by the forms existing within it and conditioning those forms.

The over-all "culture pattern" during the period covered by this exhibition has been one of increasing openness, which has encouraged formal diversity. It is analogous to a natural environment that would be propitious for almost every variety of plant and animal life. In the arts, where the appeal for validity is made to critical opinion—both contemporary and future—every kind of mutation flourishes. While scientific theories also abound, a theory must still be verified by experiment.

Beautiful scientific forms, which are analogues for nature, affirm the beauty of nature. If artistic forms can be shown to be analogous to scientific forms, they must also be true to nature. The search for analogies between the arts and sciences, therefore, is a search for criteria of truth in art and the validation of Keats's familiar lines: "Beauty is truth, truth beauty."

1. C. P. Snow's popular phrase "The Two Cultures" really indicated a contrast between the values of a scientific culture and those of the literary culture of the British "Establishment." However, it was generally misunderstood in the United States as referring to a contrast between the sciences and humanities in general.

2. Anthony Zee, *Fearful Symmetry: The Search for Beauty in Modern Physics* (New York: Macmillan, 1986), p. 3.

And, as imagination bodies forth

The forms of things unknown, the poet's pen

Turns them to shapes, and gives to airy nothing

A local habitation and a name.

William Shakespeare, *A Midsummer Night's Dream*

Every extension of knowledge arises from making conscious the

unconscious. The great basic activity is unconscious. For it is narrow,

this room of human consciousness.

Friedrich Nietszche

The pioneer scientist must have a vivid intuitive imagination, for

new ideas are not generated by deduction, but by artistically

creative imagination.

Max Planck

I. Creativity in Art and Science

In their own languages, creative scientists and artists articulate inner experiences in response to outer stimuli.[1] While physical scientists formulate their experiences in mathematical terms, artists create visual forms analogous to their affective responses to the outer world itself as well as ideas about it. Creative activity occurs when an artist or scientist invents a new form as he pushes into what John Livingston Lowes called "the surging chaos of the unexpressed."[2]

The primary purpose of a work of art, it is often said, is to delight, while that of a scientific model or theory is to provide knowledge. The work of art, however, also provides knowledge, and scientists have long recognized that aesthetic satisfaction plays an important role in their activities. The work of art provides insight into the only thing anyone can have certain knowledge about: his or her own experiencing of the world; and before a scientific theory is proved, it is often supported simply because it is beautiful.

Works of art articulate experience in their own formal languages. They are not made by translating verbal statements into visual forms, and contrariwise, they cannot be fully interpreted by the spoken or written word. The form of a painting or a sculpture is not, like a pot, made to hold its content: it is itself the form of its content.

The language of the painter, unlike verbal language, does not usually depend upon symbols with precise denotations. Rather, the associations attached to the artist's formal vocabulary are broad and open, though compelling. Paint (or any other material) can suggest affective experience when an analogy exists between the way that the work is ordered and the psychic structure of a particular experience. Contributing to such an analogy are the associations that formal elements commonly have with experiences in everyday life. Reds and yellows, to take the simplest kind of example, seem warm; blues and greens, cool. Horizontal lines suggest rest; diagonal lines, imbalance; and right angles, stability. Black indicates darkness and (in most Western cultures) death; or it implies mystery and fear. A black shape with blurred edges and some variations of value might suggest a murky atmosphere or even an opaque state of mind; it may seem ominous, somber, weighty, or enigmatic. Such associations, partly determined by cultural patterns, help to provide the import of a work of art.

Each perceiver, of course, experiences a work somewhat differently, depending upon his or her personality structure and background of experience. The possible variations of that experience, however, are limited. Anyone claiming to experience one of Monet's Argenteuil landscapes as stark or brutal, one of Mondrian's classic abstractions as lurid or frivolous, or one of Franz Kline's dramatic black-and-white canvases as elegant and charming obviously should not be taken seriously. The full experience of a work of art, or of a scientific model, involves both knowledge of its content and delight in its form. The poet John

Ciardi has remarked: "Nothing is more powerfully of man than the fact that he naturally gives off forms and is naturally enclosed by them. To acquire knowledge of aesthetic form is to acquire knowledge of man."[3]

Susanne Langer used the terms "art symbol" and "expressive form" to indicate that the form of a work of art has import—that it "expresses . . . an idea of feeling"—but that this cannot be verbally defined.[4] The term "visual metaphor" is often used, since it seems less specific and limiting than "symbol."[5]

Since artists no less than scientists must begin any experience with sensory perceptions of the phenomenal world, it would seem appropriate to ask how we know this world. Common sense answers along the following lines: (1) The external world is made up of substances having qualities such as hardness, roughness, sharpness, brightness, and hue. (2) These are combined in various ways to form physical objects such as tables, mountains, clouds, and lions. (3) We know such things through the data supplied to our minds by our sensory receptors. (4) The physical objects that we perceive are really "out there" in the world just as they appear to us after our minds have structured the information submitted by our sense organs.

If we wish to live happy and healthy lives, we must act as if these common-sense propositions are true. Most contemporary philosophers and theoretical scientists, however, no longer accept them as reliable guides to the truth about reality. Instead, they recognize that our picture of the outer world depends partly upon the nature of our nervous system, which perceives and interprets the world, as well as upon the language that we use to articulate our experience of it.

The classical physicist described a mechanically structured world of characterless events in space and time. He believed that he was not, and should not be, mixed up with what he observed in his research. He produced a picture of a cold, colorless, and silent world. Today's physicist, however, recognizes that strict deterministic causation—the traditional basis for science's picture of reality—is inadequate to describe or explain either the subatomic world or the far reaches of the universe. To deal with the internal elements of the atom and its structure, quantum theory was developed; and to deal with the structure of the universe, Einstein developed the special and general theories of relativity.

In working with quantum phenomena, scientists recognized that they had to take into account the physical processes by which they gained knowledge of them. British astronomer and physicist Sir Arthur Eddington described the process of observation as follows:

Consider how our supposed acquaintance with a lump of matter is attained. Some influence emanating from it plays on the extremity of a nerve, starting a series of physical and chemical changes which are propagated along the nerve to a brain cell; there a mystery happens, and an image or sensation arises in the mind which cannot purport to resemble the stimulus which excites it.

Everything known about the material world must in one way or another have been inferred from these stimuli transmitted along the nerves . . . . The mind as a central receiving station reads the dots and dashes of the incoming nerve signals . . . . But a broadcasting station is not like its call-signal; there is no commensurability in their natures. So too, the chairs and tables around us which broadcast to us incessantly those signals which affect our sight and touch cannot in their nature be like unto the signals or to the sensations which the signals awake at the end of their journey . . . . It is an astonishing feat of deciphering that we should have been able to infer an orderly scheme of natural knowledge from such indirect communication.[6]

Eddington's "lump of matter" has been replaced with Einstein's concentrations of energy, and we have had to recognize that the qualities our senses seem to reveal—sounds, odors, textures, temperatures—are simply the way our minds interpret the stimulations of our sense organs. While something must start the chain of physical, chemical, and psychological events that results in perception, it seems that we can have no direct knowledge of that "something."

If I stand a few feet in front of a fire, for example, I experience heat, and common sense tells me that the heat is in the fire. If, however, I move closer to the fire, I experience pain, and the pain is clearly in me. But since the pain is only a more intense degree of my pleasurable sensation of warmth, I must infer that the heat is also a sensation of mine and not actually in the fire.[7]

Contemporary scientists have similarly given up the comfortable picture of a universe made up of material objects moving according to the mechanical law of cause and effect in absolute space and time. Eddington once told the following story to indicate how our senses limit our view of reality:

There was once a fisherman who was a keen observer of nature. He observed, and after twenty years he suddenly realized that he had discovered a new law of nature. The law of nature was that all fish are longer than four inches, but the reason was . . . his net was a four inch net.[8]

And the physicist John Archibald Wheeler has commented: "What is so hard is to give up thinking of nature as a machine that goes on independent of the observer. What we conceive of as reality is a few iron posts of observation with papier-mâché construction between them that is but the elaborate work of our imagination."[9]

To indicate how the scientist becomes an integral part of his experiment, helping to determine the character of the reality that he perceives and defines, Wheeler devised an elaborate "thought experiment." Imagine . . . .

a game of "twenty questions" in which one player leaves the room while the others select a word he is to guess when he returns. While he is gone, the other players decide to alter the rules. They will select no word at all; instead, each of them will answer "yes" or "no" as he pleases—provided he has a word in mind that fits both his own reply and all the previous replies. The outsider returns and unsuspecting begins asking questions. At last he makes a guess: "Is the word 'clouds'?" Yes, comes the answer, and the players explain the game.[10]

The word "clouds" was arrived at because of the questions asked, just as an image of the world comes into being because of the questions man puts to nature. Different questions would lead to a different word, and to a different picture of the world. Scientists and artists alike depend on inferences from sensory experience to tell them what they are experiencing, and both use imagination to develop their pictures of reality.

There are, of course, failures in both fields—bad, or unsuccessful, works of art, and wrong theories in science. Albert Michelson and Edward Morley, in their famous experiment in 1887, for example, failed to demonstrate any drag as the earth moved through a luminiferous ether that, theoretically, filled space. They were left with a picture of a vast universe of absolute space without any medium through which light waves could travel. Albert Einstein took this picture of a universe in disarray and restructured it until, in 1905, with his special theory of relativity, he presented an elegant model of a universe in which the concepts of space and time were relative and were joined in a four-dimensional continuum. He proposed that motion is relative to a specific frame of reference; the speed of light is a limiting factor on velocity; mass increases with velocity; objects contract in the direction of their motion; events appearing to be simultaneous to an observer in one system do not necessarily appear simultaneous to an observer in another system; and mass and energy are equivalent and interchangeable. This spectacular, new picture of the universe was later confirmed by experiment. However, its beauty was sufficient for Einstein, and for many other scientists, to take it seriously even before it had been proven.

In various fields people have described the creative experience as being involved in something like Lowes's "surging chaos of the unexpressed." The philosopher and mathematician Alfred North Whitehead, for example, referred to " . . . the state of imaginative muddled suspense which precedes successful inductive generalization."[11] Joseph Conrad alluded to a similar state of pre-formulated experience in his novel *Lord Jim* when his narrator, Marlow, speaking of a scene of horror, says:

For a moment I had a view of a world that seemed to wear a vast and dismal aspect of disorder, while in truth, thanks to our unwearied efforts, it is as sunny an arrangement of small conveniences as the mind of man can conceive . . . . though I seemed to have lost all my words in the chaos of dark thoughts I had contemplated for a second or two beyond the pale. These came back, too, very soon, for words also belong to the sheltering conception of light and order, which is our refuge.[12]

Leaving the sunny shores of Conrad's "sheltering conception of light and order" and plunging into what Brewster Ghiselin terms "a working sea of indecision," all creative people struggle to formulate their unique experiences. Vague intimations of significance are resolved as structures referring to such experience metaphorically are developed. Stephen Spender described this phase of the creative act as: "a dim cloud of an idea which I feel must be condensed into a shower of words."[13]

When a successful scientific theory or work of art is generally accepted, and leads to a style, a movement, or a new view of reality, it becomes a paradigm. A romantic view of nature, for example, was no more a part of the experience of primitive man than were the morphological categories of the biologist. The setting sun must have caused fear of the coming darkness and its attendant dangers rather than wonder at the beauty of the event. We have been taught to experience nature as "picturesque" and "poetic" by painters such as John Constable and J. M. W. Turner as well as by poets such as William Wordsworth just as surely as we were taught to view it as mechanically ordered and causally connected by philosophers and scientists such as Copernicus, Galileo, René Descartes, and Isaac Newton.

Only when Romantic painters and poets began to see grandeur in mountains, for example, did mountains become picturesque. Mountain climbing for sport is, in fact, a Romantic invention. And the modern concept of romantic love was invented by the eleventh-century troubadours of Provençe, Spain, and northern Italy. In the preface to Poincaré's *Science and Hypothesis*, J. Larmor wrote: "New ideas emerge dimly into intuition, come into consciousness from nobody knows where, and become the material on which the mind operates, forming them gradually into a consistent doctrine, which can be welded onto existing domains of knowledge."[14]

The composer Roger Sessions identified more precisely what he experienced and articulated in his musical creations:

"Emotion" is specific, individual and conscious; music goes deeper than this, to the energies which animate our psychic life, and out of these creates a pattern which has an existence, laws, and human significance of its own. It reproduces for us the most intimate essence, the tempo and the energy, of our spiritual being; our tranquility and our restlessness, our animation and our discouragement, our vitality and our weakness—all, in fact, of the fine shades of dynamic variation of our inner life.[15]

In a letter stating remarkably similar notions, Einstein described his own creative process:

(A) The words or the language, as they are written or spoken, do not seem to play any role in my mechanism of thought. The psychical entities which seem to serve as elements in thought are certain signs and more or less clear images which can be "voluntarily" reproduced and combined .... Taken from a psychological viewpoint, this combinatory play seems to be the essential feature in productive thought—before there is any connection with logical construction in words or other kinds of signs which can be communicated to others.

(B) The above mentioned elements are, in my case, of visual and some of muscular type. Conventional words or other signs have to be sought for laboriously only in a secondary stage, when the mentioned associative play is sufficiently established and can be reproduced at will.[16]

In all fields creators invent forms that challenge the arrangement of "sunny . . . small conveniences" that have been constructed over many centuries. Monet, for example, paid scant heed to linear perspective, which had served painters for over five hundred years as a way to suggest space behind the flat picture surface. Cézanne then suggested space by overlapping and interlocking the shapes of objects located at various distances from the picture plane, thus relating them to one another and to the picture surface. He also violated perspective and defined objects by using multiple-point perspective, thus substituting relative for absolute space. Arnold Schönberg avoided traditional musical structures in creating atonal compositions; and Marcel Proust and James Joyce gave up the accepted form of the novel to develop styles of writing based on deep memories and stream of consciousness.

In the life sciences, Charles Darwin's theory of evolution by means of natural selection challenged the belief in divine creation by fiat. Einstein's space-time replaced the absolute space and time of traditional models of the universe. Quantum theory did away with the notion that the universe is composed of space filled with hard, elementary particles of matter. Even the absolute validity of Euclid's geometry, traditionally employed to measure and describe

7

all phenomena in a universe that appeared to be organized in line with Euclidean principles, was challenged by the non-Euclidean geometries of Karl Friedrich Gauss, Nicholas Lobatchevsky, John Bolyai, Georg Riemann, and others. Nevertheless, Euclid's axioms and Newton's laws of nature remain valid in everyday life because they continue to work in situations within range of our sensory receptors.

With the enormous expansion of knowledge in all fields during the nineteenth and twentieth centuries, certain traditional systems, such as Newton's mechanics, had to give up their claim to universal validity. It became necessary to postulate systems relevant to more open conditions. Werner Heisenberg posited the Uncertainty Principle, which states that it is impossible to determine with accuracy both the position and the momentum of a subatomic unit. This principle converted the laws of physics from supposed certainties into statements about statistical probabilities and introduced the possibility that ultimately nature may be irrational. In 1930 Kurt Gödel demonstrated that any consistent and finitely describable mathematical system will generate statements that it cannot prove to be true. In addition, Chaitin's Theorem, developed by Gregory Chaitin, proves that logic is limited in what it can tell us about the world.

Traditionally the physical sciences isolated systems in laboratory or quasi-laboratory situations and studied them without considering their normal environment. Causality provided the basic rule for establishing laws pertinent to the systems being considered. All the causes and effects related to such systems can be known. Heisenberg recognized, however, that certain subatomic systems cannot be isolated and studied in this way.

With the increase of physical knowledge on the atomic level, it was discovered that there are systems that cannot be successfully isolated and that any study that is made of them must inevitably interfere with them. The experimenter himself cannot avoid coming into a position of direct relationship to the system and cannot carry out any experiment on it without changing its actual state. Such, for example, is precisely the case with the system of elementary particles . . . . the experimenter (is) in a position actually inside rather than outside the experiment. Thus, while investigating the system and influencing it, he, at the same time comes under its influence . . . . Such systems . . . . we call Open-Systems.[17]

Certain kinds of modern art—such as the Abstract Expressionist painting of Jackson Pollock, Franz Kline, and Philip Guston—focus attention on the fact that often the artist also is "inside" the work he is creating. Indeed, during the period of creation, the artist and his work are involved in a fluid relationship: as the artist works, the work itself constantly confronts him with problems and forces him to make decisions that change both artist and painting. Thus, the creative act becomes what modern physics and general systems theory call an "open system;" the artist "closes" it only as he completes the work. Paradoxically, then, the painting that an artist is creating is, in fact, the subject and theme of his creation—it is not a matter of the artist having an idea or an experience and then finding a form to express it. In short, the form of a painting *is* its content, and its content *is* its form.

During its creation the work evolves from a state of disorder towards order. Picasso once remarked: "A picture is not thought out and settled beforehand. While it is being done it changes as one's thoughts change . . . . Colors, like features, follow the changes of the emotions."[18] Finally, the rate of change slows down until the form being created achieves equilibrium and a point is reached where, as Guston remarked, "The air of the arbitrary vanishes and the paint falls into positions that feel destined."[19]

The completed work of art enters into a new "open system" each time it is encountered by a different perceiver. When such an involvement is resolved in a satisfying aesthetic experience, the system is closed anew.

The problem of communication in modern art is especially difficult because of the nature of what is expressed. The usual question—"What does it mean?"—can only be answered that it means itself. The pragmatic questioner suspects that he or she is being taunted by some supernaturalistic will-o'-the-wisp. But the work of art does not refer to ideas or emotions that have been, or can be, determined and expressed in logical, verbal terms. Rather, it communicates knowledge about the experience of ideas or emotions. A painting by Renoir, for example, does not mirror a world that is necessarily joyful; it gives us insight into the artist's experience of joy in perceiving the world.

Sir Herbert Read once remarked upon the absurd spectacle of an ardent young snob trying to cultivate an emotion before a great work of art in which all the artist's emotion had been transmuted to perfect intellectual freedom. Were this not so—were the perceiver of works of art to actually experience the feelings referred to by those works—opera houses, theaters, art galleries, and concert halls would become scenes of emotional orgies.

Many artists and scientists accept the idea that they—and by implication, all mankind—do not always completely control, nor are they completely controlled by, the situations with which they are dealing. They recognize the key role of intuition and imagination in the creative process. The physicist Freeman Dyson draws an analogy between working out a pure mathematical solution and building a bridge by starting at both ends: "You make a great leap and you somehow know, somehow subconsciously you know, that the architecture is going to fit. There has to be this imaginative leap before you can even start . . . ."[20]

In addition to relying on intuition and imagination in striving after beauty and knowledge, creative artists and scientists share a respect for—and take aesthetic pleasure in—craftsmanship. It is a given in the arts, and Dyson, speaking for the scientist, reports:

"The aesthetic pleasure of the craftsmanship of performance . . . is also very strong in science. And if one is handling mathematical tools with some sophistication it is a very nonverbal and very, very pleasurable experience just to know how to handle the tools well. It's a great joy."[21]

If the artist and the scientist are successful, each emerges from the creative act with a form—a work of art or a scientific model or theory—that articulates in appropriate terms its creator's experience. Indeed, it provides knowledge that cannot be isomorphically translated into logical, verbal language but can only be obtained through the direct apperception of the work itself. And so, each adds something new to the corpus of human knowledge about the world.

1. See John Dewey, "Having an Experience," in *Art as Experience* (New York: Capricorn Books, G. P. Putnam's Sons, 1958), pp. 35-57.

2. Brewster Ghiselin, ed., *The Creative Process* (1952; reprint, Berkeley and London: University of California Press, 1985), p. 4.

3. John Ciardi, "Poetry as Knowledge," *Saturday Review*, 22 July 1961, p. 39.

4. Susanne K. Langer, *Problems of Art* (New York: Charles Scribner's Sons, 1957), pp. 124-27.

5. Ibid., pp. 104-07, 139.

6. Quoted in C. E. M. Joad, *Guide to Philosophy* (New York: Dover Publications, 1936), pp. 34-35.

7. Ibid., p. 26.

8. Quoted by Chen Ning Yang, in Deane W. Curtin, ed., *The Aesthetic Dimension of Science* (New York: Philosophical Library, 1980), p. 118.

9. *Newsweek*, "Science," 12 March 1979, 62.

10. Ibid.

11. Quoted in Ghiselin, *Creative Process*, pp. 4-5.

12. Ibid., p. 12.

13. Ibid., p. 119.

14. Quoted by William N. Lipscomb, Jr., in Curtin, *Aesthetic Dimension*, p. 9.

15. Quoted in Ghiselin, *Creative Process*, pp. 36-37.

16. Ibid., pp. 32-33.

17. Mihajlo D. Mesarović and Edward B. Henning, "Analogy in the Creative Processes and the Objects of Creation in Art and Sciences," *Dialectica* 17, No. 2/3, (1963): 161-62.

18. Pablo Picasso, from an interview with Picasso by Christian Zervos (1935). In *Painters on Painting*, selected and edited by Eric Potter (New York: Grosset and Dunlap, Universal Library, 1963), p. 202.

19. Philip Guston, quoted in Sam Hunter, *Modern American Painting and Sculpture* (New York: Dell, 1959), p. 159.

20. Quoted in Curtin, *Aesthetic Dimension*, p. 142.

21. Ibid., p. 139.

The measure of the success of a scientific theory is, in fact, a measure of its aesthetic value, since it is a measure of the extent to which it has introduced harmony in what was before chaos.

J. W. N. Sullivan

My work always tried to unite the true with the beautiful; but when I had to choose one or the other, I usually chose the beautiful.

Hermann Weyl

Aesthetic value will be taken here to mean the ability of any action, object, or combination of actions and objects to provide delight in contemplation by reason of formal structure, content, or both in combination.[1] The central issue in art, it is also an important one in science. Matters of technique, style, and history in art are subordinate to the questions: Is the work good? If so, does the goodness reside in the work, in the mind of the beholder, or in both? In science the main question is: Is it true? And in this case, Keats's observation that truth and beauty are one is accepted by many theoretical scientists today.

Attempts by philosophers to answer questions about the nature of aesthetic value have led to three basic positions—(1) absolutism: value is objective and is located in nature, in the work of art, or in the scientific theory; (2) relativism: value is subjective and is located in the mind of the perceiver; and (3) contextualism: value is relative to biological, psychological, and social contexts and is located in the relationship between the perceiver's mind and the object.

The absolutist says: "The work *is* beautiful, I merely recognize it." If human life should disappear while the work continues to exist, he believes that the work will remain beautiful. The extreme relativist says: "The work *seems* beautiful to me at this moment." He believes that if human life should disappear, nothing would be beautiful, since there would be no mind to experience it. The contextualist says: "The work seems beautiful to most people of knowledge and taste in this culture." He believes that certain values are stable only within biological and cultural contexts, and that without human life, questions about beauty are meaningless.

In science the absolutist believes that knowledge about reality is objective; the extreme relativist believes that knowledge is subjective; and the contextualist believes that truth is located in the relationship between the observer's mind and the exterior world (the exterior world may not exist in the form that our senses present it to us, he acknowledges, but something is there that stimulates our senses in particular ways).

Plato is a distant ancestor of absolutism. He proposed that Ideas or Forms are independent of, and more real than, the objects of the sensible world. Platonic Forms are perfect and eternal but accessible only to the mind.

The British art critic Clive Bell's concept of "significant form" indicates his belief that certain creative people are capable of discerning the reality behind appearances. By disentangling this reality from the tangible material that cloaks it in the world, and by articulating his vision in a work of art, Bell argues that the artist provides the means for us to gain knowledge of the pure Form of Beauty.

Leo Tolstoy, on the other hand, was an extreme relativist who argued that art is the communication of personal emotion, and that we can tell which art is great by noting how many people are moved by it, especially to feelings of brotherhood. Since Russian folk songs, for example, stir more people in this way than Mozart's quartets, Tolstoy concluded that folk songs are the superior art. According to this argument, it follows that *Uncle Tom's Cabin* has more merit than Tolstoy's own *Anna Karenina*, and that Norman Rockwell's magazine covers surpass Cézanne's paintings.

Absolutism was the dominant point of view in Western art until the nineteenth century. Except for some medieval art, the Classical tradition, deriving from ancient Greek and Roman art, was the touchstone by which most Western art was usually judged. Even giants such as Giovanni Bellini and Albrecht Dürer were generally ranked below more doctrinaire Classicists such as Eustache Le Sueur and Charles Le Brun.[2]

Absolutism also prevailed in philosophy and science. From Copernicus, Galileo, and René Descartes through John Locke, Isaac Newton, and Georg Hegel to Michael Faraday and H. L. F. von Helmholtz, scientists and philosophers had posited absolute space, absolute time, and absolute truth.

During the nineteenth century certain scientific "facts" began to be questioned, and at the same time, the supremacy of the Neoclassical style in art was challenged. The newly dominant middle classes in France had resurrected and perpetuated the Academy, since they realized that the arts and sciences had to be marshalled in defense of their Revolution. Eugène Delacroix, and then Gustave Courbet, Claude Monet, and Paul Cézanne were among the many artists who refused to make the kind of art that would have assured their official success. They chose instead to make art that presented new visions of the world. Gradually, it became clear that these were the most creative artists of their time.

The Impressionists, for example, gave up strict rectilinear perspective as a means of achieving an illusion of space on a flat surface, showering multicolored brushstrokes onto their canvases in an attempt to simulate light and atmosphere. In other words, they developed an illusion of space *empirically* rather than by the logical system of linear perspective.

Cézanne then replaced the illusion of absolute space with that of relative space, which was not objectively fixed. Shunning the empirical approach of the Impressionists, Cézanne constructed a complex space based on overlapped planes, distorted perspective, shifting viewpoints, and balanced visual tensions.

Early in the twentieth century, the Dada artists went so far as to deny the validity of the concept of aesthetic value. Nevertheless, works by Dadaists such as Marcel Duchamp, Max Ernst, and Jean Arp affirmed that aesthetic value is discernible even in what was intended to be "anti-art." Obviously, then, it seemed that art would have to be defined simply as: whatever the artist does. Such a definition precludes any a priori characteristics; rather, it suggests that works of art continually redefine art as artists invent new forms of expression. Far from destroying art, as they intended, the Dadaists actually extended its boundaries; they called traditional notions about taste into question by demonstrating that art does not depend upon particular kinds of subjects, materials, and techniques. Jean Arp's and Max Ernst's collages—made up of torn bits

13

of paper, leaves from books and magazines, and pieces of wood—manifest the triumph of aesthetic sensibility over brute matter. Along with Duchamp's "found objects" and "found objects assisted," they attest to the important role of choice in the creative act. Such works affirm that creativity in art depends upon judgment—an act of visual intelligence and of free will—as well as upon craftsmanship.

The perceiver of a work of art measures its aesthetic value by his own values, but, at the same time, his values are modified by the work. The judgment that he makes eventually acts as his own judge. The witty and sarcastic attacks on Impressionism by the French critic Albert Wolff,[3] for example, survive only as evidence of his inability to set aside conventional criteria. By the same token, Bishop Wilberforce's attempt to destroy Darwin's theory of evolution with ridicule attests to the bishop's inability to overcome orthodoxy.[4]

Late in the nineteenth century, as the prestige of official, academic art waned, new styles proliferated and relativism began to replace absolutism as the prevailing attitude toward aesthetic value. In 1887 the scientists Albert Michelson and Edward Morley failed in their attempt to measure the Earth's movement through an invisible, luminiferous ether that scientists at that time believed existed. As a result, the notion of ether was given up, setting the stage for the development of Albert Einstein's theories of relativity.

In the early twentieth century, relativism in the arts developed concurrently with Einstein's relativity theory in physics. Although a close parallel between these developments cannot be drawn, it is true that such seemingly objective things as time, space, and motion were now held to be relative, as was aesthetic value. "Beauty is in the eye of the beholder" was a fashionable cliché, but because of the fate of judgments made by critics such as Wolff, Louis Leroy, and Royal Cortissoz, the question of aesthetic value was usually avoided. Some critics opted for merely reporting what was happening in the art world and describing works of art, while others pointed out stylistic influences and discussed techniques. At the opposite pole, other critics followed the advice of Anatole France and simply recounted "the adventures of (their) soul(s) among masterpieces."

Value judgments are always indicated by the selection of certain works of art for collections, exhibitions, articles, books, and lectures. By the same token, value judgments are implicit in the selection of scientific theories to be included in textbooks, curricula, seminars, or professional journals. When a theory has not yet been proven by experiment, its selection is often due to its power to present a beautiful vision of reality. Werner Heisenberg, for example, in resolving certain difficulties with quantum theory, wrote: "I had the feeling that, through the surface of atomic phenomena, I was looking at a strangely beautiful interior . . . ."[5] The French mathematician and physicist Henri Poincaré asserted: ''The scientist does not study nature because it is useful to do so. He studies it because he takes pleasure in it; and he takes pleasure in it because it is beautiful. If it were not beautiful, it would not be worth knowing and life would not be worth living . . . .''[6]

Biographer and science author J. W. N. Sullivan[7] commented on certain of Poincaré's observations:

Since the primary object of the scientific theory is to express the harmonies which are found to exist in nature, we see at once that these theories must have an aesthetic value. The measure of the success of a scientific theory is, in fact, a measure of its aesthetic value, since it is a measure of the extent to which it has introduced harmony in what was before chaos.

It is in the aesthetic value that the justification of the scientific theory is to be found, and with it the justification of the scientific method . . . . The motives which guide the scientific man are, from the beginning, manifestations of the aesthetic impulse . . . . The measure in which science falls short of art is the measure in which it is incomplete as science . . . .[8]

When Erwin Schrödinger, in his capacity as editor, refused to publish the first version of Paul Dirac's wave equation because it was not supported by empirical data, Dirac commented: ''It is more important to have beauty in one's equations than to have them fit experiment . . . .''[9] Many scientists were convinced from the beginning that Einstein's general theory of relativity, which he completed in 1915, was simply ''too beautiful to be false.''[10] For the same reason, Einstein had remained certain that his special theory of relativity, which he enunciated in 1905, was true even when German physicist Walter Kaufmann's experiments seemed to demonstrate that it was false.[11]

In defining the aesthetic value of scientific models and theories, scientists use terms such as unity, order, diversity, elegance, symmetry, broken symmetry, and balance—all of which are familiar in the arts. While the Ptolemaic universe remained possible after the advent of the Copernican system, it was rejected because as it was extended by ever-growing numbers of cycles and epicycles it became increasingly complicated, ungainly, and therefore ''ugly.''

If aesthetic value is an important consideration for the theoretical scientist, knowledge is important for the creative artist. The artist invents aesthetic forms that express compelling subjective experience. When he succeeds, insight into his experience is made possible through the form of the work of art, and knowledge of the experience thus becomes available to others. When this knowledge is significant, it becomes part of the corpus of human experience. In this way Aeschylus, Giotto, Mozart, Rembrandt, Cézanne, and Picasso, no less than Euclid, Newton, and Einstein, added new dimensions to human experience. Like Euclid's axioms, paintings by Caravaggio, Rembrandt, and Courbet remain effective even after Cézanne and Picasso created new "knowledge" in art because they still stimulate satisfying aesthetic experience in most people. Paintings by such nineteenth-century artists as Jean Broc, Charles-François Jalabert, and Alfred Dehodencq, on the other hand, like Ptolemy's model of the universe, are interesting only as historical documents.

There is, however, a significant difference in how the artist and the scientist test the validity of their work. Opinions—of critics, collectors, art historians, and other artists—establish the aesthetic status of the artist's work, whereas the scientist himself must produce the hard facts that substantiate his theory. The success of a work of art on the commercial market depends on the critical acclaim of others, but the final test of the scientific theory is achieved only through direct experiment.

The skeptic insists that aesthetic evaluations derive from responses to actual works of art and science and therefore should be logically defensible. Attempts to meet such demands are frustrating, for no matter how pronounced the aesthetic experience may be, any effort to rationalize it must surely fail. Unraveling the tangled skein of visual and psychological threads and weighing the many imponderables involved in an aesthetic experience is impracticable. Even if it were not, no logical explanation could possibly encompass the character, subtlety, and intensity of such an experience.

If we cannot clearly define the aesthetic quality of a work of art or, indeed, of a scientific model or theory, we must still begin discussing it from where we are—in a world that communicates largely by means of reasonable verbal statements. We must, therefore, be content to indicate how to decipher the form of a work of art or of science, thus making it possible for others to "read" the work and experience its aesthetic quality directly.

It is helpful, for example, to discuss such things as Monet's juxtaposed patches of variegated hues that suggest sunlight reflected from different surfaces at particular times of day and season. It is useful to point out how he suggested space by means of aerial perspective, and to contrast this with Cézanne's treatment of space by overlapping and integrating planes and by distorting perspective.

The aesthetic quality of a scientific theory or model is dependent, to a large extent, upon its mathematical form; still, certain verbal concepts might help to comprehend its beauty. For example, Einstein constructed the special theory of relativity in an effort to bring together electrodynamics and mechanics as a step toward revealing the harmony that he believed to be inherent in nature. He postulated that mass is but a form of energy, a theory that has since all too effectively been demonstrated. Another concept to emerge from the special theory of relativity is that time is a dimension that must be added to the other three dimensions in any discussion of existence. A space-time continuum thus replaces the concept of three spatial dimensions and a separate, universal flow of time. Verbal discussion of such ideas might well result in a dawning appreciation of the elegance and balance of Einstein's theory, even if one does not fully comprehend its mathematics.

Comparing works of art or scientific theories with each other aids in understanding and evaluating them. To contrast Cézanne's blunt, broad brushwork with Monet's flickering stroke, for example, suggests that the latter's approach was analytical, while the former's was constructive. It is also enlightening to compare the ways in which artists such as Monet, Cézanne, and van Gogh, or scientists such as Niels Bohr and Einstein, interpreted the same information. Such comparative studies reveal personal styles and indicate that the work of art or the scientific theory discloses its creator's subjective experience of the world.

No matter how unique it seems, every artist's vocabulary of visual form is inevitably derived in part from older art. For example, the glowing light of J. M. W. Turner's paintings and watercolors, John Constable's flickering white "snow," Eugène Delacroix's rich palette, and Courbet's homely subjects and painterly method all contributed to Impressionism. Nicolas Poussin's carefully structured composition, on the other hand, is joined with Impressionist color and painterly brushwork to establish the basis for Cézanne's mature style.

Paradoxically, works of art often are judged by values that they themselves create. When we consider Cézanne's paintings to be of superior merit in relation to Western art of the late nineteenth century, we are actually evaluating Cézanne's paintings by standards that they themselves set. Similarly, when we judge the human race to be superior to other forms of animal life, it is because we are applying criteria based on human values. Evolution in life forms as well as art defines its own criteria as it goes along.

When Einstein was queried about the difficulty of measuring movement in a relativistic universe, he replied that it was only necessary to "choose a star." That is, to ascertain the relative speed of a body in space one has only to select another body, assume it to be stable, and measure the movement of the first body against it. Measuring the aesthetic value of a work of art may be more abstruse than gauging the velocity of a body in space, but one can become sensible of the aesthetic value of a painting or sculpture by comparing it with other works with which it has some things in common and whose values are established.

New forms and new values are constantly being produced by creative artists. As mentioned above, Cézanne's paintings derived certain elements from Poussin and other elements from Impressionism in general. Cubism carried Cézanne's concepts and methods beyond where he left them, and Mondrian then developed a severely formal style based upon the Classical elements in Cubism, while eliminating the last evidence of Impressionism. The Futurists, on the other hand, jettisoned the Classical tendencies of Cubism and developed a style glorifying the dynamic character of the modern world. Each development brought with it new forms that were fractionally encompassed by the old, and discarded elements of the old that were not useful.

Science is also cumulative. Auguste Comte indicated that each science is based on information accumulated by earlier sciences, and Isaac Newton declared that he had accomplished much because he "stood on the shoulders of giants." Yet, invention is as important in the sciences as in the arts. When Linus Pauling once described his theory of electroneutrality in molecules and reactions to a group of graduate students, one of them asked him what he had derived it from. Pauling replied that there was no derivation. When the student then asked how he had arrived at the principle, Pauling replied: "I made it up!"[12]

Comprehending the meaning, and gauging the aesthetic value of works of art and of science involve comparisons within a broad cultural context that conditions the minds of both creators and perceivers. New meanings and values are constantly being invented and accepted or rejected by human beings in a dynamic process generated by their decisions and actions.

1. Based on a definition by the Earl of Listowel, *A Critical History of Modern Aesthetics* (London, 1933), p. 210. Quoted in Thomas Munro, *The Arts and Their Interrelations* (New York: Liberal Arts Press, 1949), p. 95.

2. See, for example, Roger de Piles's evaluation of 15th-, 16th-, and 17th-century painters in Elizabeth G. Holt, *A Documentary History of Art*, 2 vols. (Princeton, NJ: Princeton University Press, 1958), 2: 185-87.

3. Quoted in John Rewald, *The History of Impressionism* (New York: Museum of Modern Art, 1973), pp. 368-70.

4. In 1860 Bishop Samuel Wilberforce, who was regarded as a master of all branches of natural knowledge, was selected by orthodox forces to attack Darwinism at the Oxford meeting of the British Association. He was effectively answered and rebuked by Thomas Huxley.

5. Quoted in Deane W. Curtin, ed., *The Aesthetic Dimension of Science* (New York: Philosophical Library, 1980), pp. 6-7.

6. Ibid., p. 7.

7. Sullivan wrote *The Limitations of Science* (1933) and biographies of Newton and Beethoven. He was also the subject of a biography by Virginia Woolf.

8. Quoted in Curtin, *Aesthetic Dimension*, p. 8.

9. P.A.M. Dirac, "The Evolution of the Physicist's Picture of Nature," *Scientific American* 208, no. 5 (May 1963): 47.

10. Richard Morris, *Dismantling the Universe* (New York: Simon and Schuster, 1983), p. 182.

11. Ibid., pp. 67, 80, and 114.

12. Quoted in Curtin, *Aesthetic Dimension*, p. 2.

What is the good of prescribing to art the roads that it must follow? To do so is to doubt art, which develops normally according to the laws of Nature, and must be exclusively occupied in responding to human needs.

Feodor Dostoevsky

Imagination, not reason, creates the novel. It is to social inheritance what mutation is to biological inheritance; it accounts for the arrival of the fittest. Reason or logic, applied when judgment indicates that the new is promising, acts like natural selection to . . . insure the survival of the fittest.

R. W. Gerard

III. Evolution by Social Selection in the Arts

The idea that art reflects social conditions is a proposition become platitude and finally cliché; yet exactly how this works is still not clear. Why have some periods of great social and political turmoil—for example, fifteenth-century Italy—produced relatively coherent art styles? And why have some fairly stable periods—for example, the last quarter of the nineteenth century in France—given birth to widely divergent styles?

Art historians and theoreticians such as Alois Riegl, Max Dvořák, Frederick Antal, and Arnold Hauser have described and analyzed the economic and social structures of certain periods of history and have suggested that contemporaneous art styles reflect class reactions to those conditions. They have indicated that class psychology plays a role in determining art styles, but they have not explained how class attitudes can be transformed into actual works of art of particular kinds. Nor have they given equal attention to the idea that art, in turn, influences society.

Antal cites two stylistically different paintings—one by Masaccio (1425), the other by Gentile da Fabriano (1426)—both done in Florence, and asks: "How could two such widely differing pictures have been painted in the same town and at the same time?" He concludes that they could have been painted at the same place and time only because there were different social groups patronizing the arts in Florence at the time: "We can understand the origins of co-existent styles only if we study the various sections of society, reconstruct their philosophies and thence penetrate to their art."[1] But the question then arises: how can a social group influence the creative acts of artists who are not members of that group? There is no justification for assuming a causal relationship between such a group and an art style simply because they occur at the same time and place.

Unquestionably, art is at least partly a social phenomenon, but it does not simply mirror other social events. It is one of many components within a social complex and causal connections between it and other elements are not easily perceived.

It is proposed here that the relative unity of most period-styles prior to the nineteenth century was due to the selection of art works by ethnically, socially, economically, and psychologically unified patron-groups. The extreme stylistic diversity of the modern period, on the other hand, seems to derive largely from an artist-dealer-collector relationship that has replaced the traditional one between artist and patron, thereby greatly reducing the influence that the purchaser of art formerly had on the character of the works themselves.

In examining how art and society influence one another, it is convenient to begin by considering certain ideas developed by Charles Darwin. In 1859 Darwin proposed that natural selection was the chief agent of change in the evolution of living species. He also recognized the role of genetic effects, even though he could not explain the mechanism that produced such effects.[2] (The explanation was provided by Dutch botanist Hugo De Vries in 1901 when, after rediscovering the studies of Fr. Gregor Mendel, he developed a theory of mutation, which contributed to the new science of genetics.) Darwin's theory had a great impact not only in biology but also in all areas where evolutionary change was a consideration. From then on, selection of one kind or another was an important element in speculation about the process of evolution.

In considering how socially and economically coherent groups select works of art, however, it must first be determined how such groups are unified in their aesthetic needs and desires. Human nature appears to be erected on a basic structure of hungers and drives common to all animal life. What is distinctly human derives in large part from the ability to operate by means of symbols, signs, and forms that are created and organized in various ways to make up "language." Thus, education—broadly speaking, the transmission of knowledge, traditions, and values from generation to generation—becomes possible.

Societies, however, are usually made up of diverse, often antagonistic, groups, and the transmitted information varies from group to group. The education of the feudal lord, for example, was quite different from that of the serf or the craftsman, the merchant or the banker. Furthermore, each group's relations to prevailing economic, social, and political realities are unique. Conditions that are comfortable and seem to be the natural order of things to one group may be unpleasant and seem to be unjust to another.

The varying relations of such groups to the social environment causes differences in their psychological states, and, therefore, in their aesthetic needs and desires. If an artist should belong to one of the social groups supporting the arts, it could logically be argued that the works he creates also give expression to the group psyche. Since artists rarely come from the same social strata as the major art consumers, however, they seldom share the same dreams or the same psychological—and therefore aesthetic—needs and desires as their patrons.

Styles in art normally have been perpetuated by artists who trained in studios and schools where successful styles were dominant. Individual variations have occurred, of course, and the success of some of these has been determined by the support they received from socially, economically, and psychologically coherent consumer groups. I propose that such groups have influenced artists and their works in three ways: by stipulation, by attraction, and by selection.

Stipulation refers to any command given to the artist. In painting it includes such things as size, subject, number and type of images, colors, and even composition. Often a determining factor in the past, stipulation in the Western world today occurs mainly in advertising art, architecture, commercial films, television, and commissioned portraits. It was a major factor in the official painting of Nazi Germany, however, and it is still important in the Soviet Union and in other restrictive societies.

Attraction indicates the ability of a social group to appeal to artists by a moral and intellectual climate that they find sympathetic. During the Middle Ages in Western Europe, for example, artists were attracted by Christianity and willingly created art that expressed the Christian faith. During the seventeenth century, Dutch bourgeois society, based on commercialism, attracted artists to the ideals of middle-class life. Many of the artists were so close to the burghers socially that they shared their attitudes. During the late eighteenth century, artists such as Jacques-Louis David and Antoine-Jean (Baron) Gros were attracted by the aims and ideals of the revolutionary French middle classes and the Republic. Later, they were swept up by enthusiasm for Napoleon and the Empire. In the twentieth century, artists such as Ben Shahn, William Gropper, and Raphael Soyer in the United States and Diego Rivera, José Clemente Orozco, and David Siqueiros in Mexico were attracted to the moral position of the dispossessed agricultural and industrial classes.

Selection refers to the choosing of works of art. Everyone selects art of some kind, even if it is only wallpaper or a movie; but only those on an upper economic level can afford to become major patrons or collectors of art. When patrons have psychological needs and desires in common, they form a group taste, which is manifested in a style that develops in response to the choices they make. In the seventeenth century, certain Italian, French, and Flemish artists, or their works, were selected both by the Catholic Church, which was seeking to dramatize the ideals of the Counter-Reformation, and by secular rulers, whose growing power was challenging that of the Church, the Baroque style manifested their choices. In the eighteenth century, the elegant rococo style was determined largely by the selections of nobles who had been reduced from powerful lords of their own domains to courtiers.

The development of two or more styles at the same time and place, either coexisting or overlapping and supplanting one another, usually occurs, as Antal suggests, when there are competing social groups with different psychological and aesthetic needs as well as enough wealth to become patrons. The first clear instance of this kind of conflict occurred during the reign of the monotheistic Egyptian pharaoh Amenhotep IV, between 1372 and 1358 BC, when the young ruler and his supporters tried to limit the power of the priests of the god Amen. Coincidental with this conflict, a graceful, curvilinear style based on certain naturalistic tendencies that had long been an undercurrent in Egyptian art emerged as the dominant style. Elements of the new style persisted for awhile after the death of Amenhotep, but the power of the priests and the old religious forms were restored and a stiffer, more formal, style, in keeping with tradition, was eventually reestablished.[3]

In late thirteenth- and early fourteenth-century Florence, middle-class merchants and bankers, organized in guilds and controlling great wealth, wrested political power from the landed aristocracy. The struggle between the aristocratic Ghibelline and the bourgeois Guelph parties coincided in time and place with a conflict in painting between a traditional, flat, quasi-Byzantine style and a new way of suggesting three-dimensional form by means of modeling in light and shade, and defining space with linear perspective.

Another dramatic change occurred in late eighteenth-century France when the rise of Neoclassicism and the decline of the rococo style coincided with the growing economic and political power of the upper middle class and its final seizing of political control from the monarchy.

A conflict of styles in art also results when the conditions of a patron-group's existence are altered, causing a change in its psychological state and therefore in its aesthetic needs and desires. This occurred in France, for example, when the transition from the high Baroque style of the seventeenth century to its lighter and more elegant phase in the eighteenth century coincided with a change in the status of the aristocratic patron-group.[4] The nobles had been stripped of much of their administrative and judiciary power by Louis XIII. He and, after him, Louis XIV appointed civil administrators to take charge of local government, which had until then been the responsibility of the aristocracy. Many nobles moved from their provincial châteaux to the cities, where they often became courtiers. The enhanced power of the throne found expression in the academies and in the classical Baroque styles of Nicolas Poussin, Charles Le Brun, Laurent de La Hyre, Eustache Le Sueur, and others.[5] The emasculated nobility and the two weaker kings who followed Louis XIV favored a more delicate and elegant style. Jean Antoine Watteau's masterwork *A Pilgrimage to Cythera* is often said to represent an escapist dream for an aristocracy reduced in power and threatened by the burgeoning middle classes. Later, erotic paintings by Jean-Baptiste Pater, François Boucher, Nicolas Lancret, and others reflect the elegant lifestyles and sensuous concerns of the debilitated nobility.

Stylistic diversity normally occurs when two or more patron-groups, each with different aesthetic needs, have the power to stipulate, attract, and select works of art or artists. Competing factions, however, may support similar styles when they consider art to be a psychological weapon in ideological struggles. Nazi Germany and Communist Russia, for example, were political enemies, yet they both rewarded artists who worked in Social Realist and Neoclassical styles.

The anthropologist A. L. Kroeber has observed:

Any art rising from obscurity to its first modest achievements has to make certain choices and, therefore, commitments; and as its condition develops further momentum increases, and it is usually more profitable to improve, refine, extend these commitments than to start all over again with contrary or unrelated choices . . . . The frame helps strongly to channel the course of development.[6]

The channel changes course to some degree, however, for no pupil produces work exactly like that of his master, and no artist produces two works exactly alike. Still variations are normally slight and remain within the overall configuration of the channel, particularly in a highly structured and conservative society such as that of ancient Egypt. In less restrictive environments, more daring changes occur and, if successful, become paradigms for new styles. The innovations of Giotto, Michelangelo, and Caravaggio, for example, like successful biological mutations, introduced new tendencies that were encouraged by a changing social environment.

The analogy with biological evolution is not exact, however, for physiological variations are far more random than cultural variations. This is explained by the fact that the mechanism for biological adaptation is located in the natural selection of chance mutations that are best suited for existence in a particular environment. Cultural adaptations, on the other hand, depend on deliberate decisions by artists and selections by art consumers. The notion of cultural evolution therefore depends upon the concept of free will.

The idea of cultural selection is simple, although its operation is often complex. Works by Raphael, Rubens, Shakespeare, and Mozart were "selected" by patrons who found them especially satisfying; indeed, later generations also have found them satisfying. On the other hand, works by Federico Zuccari, Agostino Carracci, and Charles Le Brun, which were also selected by contemporary patrons, have not been confirmed by later audiences as being works of superior merit. Immediate success is no guarantee of longevity or superior aesthetic merit.

Until the nineteenth century, the dynamics of the art market were relatively simple: artists whose works were selected by contemporaneous patrons had more students, apprentices, followers, and imitators than those whose works were not selected. The stylistic traits of successful works, therefore, occurred frequently in works by younger artists. On the other hand, the desires of the art-buying public were influenced by successful contemporary works. A reciprocal flow of influence thus occurred: from those who selected works of art, to artists, and back through works of art to their audience.

The Modern Period

The system outlined above began to break down early in the nineteenth century, and by the late nineteenth and twentieth centuries the increasingly complex art scene required a new interpretive approach. Allowing for the fact that those within a forest only see a variety of individual trees, it still seems obvious that there is unprecedented stylistic diversity in the visual arts today. Furthermore, styles cannot be clearly traced to the selections of particular social groups. To what socially cohesive group of art consumers, for example, could we trace the success of Cubism or Surrealism? Which specific groups supported the art of Pablo Picasso, Jackson Pollock, or Roy Lichtenstein? Clearly, there are no typical, cohesive groups of art patrons or collectors today.[7]

24

During the nineteenth century the political triumph of the middle classes and the dramatic success of an industrial and commercial economy produced relativistic attitudes that affected all creative activity. A pragmatic moral climate (deriving from the successes of Western industry and commerce), a romantic emphasis on individual liberties (a necessary corollary of the free enterprise system), and the recognition of multiple value systems (deriving from individualism and the study of exotic cultures)—all helped to encourage a variety of styles in late nineteenth-century and early twentieth-century Western art.

At the same time, traditional values were questioned and often abandoned. Belief in a special creation, for example, was challenged by Darwin's theory of evolution; and the ancient notions of absolute time and of absolute space filled with ether were given up following the experiment by Michelson and Morley.

In the arts, absolutism had persisted because the bourgeoisie's insecurity in cultural matters had led it to resurrect the Academy and support Neoclassicism in art. Furthermore, realism was often associated, in the public mind, with socialism (or anarchism), thus arousing the opposition of the bourgeoisie. At the same time, however, new knowledge about exotic cultures and an emphasis on individual freedoms were contributing toward a general weakening of traditions. Official support for an Academy of Fine Arts (which habitually rewarded insipid painting and sculpture) drove the most adventurous and creative artists to look outside the Neoclassical tradition for inspiration and for new ways of expressing original visions of reality.[8] For the first time, artists challenged the environment by creating art not likely to be selected, thus working against their own material benefit.

New artistic perceptions were at first rejected by the culturally insecure bourgeoisie, and, contrary to romantic notions, hunger seldom stimulates creativity. Of the Impressionists, for example, only Degas, fortified by wealth and an immense pride, seems to have been indifferent to popular, official, and commercial success. Manet, Monet, Renoir, and even the financially secure Cézanne yearned for recognition and acclaim from both the public and the art-establishment. These artists did not consider ''bohemianism'' to be good in itself, but it provided a means of maintaining their identity within an intolerant society. Ironically, they were finally supported by the very group that they most scorned: the businessman who appeared in the guise of the art dealer and the art collector.

New industrial methods prompted the development of new products. The development of advertising and sales techniques stimulated new markets for these goods. The same methods were eventually adapted for the marketing of works of art. While reputable dealers, such as Paul Durand-Ruel and Ambroise Vollard, did not pressure artists to create works that would be saleable, they did support artists whose works they believed were saleable—as well as good. Finally, some dealers, concerned primarily with business, encouraged fashions in art—not unlike fashions in clothing or automobiles—with each season bringing its surprises. It is sometimes difficult today to recognize serious art within the show-and-sell atmosphere that surrounds it.

The position of the contemporary dealer and critic—between the producer and the consumer of works of art—has altered the historical dynamics of that relationship. Of the three ways mentioned earlier in which patrons traditionally influenced art, only selection plays a major role in painting and sculpture today. It is selection by dealers and critics, however, that does most to determine the success of artists, art styles, and art movements. For good and bad, the modern dealer is the artist's "patron," but he is primarily a merchant rather than a consumer.

The great and continued success of certain modern artists—Cézanne, Picasso, Mondrian, and Miró—suggests that their art satisfies deep psychological and aesthetic needs for large segments of the population regardless of social, economic, political, or other groupings. Museums and galleries have made works of art available to all, and art books, films, and reproductions have extended information about art to many people. Scarcely conceivable in such open and fluid circumstances are socially, politically, and economically cohesive groups of collectors with common psychological and aesthetic needs. The advantages of this situation are: (1) Despite many pressures on the artist, he is freer than ever before to make whatever kind of art he wishes. (2) Art consumers are distributed throughout many social strata, thus removing pressures on the artist to give form to the dreams of any particular group.

1. Frederick Antal, *Florentine Painting and Its Social Background* (London: Kegan Paul, 1948), p. 4.

2. See Charles Darwin, *The Descent of Man and Selection in Relation to Sex.* Quoted in Url Lanham, *Origins of Modern Biology* (New York: Columbia University Press, 1971), p. 181.

3. This applies only to representations of the pharaoh, the nobles, and the priests. Representations of lower-level functionaries were more realistic.

4. These brief indications of coincidental changes in society and in art styles are, of course, too simple and bald. They only indicate possible paths to pursue in further examinations of connections between art and society.

5. Although Poussin spent only two years in France after his thirtieth birthday, from his adoptive home in Rome, he was the major influence on the Classical tradition in France.

6. A. L. Kroeber, *Style and Civilizations* (Ithaca: Cornell University Press, 1957), p. 34.

7. Some critics now theorize that a new "post-modern" age has recently emerged, in which modernist art—supported by such government agencies as the NEA, corporations, and wealthy patrons—has found official sanction, thereby transforming the avant-garde into the new "Academy."

8. Paul Cézanne and Georges Seurat were two major exceptions who looked precisely to the Western Classical tradition (e.g., to Poussin and Piero della Francesca) for inspiration.

At first judged to be a minor eddy in the mainstream of Western art, Impressionism was ultimately recognized as a major tributary to the Realist tradition. From Giotto (1266/7-1337) and Jan van Eyck (1385/90-1441) to Claude Monet (1840-1926) and Edgar Degas (1834-1917), Western painting gradually developed an increasingly accurate representation of nature as it appears to the human eye. In a parallel development, philosophy and science evolved—from Copernicus (1473-1543), Francis Bacon (1561-1626), and Galileo Galilei (1564-1642) to Auguste Comte (1798-1857), Ernst Haeckel, (1834-1919), and Ernst Mach (1836-1916)—toward the presentation of an ever sharper picture of nature as it is perceived by the senses.

Most of the Impressionist painters took their canvases out of doors to record the immediate effects of atmosphere and light reflected from the various surfaces of nature. Since visual sensations are caused by light striking the retina of the eye, they juxtaposed small patches of colored pigment to achieve sensations analogous to the reflection of light from foliage, water, and clouds. Abandoning rational a priori systems such as linear perspective, these artists attempted to paint what they actually saw. Their work depends upon pure color relationships and is more concerned with momentary visual effects than are the paintings of precursors—Gustave Courbet, Eugène Boudin, Johann Jongkind, and the Barbizon painters. Impressionism thus issued from a long tradition of Realism, modified especially by Monet's particular vision. Contemporary scientific theories concerning color and the physical nature and effects of light supported the Impressionists' conviction that visual appearances are due to the effects of light on the retina.[1]

During the same period, materialism, mechanism, and positivism reached a peak in the sciences. Physical scientists such as Michael Faraday, Hermann von Helmholtz, Haeckel, and Mach subscribed to the notion that only induction provides information accurate enough to form a basis for knowledge about the physical world. Experimentation was their primary tool for substantiating such information. In the life sciences, Charles Darwin supported his theory of evolution by natural selection from accidental variations with a wealth of observed facts. In the social sciences, Karl Marx and Friedrich Engels emphasized the practice of basing theory upon facts in the study of social evolution. The philosopher Auguste Comte founded the school of Positivism, which maintains that the goal of knowledge is not to explain but simply to describe experienced phenomena. Positivism provided an appropriate theoretical basis for the empirical, mechanistic, and materialistic aspects of nineteenth-century science.[2] Early in the twentieth century, J. B. Watson in the United States and I. P. Pavlov in the Soviet Union introduced positivist methods into the field of psychology in their development of the theory of behaviorism.

In 1900, thirty-odd years after the Impressionists dissolved images of solid objects into small patches of color representing light reflections, Max Planck suggested that light is emitted in tiny packets of energy, which he labeled quanta.

No matter how objectively an artist tries to represent the appearance of nature, his personal vision is inevitably revealed in his art. Even Monet was clearly more than "just an eye." Perception, after all, is a complex psychological process dependent not only upon the physical factors of light and its recording by the retina but also upon the personality and temperament of the perceiver. The Spanish philosopher Ortega Y Gasset noted that: "The inspiration for artistic images . . . moved from the object to its visual medium, light, from there to the artist's retina, and finally to the interior of the mind itself."[3]

By the turn of the century the ideal of strict objectivity and the notion of mechanistic materialism in science were giving way before theories and events indicating that the human personality and subjective experience must be considered in any model of "reality." The Impressionists' effort to maintain an objective view of nature gave way to the subjectivity of paintings by Post-Impressionist artists.

When, working side by side, Monet and Renoir or Renoir and Cézanne painted the same motif using a similar palette and technique, each produced a unique, personal image. Paralleling such evident subjectivity in the visual arts, many scientists began to posit theories derived from their unique vision rather than from pure induction. During the first few years of the twentieth century, for example, the Dutch botanist Hugo De Vries developed the theory of mutation, which, when joined with Mendel's rediscovered laws of heredity, provided a more spontaneous, less mechanical basis for Darwin's theory of evolution by natural selection. Niels Bohr proposed a theoretical structure for the invisible atom. Einstein's theory of relativity invalidated the absolute character of time and space and indicated that one's view of an event is partly determined by one's position relative to that event. Around the same time, Sigmund Freud proposed a structure for the unconscious levels of the mind, which, he suggested, often determines a human being's experiences and actions.

Despite the joyful vision of life provided by Impressionist canvases, the artists found little contemporary public and critical support. Perhaps the critics sensed the subtle amorality of these delightful paintings that simply record the world as it is, without making moral judgments or presenting ideal visions of what it should be.

Most critics saw Impressionist paintings with eyes conditioned by the slick banalities of Salon painters such as Alexander Cabanel, Ernest Meissonier, and Jean-Léon Gerôme. For the ambitious collector, approval by these critics and the Academy provided prestige and indicated a safe investment. Lack of official and popular success, however, never caused the Impressionists to doubt the validity of their aims. Although Renoir and Pissarro wavered briefly, their doubts were prompted by problems of art, not of popularity.

Beginning in 1874 the Impressionists organized eight group exhibitions, which directly challenged the official Salons.[4] They hoped to find favor with a public that would judge their art on its own terms. For many years this hope was rudely disappointed, yet the artists refused to compromise their aims and ultimately won their war with the Academy.

The Academy had been restructured early in the nineteenth century and the means to official success lay firmly in its control. However, it was an anachronism. Lacking an artistic tradition, the bourgeoisie supported Neoclassicism, which began as an attempt to revive the verities of the ancient Roman Republic. The artists, however, were middle-class-oriented academicians. The opening encounters of the Revolution had been fought in France during the last quarter of the eighteenth century. The political struggle, in harness with the industrial and commercial revolutions, spread across Western Europe during the nineteenth century. Individual freedoms were deemed essential for laissez-faire economics and democracy. The arts, however, were viewed by the bourgeoisie as frivolous activities that had been supported by the aristocracy and, therefore, were legitimately subject to controls. The revived Academy provoked opposition from most serious and gifted artists.

The typical path to official artistic success began with study under an Academic master; led to the Prix de Rome (four years of study at the French Academy in Rome); included the acceptance of one's works and the winning of awards in the biennial Salons, followed by the purchase of one's works by the government; and, finally, appointment to a chair in the Academy of Fine Arts. Salon juries were composed largely of established academicians who used their influence to win places and awards for themselves, their friends, and their protégés.

By the third quarter of the nineteenth century the official Neoclassical style had adopted the sensuous, linear manner of Jean Auguste Dominique Ingres, with occasional grafts from the colorful and painterly technique of Eugène Delacroix. The resulting hybrid style was applied to allegorical, historical, mythological, and occasionally, moralistic genre themes by artists such as Gérôme, Cabanel, Thomas Couture, and Adolphe William Bouguereau.

Inspired by Dutch seventeenth-century paintings, artists such as Théodore Rousseau, Charles François Daubigny, and François Bonvin created landscapes and genre paintings that not only were accepted but also were occasionally rewarded with lesser prizes in the Salons.

The first Impressionist group exhibition, organized in 1874, was greeted by jeers from the public and critics such as Louis Leroy, who wrote a farcical review in *Le Charivari*. A small bomb had been exploded outside the tidy façade of the official art establishment, but the effects were devastating. It seemed unlikely that a few young malcontents could seriously disturb the imposing structure of the Académie des Beaux-Arts, yet the vehemence of the official reaction indicates that serious damage had been done.[5]

1. For example, Charles Blanc's *Grammar of Painting and Drawing* (1867); Eugène Chevreul's *Law of Simultaneous Contrasts* (1839); Hermann von Helmholtz's *Treatise on Physiological Optics (1867)*; James Clerk Maxwell's *A Treatise on Electricity and Magnetism* (1873); and Ogden N. Rood's *Students' Text Book of Color* (1881).

2. Auguste Comte (1797-1857) postulated science as a religion and predicted that positivistic scientific methods would be applied to the social sciences.

3. José Ortega Y Gasset, "On Point of View in the Arts," *The Dehumanization of Art, and Other Writings on Art and Culture* (Garden City, New York: Doubleday Anchor Books, 1956), pp. 99-120. Summarized in John Adkins Richardson, *Modern Art and Scientific Thought* (Urbana: University of Illinois Press, 1971), pp. 7-8, fn. 4.

4. The exhibitions took place in 1874, 1876, 1877, 1879, 1880, 1881, 1882, and 1886. Only twice, in 1874 and 1877, did the five main Impressionists (Degas, Monet, Pissarro, Renoir, and Sisley) exhibit together. Both times Cézanne also exhibited.

5. In the sciences, Darwin's theory of evolution by natural selection caused a comparable storm of opposition. Ironically, it was recognized eventually that both Darwinism and Impressionism embodied bourgeois values.

Claude Monet (1840-1926)

When Monet wished that he could be as one born blind who could suddenly see, he was expressing a common Impressionist desire to see the world with a fresh eye rather than by means of a structure of conventions. This empirical attitude was appropriate to the developing industrial, urban society of Western Europe, wherein nature was experienced fleetingly and episodically by mobile city dwellers on holiday in contrast to the peasant's view of the slow, methodical rhythms of nature's recurring cycles.

Monet's inductive approach to nature led him to develop certain pragmatic painting techniques that more accurately suggested direct visual perceptions than did rational devices such as linear perspective and modeling with dark and light tones. Working out of doors, he devised a patchy brushstroke so as to juxtapose a variety of colors. Paintings developed in this way were to be interpreted by the observer as representing a corner of nature seen in a particular light and atmosphere. This method permitted Monet to suggest evanescent light reflections, which could not be achieved with traditional painting techniques. As science analyzed light into colors, Monet now achieved the effect of light by assembling patches of prismatic color.

During the early 1860s Monet worked under the influence of Courbet, Jongkind, and Boudin. During the summer of 1864, at Honfleur, in the company of Boudin and Jongkind, he expressed in a letter to his friend Frédéric Bazille an attitude worthy of the most empirical scientist: "I intend to struggle, scrape off, begin again, because one can produce what one sees and what one understands . . . . It is on the strength of observation and reflection that one finds it."[1]

Five years later Monet and Auguste Renoir spent the summer painting around Bougival, a small village on the Seine near Paris, where they found festive subjects at La Grenouillère, a restaurant and bathing wharf on the river. Young workers, clerks, and women in variegated blazers and dresses and carrying parasols arrived and departed in skiffs and canoes. They ate, drank, and lounged out of doors as dappled sunlight filtered through foliage.

Seduced by this lovely, ever-changing scene, the two young artists were more than ever convinced of the validity of their intention to paint everyday subjects out of doors in natural light. During that summer of 1869 they developed fully the Impressionist method, and neither artist was ever to surpass the freshness and spontaneity of the paintings they did during these few months of shared ideals, enthusiasm, and poverty.

In 1870 the war with Prussia scattered the small group of Impressionists. Monet, Camille Pissarro, and Alfred Sisley went to England; Renoir served with a regiment of cuirassiers; Degas enlisted in the artillery; Manet served as a staff officer in the artillery of the National Guard; Bazille joined a company of Zouaves and was killed in battle; and Cézanne took refuge at the village of L'Estaque in the south of France.

While in England, Monet, Pissarro, and Sisley discovered the works of the English landscape painters John Crome (Old Crome), Joseph Mallard William Turner, and John Constable. The Impressionists had already surpassed these British artists in rendering light and atmosphere, but the experience confirmed the validity of their aims. Pissarro later wrote:

Turner and Constable, while they taught us something, showed us in their works that they had no understanding of the analysis of shadow, which in Turner's painting is simply used as an effect, a mere absence of light. As far as tone division is concerned, Turner proved the value of this as a method, among methods, although he did not apply it correctly and naturally.[2]

The young Impressionists had already realized that shadows, like lighted areas, are made up of light reflections, so they used rich colors (rather than grayed or darkened local tones) in shadowed regions. Lighter, warmer hues were used to represent sunlit zones. Thus, the shadowed side of a cottage might be painted with some dark red patches, indicating reflections from a nearby bed of roses; green patches, suggesting reflections from grass or bushes; blues and violets, for atmosphere; and the actual color of the building modified by the prevailing light. Sunlit walls of the same cottage might be painted with lighter tones of the local color with blues or violets for atmosphere.

While in England, Monet and Pissarro met Paul Durand-Ruel, a French art dealer who already owned a few Impressionist paintings. Durand-Ruel was pleased to form an association with the young successors of the Barbizon painters whom he had championed for many years.

Following the Franco-Prussian War, Monet refined the technique and style of Impressionism that he and Renoir had established at Bougival in 1869. Despite the antagonism of most critics and academicians, a few critics and collectors eventually began to defend the Impressionists. Victor Chocquet, Eugène Murer, Gustave Caillebotte, Père Tanguy, Dr. Paul Gachet, Paul Gauguin (then a young banker), and a few others even bought their paintings.

During the latter part of the 1870s writers and critics such as Edmond Duranty, Georges Rivière, and Théodore Duret published and edited articles and journals on Impressionism. Emile Zola consistently defended the Impressionists, believing that their paintings echoed the naturalism of his writing. They, in turn, considered him a sympathetic friend until his novel *L'Oeuvre*, published in 1886, demonstrated that he neither understood nor appreciated their accomplishments. Ironically, while he was writing that the Impressionist man of genius had yet to appear, Monet, Degas, and the close friend of his youth, Paul Cézanne, were creating some of their greatest paintings.

During the 1870s and early eighties Monet and his companions worked in the countryside around Argenteuil, Pontoise, Vétheuil, and other sites clustered to the north and west of Paris. They also worked in the Forest of Fontainebleau and at certain locations on the channel coast. In all of these regions they had the advantage of a limpid light and reflective atmosphere.

Throughout this period the financial plight of Monet and most of the other Impressionists remained desperate. In an effort to alleviate their difficulties, two group sales were held, but they achieved little success. Georges Charpentier opened a gallery, La Vie Moderne, in which he held one-man shows for Renoir in 1879 and for Manet and Monet in 1880; but despite low prices, sales were few. In 1879 Monet's wife, Camille, died of illness caused by the wretched conditions in which they lived. The artist himself, robust and normally optimistic, made a half-hearted attempt to commit suicide.[3]

Monet and his friends were not scornful of successful careers and money; on the contrary, they yearned for both. But they insisted on making art on their own terms.

Completely self-assured, Monet developed his art without hesitations or changes in direction. In 1877 he painted a series of views of the Gare St. Lazare in Paris. Around 1891 he again took up serial paintings: one series depicted haystacks at different times of day; another, poplar trees; yet another, the façade of Rouen Cathedral. These were intended to demonstrate how his subject changed with the light, even though the motif remained the same.

Later in the same decade Monet began a series of paintings of his gardens—especially the lily pond—at Giverny; he continued these until his death, in 1926. Many of the canvases from this series are mural size; some are intended to be seen in connected groups of three or more, which almost literally surround the viewer. Instead of objectively depicting light reflections, however, they provide insight into the artist's subjective experience of the ephemeral world of rippling water, floating lily pads, waving underwater plants, and dancing reflections of sky and clouds (cat. no. 4). These sensuous canvases loosely covered with skeins of paint were once regarded as evidence of the declining powers of the aging Impressionist master. Around the middle of the twentieth century, however, they were reevaluated and accorded a major position in the oeuvre of Monet and in the history of modern art.

Monet's attitude—and consequently his style—had changed from that of an objectively recording eye to that of a subjectively responding personality. The artist himself reported that he had "rediscovered the powers of intuition and allowed them to predominate."[4]

Edgar Degas (1834-1917)

Degas was never seriously interested in landscape painting, and therefore produced little in this genre. He once mockingly suggested that the police comb the countryside and arrest all the *plein-air* painters for desecrating the landscape with their paints and easels. His misanthropic nature and mordant wit assured that his relations with the other Impressionists were often strained. Aristocratic by nature, he had such self-confidence that he felt little need of approval from the public, the critics, the Academy, or even his own comrades. Enormously talented, he could be charming, clever, and abrasive all at the same time.

In his own words he was ''a die-hard, incorrigible reactionary.'' While this was an accurate self-appraisal of his social and political views, in matters of art his compositional innovations were revolutionary.

In the early days of Impressionism, when the artists met at the Café Guerbois, Manet and Degas—both of whom were intelligent, educated, articulate, and witty—dominated discussions. Inevitably, however, their personalities clashed and their friendship suffered interruptions. Degas, splendidly contemptuous of bourgeois values and caring nothing for official recognition, cruelly taunted Manet, whose middle-class ambition led him to refuse to exhibit with the Impressionists because he feared that such an association would jeopardize his chances for official success.

As a boy, Degas had met Ingres, and he never abandoned his respect for this Neoclassical master. He also admired Raphael and other Italian Renaissance artists. At the same time, he shared the Impressionists' contempt for the doctrinaire academicians who also owed much to Ingres and Raphael.

Although he also shared the Impressionists' interest in unposed moments of life, Degas' motifs tended to be urban figures rather than rural landscapes. Laundresses, ballet ''rats'' (cat. nos. 6, 7), scenes at the race track (cat. no. 5), and pictures of women about their toilet were among his favorite subjects. In contrast to Renoir's straightforward, pagan worship of female flesh, however, Degas viewed his subjects as a means to daring formal inventions. The women in his compositions are impersonal, pallid, and often pictured in awkward positions.

His cynicism was encouraged by his failing eyesight, surely the most terrible loss that a painter can suffer. As his sight worsened, his technique became broader and less detailed. Eventually he came to depend almost entirely on colored chalk worked in broad, dense strokes.

Degas' use of unusually high viewpoints, empty spaces, tilted planes, and images cut off by the edges of the painting owe something to photography and to Japanese prints, but his adaptations of such devices were original and daring. A master draftsman, he used line to define the characteristic, weary slouch of a resting dancer; the lift of a jockey's shoulder as he glances backward; the stretch and yawn of a laundress; or the awkward grace of a nude woman stepping out of her bath. Except for certain portraits, his attitude toward his subjects was detached and objective. Degas broadened the range of Impressionism to include urban-figure compositions; line drawing; and thoughtfully organized, balanced, compositions.

Also a sculptor of great ability, Degas is nevertheless associated in most peoples' minds with painting. His subjects were the same in both arts, as was his concentration on depicting unusual, informal attitudes (cat. no. 8). The flowing contours of his sculptures echo his concern with line drawing in his paintings. Parts of his sculptures often thrust daringly into space and are stabilized only by a carefully calculated balance.

Degas modeled his sculptures in wax and clay and allowed the surfaces to remain uneven, thus suggesting a spontaneous technique. These rough surfaces also break up the light reflected from the surface in a way that parallels the Impressionist painters' rough patches of broken color.

Degas sculpted for almost fifty years but only once exhibited a sculpture, *Little Dancer of Fourteen Years* (Figure 1)—at the 1881 Salon. This well-known work demonstrates Degas' concern for realism and his lack of interest in symbolism. To achieve the highest degree of realism, he dressed this figure in a ballet dancer's skirt, bodice, and shoes; tied the hair with a ribbon; and tinted the face. Aside from a few positive comments such as J.-K. Huysmans' declaration that it was "the one really modern sculpture" in the exhibition, it was met with animosity or indifference.

Degas treated his sculptures much as Cézanne treated his paintings—as evidence of his developing knowledge and skill. Only a few were cast in plaster and none in more permanent material. Around one hundred and fifty pieces were found in his studio after his death; of these, only about seventy were undamaged. These were cast in bronze some two years later.

James Abbott McNeill Whistler (1834-1903)

Born in Massachusetts and raised in Russia, where his father worked as a military engineer, Whistler lived his entire adult life abroad, mostly in London and Paris. Highly eclectic, and hardly the equal of Monet or Degas, he nevertheless took a major step toward abstraction at a very early date.

Whistler had little training as an artist, but he was in Paris in the 1850s and sixties and knew painters such as Gustave Courbet, Edouard Manet, and Henri Fantin-Latour, as well as the poet Charles Baudelaire. Although he well understood French Impressionism, he preferred a more intimate, subjective style based on subtle arrangements of subdued colors and tones.

Figure 1. Edgar Degas, *Little Dancer of Fourteen Years*. Bronze, ca. 1880-81 (cast ca. 1922), h. 99 cm. The Metropolitan Museum of Art, New York, Bequest of Mrs. H. O. Havemeyer, 1922.

Figure 2. James Abbott McNeill Whistler, *Nocturne in Black and Gold: The Falling Rocket*. Oil on oak panel, ca. 1874, 60.3 x 46.7 cm. Copyright 1987 The Detroit Institute of Arts, Gift of Dexter M. Ferry, Jr.

Whistler preferred London to Paris, and the misty light of England to the brilliant sunlight that engrossed the French Impressionists. He also preferred night or evening scenes to those of daylight. For example, in paintings such as *Nocturne in Blue and Gold: Old Battersea Bridge, Nocturne in Black and Gold: The Falling Rocket* (Figure 2), and *Nocturne in Black and Gold: Entrance to Southampton Water* (cat. no. 9), objects are reduced to blurred silhouettes whose substance is lost in velvety darkness.

One of the precursors of the Abstractionists, Whistler stands between the French Impressionists, who rendered reflections of light from the surfaces of nature, and Mark Rothko, who painted abstractions indicating pure light and atmosphere.

Auguste Rodin (1840-1917)

An exact contemporary of the Impressionist painters, Rodin was, in some ways, close to Romantic Realism and to Symbolism. Although elements of Romanticism, Realism, Impressionism, and Symbolism can all be found in his art, he originally shared the abuse aimed by the academic artists, the critics, and the public at the Impressionists; but the power and vigor of his works—so reminiscent of Michelangelo—plus its symbolic content, won for him popular recognition sooner than it came to the Impressionist painters. Official and popular acceptance grew into adulation and he was eventually acclaimed "the greatest sculptor since Michelangelo" and "the only sculptor of genius since Bernini." When he died in 1917 he was honored and revered as a master without peer.

In 1864, one year after Manet's *Luncheon on the Grass* was rejected by the Salon, Rodin's *Man with a Broken Nose* was rejected. Apparently both were too realistic for a jury conditioned by the Romantic and Neoclassical tendencies of such artists as Gérôme, Antoine-Louis Barye, and Albert-Ernest Carrier de Belleuse.

While working in Brussels, in the studio of Horace Lecoq de Boisbaudran, Rodin became acquainted with the powerful Baroque paintings of Peter Paul Rubens, and through Rubens, with the work of Michelangelo. In 1874 he studied Michelangelo's work first-hand in Italy. Impressed by the vitality and force of the Renaissance master's works, Rodin possessed the strength and energy to create the true descendants of Michelangelo's sculptures. At the same time, Donatello's sculptures, developing the idea of strength in repose, were also an important influence on Rodin.

The Italian Renaissance artists were primarily carvers; however, Rodin was, above all, a modeler in clay and wax whose finished work was cast in bronze. These two methods are essentially different: the carver must have an image clearly in mind before beginning to work, whereas the modeler finds it easy to change direction as he goes and his actions are more apt to be concerned with gestures of the figure.

Figure 3. Auguste Rodin, *The Thinker*. Bronze, h. 72.3 cm. The Cleveland Museum of Art, Gift of Alexandre P. Rosenberg, 79.138.

The Age of Bronze (cat. no. 10), which Rodin sent to the 1877 Salon, created a controversy when, due to its great realism, the artist was accused of using a live model to create his plaster mold. A committee of enquiry was appointed, and Rodin finally convinced its members that he was capable of creating such a figure.

In 1880 he was commissioned to do an entrance for the Musée des Arts Décoratif. Inspired by Dante's great poem, *The Inferno*, he labored for about twenty years on *The Gates of Hell*. Although he never completed it, he took from it many of his later figures, of which *The Thinker* (Figure 3) is the best known.

In 1884 he began work on a large group-sculpture, *The Burghers of Calais*, commissioned by the town of Calais to commemorate an heroic event in the town's history: during the Hundred Years' War, a group of leading citizens in Calais offered their lives to English forces in exchange for the safety of their city. The subject was well suited to Rodin's romantic temperament. He completed the sculpture in 1886, but it was 1895 before it was accepted and erected in Calais.

While Rodin's larger works are often symbolic, even allegorical, and seem somewhat pretentious to modern taste, his small studies of arms, legs, hands, and feet emphasize his concern with the gesture of a figure or of a limb. They reflect the first evidence in sculpture of an attitude that became dominant around the mid-twentieth century: that is, to regard the work of art as visual evidence of the artist's ongoing decisions as he struggles to articulate his experience in response to his chosen motif. This approach does not produce finished images that present the artist in a carefully considered way; rather, it produces ingenuous images that reveal the artist's struggle to invent forms and discover their meaning. Such works contributed much to the mainstream of modern Western sculpture; their influence can be discerned in artists as different as Picasso, Julio Gonzalez, Henry Moore, Alexander Calder, and David Smith, among others.

1. Letter from Monet to Bazille, July 15, 1864; see G. Poulain, *Bazille et ses amis* (Paris, 1932), p. 34. Quoted in John Rewald, *The History of Impressionism*, 4th ed. (New York: Museum of Modern Art, 1973), pp. 110-11.

2. Letter from Pissarro to his son Lucien, May 8, 1903, quoted in Rewald, *Impressionism*, p. 258.

3. Later, Monet described to Georges Clemenceau his horror at realizing that as he contemplated Camille on her deathbed, he noticed, above all, the unusual coloring of her flesh. He decided on the spot to paint her one last time. See G. Clemenceau, *Claude Monet* (Paris, 1928), pp. 19-20. Quoted in Rewald, *Impressionism*, p. 431; in Jean Martet, *Georges Clemenceau*, trans. Milton Waldman (London, 1930), p. 203; and in Richardson, *Modern Art*, p. 23.

4. George Heard Hamilton, *Painting and Sculpture in Europe, 1880 to 1940*, The Pelican History of Art (Baltimore: Penguin Books, 1967), p. 18. See also Roger Marx, "Les Nymphéas de M. Claude Monet," *Gazette des Beaux-Arts*, I (1909): 523-31.

The Post-Impressionists

Impressionism was a unified style compared with the art that followed it. Four of the major Post-Impressionists—Paul Cézanne, Georges Seurat, Paul Gauguin, and Vincent van Gogh—gave up the Impressionists' objective goals and empirical methods. Each adapted the rich colors and broken brushstroke of Impressionism for the expression of his own subjective experiences. The complex order of Cézanne's compositions provides a structure for his blunt, virile brushstrokes; Seurat's intricate "machines" were logically constructed with an infinite number of colored dots; pools of resonant color and a pattern of incisive contours make up Gauguin's decorative and symbolic compositions; and van Gogh's impetuous brushstroke, brilliant hues, and distortions of drawing all foster the emotional expressiveness of his canvases. These four Post-Impressionist painters created the bases for the main styles and movements of the first half of the twentieth century: Fauvism, Expressionism, Cubism, and Surrealism.

Paul Cézanne (1839-1906)

A contemporary of the Impressionists, Cézanne spent most of his career working in isolation within range of his home in Aix-en-Provence. Although he was a creative artist of the first magnitude, he had no theoretical program around which disciples could rally and he was temperamentally unsuited to lead a group. Until late in his career, he had no followers, few friends, and hardly any defenders.

Few artists younger than the Impressionists had even heard of Cézanne, until the mid-eighties when Emile Bernard and some other young artists saw several of his paintings at the shop of Père Tanguy, an old color-grinder who occasionally showed Impressionist paintings and sometimes traded supplies for them. In 1890 Bernard published a pamphlet on Cézanne, and in 1891 he and Louis Anquetin openly proclaimed their admiration for this artist in the journal *Echo de Paris*. Most of the Impressionists had disapproved of his early work, but they now recognized his great creative accomplishments. Once aloof and severely critical, Degas even bought one of his paintings. It was not until the birth of Cubism in 1908, however, that his true legacy was established.

Cézanne was introduced to the incipient Impressionists in Paris in 1861 by his close boyhood friend Emile Zola, a defender of these young artists whose paintings he regarded as counterparts of his own naturalistic novels. Cézanne's inability to hold his own in witty café discussions with Manet and Degas, plus his gauche appearance and provincial manners (which he exaggerated in the presence of the fastidious Manet), earned him an undeserved reputation as an uncouth peasant type. He neither boycotted the annual Salons, as did Monet and Degas, nor modified his art to win acceptance, as did Manet. He submitted his work every year, hoping for its acceptance but expecting refusal.[1] He always submitted one of his most innovative canvases, convinced that its rejection would ultimately demonstrate the incompetence of the jury to judge his work.

In 1870, to escape service in the war with Prussia, Cézanne retired to L'Estaque, a small Mediterranean port near Marseilles, where he began painting out of doors. Two years later he joined Pissarro in Pontoise and, influenced by the older artist, attempted to work in the Impressionist manner. At the insistence of Pissarro, and over the objections of Degas and Monet, he exhibited in the first show by this group in 1874. The third group exhibition, in 1877, was the only other time he exhibited with the Impressionists, thus subjecting a number of them to the embarrassment of exhibiting with such an "ungifted fellow." It would seem that he was right not to join in their other exhibitions, for his solidly constructed, complex compositions are the antithesis of Impressionism's empirical realism and lack of concern for pictorial structure.

The Impressionists recorded their retinal sensations of light reflected from the surfaces of nature, whereas Cézanne defined the order that he conceived as underlying nature's surface. Impressionism proceeded by inductive methods; Cézanne, by intuition. Impressionism rejected formalism, Cézanne emphasized it. The Impressionists selected corners of nature as motifs, although light was their real subject. Cézanne also took motifs from nature, but his subject was always his inner sense of an integrated structure beneath their surfaces. Monet painted subjects such as the façade of Rouen Cathedral and haystacks many times because when the light changed, his subject changed. Cézanne painted many versions of the Mont-Sainte-Victoire—one of which is in Cleveland (cat. no.13)—because he found ever more effective ways of recording his vision of underlying order. The Impressionist's world was in constant flux; Cézanne's world was immutable and dependent upon balanced tensions. Impressionist paintings are delightful; Cézanne's, majestic.

Cézanne created a "language" of visual form appropriate for the articulation of his "little sensation" before nature. This sensation involved both an acute, sensuous, subjective response to his motif and an intense will to form. It was essential that he work in contact with nature, else he would surely have foundered between the excessive urges of his emotions and the restraints of his intellect.

His paintings seem to have been of little interest to Cézanne once they were completed. Sometimes he left them in the countryside where he had been working; sometimes he allowed them to be used to clean his studio; and sometimes he permitted his young son to cut them up. Since his main concern was the invention of appropriate means to express his subjective experience of reality, he regarded the finished paintings merely as evidence of that process. He was fearful, however, that other painters would steal his discoveries and try to use them to advance their own careers. This fear was realized in the early twentieth century when hordes of "Cézannesque" artists aped his methods, pathetically mistaking means for ends. In the hands of numerous, less gifted painters, devices such as modeling with color and developing images in terms of geometrical forms were hardened into a new "academic" system. Cézanne had foreseen just such a danger when he wrote to the young Georges Rouault: "If they organize my triumph, do not believe in it; if they try to create a school in my name tell them that they have never understood, never loved what I have done."[2]

Beginning in 1908, however, Pablo Picasso and Georges Braque adapted Cézanne's innovations for the invention of Cubism, a style that altered the course of modern art. Cézanne's pictorial vocabulary was invented as an efficient means of expressing his "little sensation," and his meaning was affected, in turn, by his pictorial "language." His transparent watercolors, for example, with their broad, patchy brushwork, summarize the artist's concept of the essential form of a landscape or still life without developing surface details or suggesting textures. They resulted from Cézanne's attempt to condense the structure of a particular landscape. These studies, in turn, influenced his late, thinly painted, highly structured, nearly abstract oil paintings.

Meyer Schapiro pointed out that on the surfaces of Cézanne's canvases:

The visible world. . . .is recreated through strokes of color among which are many that we cannot identify with an object and yet are necessary for the harmony of the whole. If his touch of pigment is a bit of nature (a tree, a fruit) and a bit of sensation (green, red), it is also an element of construction which binds sensations or objects.[3]

Picasso aptly remarked that it is the drama of Cézanne that makes him a vital and exciting figure for us.[4] That drama is the heroic struggle by a highly imaginative, emotional human being to control his intense feelings while creating visual forms that reflect his sense of order in nature.

Georges Seurat (1859-1891)

Seurat also adapted Impressionist technique to a complex pictorial structure. Where Cézanne sought to control a Romantic temperament, however, Seurat was inherently methodical and rational.

Born in Paris in 1859, Seurat spent two years studying at the Ecole Nationale des Beaux-Arts with Henri Lehmann, a pupil of Ingres. He then put in a year of military service before returning to his studies. His father was a minor legal official with an adequate income. Most important, however, both parents were interested in art and encouraged his career. Seurat was thus spared financial worries, nor did he have to endure the opposition of his father, as did Cézanne and Pissarro.

Seurat admired the work of Ingres, Delacroix, Veronese, and Piero della Francesca and was interested in the many color theories that abounded in the nineteenth century—especially that of the scientist and poet Charles Henry.[5] Applying his own eclectic theory and his methodical technique to painting meant that he worked slowly (he took two years to finish *La Grande Jatte*) but constantly, as though sensing that he would have just a few years to accomplish his aims.

Like Degas and Ingres, Seurat was introverted and proud—one might almost say haughty. Like Cézanne, he worked alone, developing his methods and theories in secret, afraid that others would appropriate his discoveries. He complained that he had too many followers of poor talent, yet his closest colleague, Paul Signac, constantly recruited more artists for the Pointillist movement.

Seurat's theoretical contributions lay in two directions: a practical scientific analysis of light through the use of color and the notion that the formal elements of color, line, and composition can express feelings.

The first of these two problems he attacked in earnest following the exhibition of his first major canvas, *The Bathers*, at the exhibition of the "Groupe des Artistes Indépendants" in 1884. Measuring almost seven by ten feet, this large painting had been rejected by the Salon jury that year. Paul Signac, then a young painter interested in the Impressionists' intuitive experiments using color to suggest light, was impressed by the picture and sought out Seurat to acquaint him with Impressionist ideas and methods. Following the exhibition, Seurat repainted part of his composition, eliminating earth tones and substituting prismatic hues. From that moment on, he carefully studied various scientific color theories and then developed his own theory, which he put in a letter to Maurice Beaubourg written shortly before his death:

Esthetic

Art is harmony.
Harmony is the analogy of opposites, the
analogy of similar elements, of *value, hue,*
and *line*, considered according to their
dominants and under the influence of
lighting, in gay, calm, or sad combinations.

The opposites are:

For *value*, a more luminous for a darker one.
    light

For *hue*, the complementaries, i.e., a certain red
opposed to its complementary, etc.
    red-green
    orange-blue
    yellow-violet

For *line*, those forming a right angle.[6]

Figure 4. Georges Seurat, *Sunday Afternoon on the Island of La Grande Jatte*. Oil on canvas, 1884-86, 207.6 x 308 cm. Helen Birch Bartlett Memorial Collection, 1926.224,

Figure 5. Georges Seurat, *Le Chahut*. Oil on canvas, 1889-90, 169 x 139 cm.

In *Sunday Afternoon on the Island of La Grande Jatte* (Figure 4), for example, a section of the grassy area in shadow is dominated by the local color—the green of the grass—with scattered strokes of orange to suggest the effect of filtered sunlight; dark violet, to introduce the complement of the yellowish green of the grass; and blue, which becomes denser toward the line of demarcation between the shadowed area and a sunlit section of grass. Thus, Seurat combined local colors, the effect of illumination and of shadows in accordance with the laws of contrast, gradation, and irradiation.

He also experimented with different moods suggested by formal arrangements. The somnolent air of *La Grand Jatte*, for example, is established with long, repeated horizontal lines and planes. Vertical figures and trees form stable right angles with the horizontals and repeated regular curves and balanced tones all add to the composition's quietude and stability. The forced gaiety of *Le Chahut* (Figure 5), on the other hand, is suggested by the many upsurging diagonals and light, warm colors.

In his letter to Beaubourg, Seurat also mentioned the symbolic possibilities of line, color, and composition:

Gaiety of value *is the light dominant of* hue *the warm dominant; of* line, *lines above the horizontal.*

Calmness of value is the equality of dark and light; of hue, of warm and cool; and the horizontal for line.

Sadness of value is the dark dominant; of hue, the cool dominant; and of line, downward directions.[7]

Thus, Seurat indicated emotions by applying a logical formula to his painting. He denied that the poetry that others claimed to see in his work was really there. ''I apply my method,'' he said to Charles Angrand, ''and that is all there is to it.''[8] The poetry is really there, however, for it was not his method that was responsible for the quality of his work, it was his genius. Other artists adopted his painting theories and techniques, but none achieved the poetic quality of Seurat's canvases.

During his short career Seurat completed only seven major figure compositions: *The Bathers, Sunday Afternoon on the Island of La Grand Jatte, The Side Show, Le Chahut, The Models, The Circus*, and *Young Woman Powdering Herself*. During the summer months he painted limpid, richly nuanced seascapes and landscapes, and did oil sketches for larger compositions.

Seurat thought of progress in terms of scientific method, and he painted his pictures as a scientist might develop a theory. Beginning with observations of nature, he questioned his assumptions and revised his concepts as the work developed. His creative process was always under the control of a systematic methodology. Even more than the Impressionists, he tried to achieve the luminosity of light by methodically organizing colors on the surface of the painting.

Seurat's paintings, like the scientist's hypotheses, represent, rather than reproduce, reality. They are fantasies that, at the same time, describe nature. Despite his devotion to theory and to rules, he was boldly inventive. Indeed, his method seems to have relieved him of uncertainties, permitting him freedom within loose limits.

Vincent van Gogh (1853-1890)

The eldest son of a Dutch Calvinist clergyman, Vincent van Gogh was a passionate observer of human problems who wanted only to alleviate the sufferings of the poor. At first he tried to fit into an acceptable social pattern. At sixteen he joined the firm of Goupil and Co., international art dealers, who had bought his uncle's business. He was unsuited to sell paintings, however, for he reacted intensely to works of art and expressed himself freely to potential customers. Beginning at the Hague branch of Goupil's, he moved briefly to their Brussels gallery and then in 1873 was transferred to London. In 1875 he was reassigned to Paris, where his unorthodox business procedures and violent arguments with his fellow workers finally caused his dismissal.

In 1877 Vincent entered school to prepare for a career as a minister. After failing the examinations, he volunteered as a lay preacher in the Borinage, the poverty-stricken coal mining district of Belgium. He was quickly dismissed from this post, but he remained in the area and began to draw the miners and their families and to make copies of Jean François Millet's paintings of peasants. Finally he left the Borinage to study with his cousin by marriage, Anton Mauve, a popular landscape painter in The Hague. His paintings of this period are dark, intensely sympathetic renderings of peasants and miners carrying out the everyday tasks of their dull lives. *The Potato Eaters* (Figure 6) has the typically impassioned brushstroke, dark values, and strong but awkward drawing of this period. Van Gogh wrote: ''I have wanted to make it clear how these people, eating their potatoes, under the

Figure 6. Vincent van Gogh, *The Potato Eaters*. Oil on canvas, signed, 1885, 82 x 114 cm. Vincent van Gogh Foundation, Rijksmuseum Vincent van Gogh, Amsterdam.

lamplight have dug in the earth with those very hands they put in the dish, and so it speaks of *manual labor*, and how they have honestly earned their food."[9]

Following the sudden death of his father, Vincent went to study at the academy in Antwerp and was overwhelmed by his first encounter with the paintings of Rubens. At the same time, he also discovered Japanese prints. The following year his brother Theo, who was now a successful art dealer at Goupil's, brought him to Paris. He studied first at Cormon's Studio but found the academic atmosphere oppressive, relieved only by the presence of a fellow student, Henri de Toulouse-Lautrec. Vincent spent almost two years in Paris working under the influence of the Impressionists, which led him to lighten his colors and his touch with the brush, and gave him, temporarily, a more objective style.

The agitated tempo of Paris was too much for van Gogh's already overstrained nervous system, however, and in February 1888 he left for the south of France. The next two years, spent in Arles, were the most intensely creative of his career. Like Cézanne, he had gone through an Impressionist period but found the dissolution of form into light reflections an unsatisfying goal. Where Cézanne developed complex formal structures, however, van Gogh pursued his natural tendency toward emotional expressiveness. The extreme distortions in the paintings that he did in Arles, Saint-Rémy (cat. no. 14), and Auvers during the last three years of his life had great influence on early twentieth-century Fauvism and Expressionism. Distortions of formal elements for expressive purposes were not new, but van Gogh's expressionism was more extreme than that of earlier artists. For example, he wrote to Theo about *Night Café*: "I have tried to express in this picture the terrible passions of humanity by means of red and green. The room is blood red and dark yellow with a green billiard table in the middle . . . . Everywhere there is a violet and blue in the figures of the little sleeping tramps, in the empty dreary room . . . . The color is not true . . . it is a color suggesting some emotions of an ardent temperament.[10]

During his stay in Paris, van Gogh had been impressed by the witty and urbane Paul Gauguin, and he urged him to come to Arles, where the two of them could form the nucleus of a "Studio of the South." Gauguin, living in poverty in Brittany, agreed, and in October of 1888, financed by Theo van Gogh, he traveled to Arles. From the beginning, the arrogant and sardonic Gauguin antagonized the intensely nervous and sincere van Gogh. For a short time they managed to work together and van Gogh even completed a few works under Gauguin's influence. However, after three tempestuous months that culminated in a violent quarrel during which Vincent attempted to attack Gauguin with a razor and finally slashed off his own ear, Gauguin fled back to Paris.

In May of 1889 Vincent entered an asylum at Saint-Rémy near Arles. Here he alternated between periods of lucidity, during which he worked hard, and periods of complete collapse. The following spring Theo brought him to Auvers, near Paris, and put him in the care of Dr. Paul Gachet. Gachet had been among the first to appreciate and patronize the Impressionists, and under his sympathetic eye Vincent completed the last paintings of his short, tragic life. Among these works is an admirable portrait (cat. no. 15) of the daughter of the Ravoux family with whom he was staying.

The end was near, however, for Vincent realized the hopelessness of his future and bitterly regretted the trouble that he caused Theo and his bride. Finally, on the evening of July 27th, the artist shot himself and two days later died.

Paul Gauguin (1848-1903)

Paul Gauguin's father was a journalist from Orléans with strong Republican convictions. His maternal grandfather was a painter and lithographer; his maternal grandmother was a militant socialist who was related to the Borgias of Aragon, several of whom had served as viceroys to Peru. As a consequence, when Louis Napoleon brought off a coup d'etat in 1851, his parents fled with their three-year-old son to Peru. His father died on the journey, however.

After living in Lima for four years, the family returned to France. Gauguin attended a religious school in Orléans and at seventeen joined the Navy. His mother died when he was twenty-three, and he returned to Paris to enter a stockbrokerage firm. Soon after, he married.

As his income increased, Gauguin decided to collect Impressionist paintings. He and another stockbroker, Emile Schuffenecker, began to paint on weekends, and in 1876 Gauguin had a painting accepted in the Salon. Camille Pissarro investigated this curious stockbroker who painted and bought Impressionist pictures. The older painter undertook to teach him Impressionist theories and practices and insisted that Gauguin exhibit with the Impressionists in their group shows.

By 1880, to his wife's chagrin, Gauguin had adopted painting as a career and had moved his family to Rouen, where he expected to live more cheaply. He then moved his family to Copenhagen to live with his wife's family, but finding life there unbearable returned to Paris with his son Clovis.

Convinced that Europeans lived according to a fabric of outmoded conventions, and that official art in France was a tissue of falsehoods, Gauguin sought out one of the most primitive cultures in France—at Pont-Aven, a village in Brittany—where he believed he could reinvent the art of painting by being simple, direct, and true to his basic feelings. After a couple of months, however, he returned to Paris, disappointed at the extent to which conventional civilization had penetrated Brittany. A year later he embarked for Panama with his friend Charles Laval, but because of a typhus epidemic there, they moved on to Martinique, where he found lush, tropical colors; a brilliant sun; and a more primitive society than that in Brittany.

Soon, he returned to Pont-Aven, where he had become a celebrity. Happier in Brittany this time, he wrote to his friend Schuffenecker: "I love Brittany. I find wildness and primitiveness there. When my wooden shoes ring on this granite, I hear the muffled, dull, and powerful tone which I try to achieve in my painting."[11] About this time, he became aware of Japanese prints, with their firm contour lines that surrounded decorative shapes of flat color.

One of the many young painters who visited Gauguin at Pont-Aven was Emile Bernard, who was bursting with theories acquired from the Symbolist writer G.-Albert Aurier. As a result of this meeting, Gauguin's painting began to take on firmer form, reflecting Bernard's theories. Subsequently a dispute arose between the two as to which of them was responsible for the original development of Synthetism.[12]

Gauguin was corresponding with Vincent van Gogh in Arles. Struggling with the symbolism of color, van Gogh found many of the ideas expressed in Gauguin's letters related to his own efforts. So at Vincent and Theo van Gogh's urging, Gauguin joined Vincent in Provence. The tragic story of the short-lived association of the two in Arles is well known. Gauguin's self-centered egoism, his cold willingness to sacrifice anyone for his art, and his domination of those around him assured conflict with the rough-mannered, volatile, and sensitive van Gogh.

Gauguin returned to Paris and with close friends organized an exhibition, "Impressioniste and Synthetiste," at the World's Fair of 1889. Nothing was sold, however, and the scant notices the exhibition received came from critics such as Félix Fénéon and Aurier, who were already well aware of these painters. The only satisfaction for Gauguin was that many younger artists were interested in the exhibition.

Two years later, Gauguin sold thirty paintings at an auction of his works in order to raise money to go to Tahiti, since Georges Clemenceau (then editor of *La Justice*) had supported a petition by which the government would send him there on a special mission, without salary. In late June, 1891, after a three-month voyage, he arrived in the South Seas island and settled near the shore.

Important changes now began to occur in Gauguin's painting. He modified the modeling of his forms and enriched his flat, colored shapes by merging various hues within them. Contours became sensuous, with interrelated, decorative curves. Gauguin wrote:

In order to explain my Tahitian art, since it is held to be incomprehensible: as I want to suggest an exuberant and wild nature and a tropical sun which sets on fire everything around it, I have to give my figures an appropriate frame. It really is open-air life, although intimate; in the thickets and the shaded brooks, those whispering women in an immense palace decorated by nature itself with all the riches Tahiti holds. Hence these fabulous colors and this fiery yet softened and silent air.

But all this does not exist!

Yes, it exists as the equivalent of the grandeur and profundity of this mystery of Tahiti, when it must be expressed on a canvas one meter square.[13]

In May of 1893 Gauguin returned to France to find that Cézanne and the Nabis (a group of young artists) were gaining in fame. The dealer Durand-Ruel was beginning to have success in selling Impressionist canvases, and he seemed interested in Gauguin's pictures. Best of all, Gauguin received a modest inheritance from an uncle in Orléans. He soon squandered it, however, in flamboyant living with a Javanese mistress, Annah, and it was not long before misfortune overtook him: an exhibition of his Tahitian works at Durand-Ruel's was a financial disaster, his ankle was broken in a brawl with some sailors in Brittany, and Annah ransacked his studio in Paris.

Despondent, Gauguin returned to Tahiti in July 1895. From this point until his death (1903), his life was one of constant work and suffering. He was ill with syphilis and spent time in prison. In 1898 he failed in a suicide attempt. In 1901 he left Tahiti for the Marquesas Islands, where he painted some of the most sensuous, colorful, and imaginative works of his career, including *L'Appel* (cat. no. 17).

Henri Rousseau (1844-1910)

Five years younger than Cézanne and fifteen years older than Seurat, Rousseau is of the Post-Impressionist generation. Although his paintings demonstrate that he shared their subjective approach to the creative act, he always insisted that he worked from nature. He also was as intuitively concerned with tightly ordered composition as was Cézanne and Seurat. Unlike them, however, he never used the patchy Impressionist brushstroke; indeed, it was antithetical to his tight, highly finished, detailed technique. Guillaume Apollinaire went so far as to label Rousseau the Uccello of the twentieth century.

Following two enlistments in the French Army, Rousseau served for fourteen years as a customs inspector, and then retired, at about age forty, to devote himself to painting. Like most untrained artists, he was obsessed with recording the details of his subjects. In all probability, the main influence on his art was the many anonymous folk paintings that flooded Europe and the New World during the nineteenth century. He himself reported, however, that he ''worked alone without any master but nature and some advice from Gérôme and Clement.''[14]

Rousseau's technique was similar to that of all folk painters, but his exotic subject matter recalls Gauguin, and his innate sense of formal structure relates him to Cézanne and Seurat. Furthermore, the dreamlike scenes of his paintings, their enigmatic and poetic subjects, as well as their logically unrelated images, precede similar concerns by the Surrealists in the twentieth century.

Although Rousseau publicly claimed to achieve realism by observing nature, he privately confessed that formal reasons accounted for the placement of many objects in his paintings.[15] For example, he admitted to Andre Salmon that in *The Dream* (Figure 7), the sofa on which the nude female figure reclines in the middle of a jungle "is there only because of its glowing red color."

The meticulously detailed surfaces of Rousseau's canvases do not conceal the underlying formal order of his paintings—an order that reveals a vision of the world that is as structured and poetic as Seurat's, Max Planck's, and Albert Einstein's.

Figure 7. Henri Rousseau, *The Dream*. Oil on canvas, 1910, 204.5 x 299 cm. Collection, The Museum of Modern Art, New York, Gift of Nelson A. Rockefeller.

1. Only once was this expectation disappointed. In 1882 Antoine Guillemet, who as a juror that year had the right to choose one of his pupils' works to be included without judgment, selected a painting by Cézanne, even though their relationship had never been one of pupil and teacher.

2. Bernard Dorival, *Cézanne* (Paris: Pierre Tisne, 1948), p. 105.

3. Meyer Schapiro, *Cézanne* (New York: Harry N. Abrams, 1965), p. 10.

4. Alfred H. Barr, Jr., *Picasso: Fifty Years of His Art* (New York: Museum of Modern Art, 1980), p. 274.

5. Other color theories that interested Seurat include those by: Michel Eugène Chevreul, Charles Blanc, David Sutter, James Clerk Maxwell, Hermann von Helmholtz, and Ogden Rood.

6. William Innes Homer, *Seurat and the Science of Painting* (Cambridge: M.I.T. Press, 1964), pp. 186-87.

7. Ibid, p. 187.

8. John Rewald, *Post-Impressionism: From Van Gogh to Gauguin* (New York: Museum of Modern Art, 1977), p. 104.

9. Van Gogh, letter dated 30 April '85 to his brother Theo. Reproduced in *Van Gogh: A Self-Portrait*, letters selected by W. H. Auden (Greenwich: New York Graphic Society, 1961), p. 237.

10. Rewald, *Post-Impressionism*, p. 210.

11. Ibid., p. 171.

12. Synthetism rejected the analytical creative process of Impressionism in favor of a synthetic procedure in which nature was represented by broad, flat areas of color with definite edges. Color, drawing, and spatial relations were distorted for the sake of decoration and expression. Content was communicated by formal means. Maurice Denis suggested that works of art be regarded as metaphors for the artists' feelings.

13. Rewald, *Post-Impressionism*, p. 487.

14. Quoted in Daniel Catton Rich, *Henri Rousseau* (New York: Museum of Modern Art, 1942), p. 14.

15. Ibid., pp. 69, 73.

The Inventors of Cubism: Picasso and Braque

Analytical Cubism, 1908-12

The most radical and influential movement in twentieth-century art was Cubism. First appearing in 1908 in paintings by Pablo Picasso (1881-1973) and Georges Braque (1882-1963), it transformed the dominant intention in art from that of rendering natural objects and phenomena to that of creating purely aesthetic objects by investigating the materials and means of art itself. Many abstract styles and movements developed out of the Cubist inventions of Picasso and Braque. Even Surrealism, which emerged during the teens and early twenties in opposition to the formalism of Cubism, is in some ways indebted to it. The main phases of this movement—Analytical Cubism (1908-12) and Synthetic Cubism (1912-25)—overlap and contain variations within themselves.[1]

During the first decade of the twentieth century, relativity and quantum theories were developed in the physical sciences to challenge the absolute reign of Newtonian physics. Traditional notions such as absolute space and time, elementary solid particles, the causal nature of physical phenomena, and the ideal of an objective description of nature lost validity when extended to the far reaches of the universe and to the subatomic world. Neither artistic traditions—such as rectilinear perspective to indicate space, and the modeling of forms to suggest volume—nor traditional scientific concepts could be applied in the new regions being explored by artists and scientists.

Analytical Cubist paintings done by Picasso and Braque between 1908 and 1912 were developed by analyzing the forms of natural objects and also, of course, by invention. Synthetic Cubist paintings, done from 1912 on, are not based upon the artist's direct visual experience of nature, although they invariably refer to subjects from the natural world. Like all verbal designations—even the most scientific—the terms Analytical and Synthetic Cubism are only approximately true, but they are useful.

The immediate harbinger of Cubism was a large canvas by Picasso entitled *Les Demoiselles d'Avignon (The Young Ladies of Avignon;* Figure 8), painted in 1906-7. (The title refers to a brothel on a street named Avignon in Barcelona.) Picasso began the painting as an allegory, a "memento mori," perhaps as a challenge to Henri Matisse's *Joie de Vivre (The Joy of Life;* Figure 9), which had created a sensation in the Salon d'Automne of 1906. During its creation, the *Demoiselles* underwent numerous changes, losing its obvious allegorical character as it became increasingly formalistic. It displays two distinct styles and influences: that of early Iberian art, which Picasso acknowledged had influenced the three figures on the left side of the composition, and that of African masks and sculptures, which he denied had influenced the two figures on the right.[2]

Of all the people to whom Picasso showed the canvas in 1907, only Braque responded to it positively. Although he belonged to a group of artists led by Matisse, called Les Fauves (The Wild Beasts),

Figure 8. Pablo Picasso, *Les Demoiselles d'Avignon.* Oil on canvas, 1907, 243.8 x 233.7 cm. Collection, The Museum of Modern Art, New York, Acquired through the Lillie P. Bliss Bequest.

Braque looked to Cézanne for inspiration and was more concerned with structure and formal order than the other members of that group. After seeing Picasso's *Demoiselles*, Braque broke with Fauvism, painted a figure titled *Great Nude*—which seems clearly to be indebted to Picasso's picture—and soon thereafter began a five-year collaboration with the Spanish painter.

By 1907 Picasso was edging Matisse for leadership of the Parisian avant-garde. He had enjoyed some financial success and had developed a following among the young Spanish artists and poets living in Paris. Having already gone through a period in which he was influenced by Toulouse-Lautrec, he passed through his "Blue Period" and his "Rose Period." In addition to many Spanish companions, Picasso now acquired French friends such as the poets André Salmon, Max Jacob, Guillaume Apollinaire, Pierre Reverdy, and Maurice Raynal, and an amateur mathematician named Maurice Princet.

Accounts by his mistress, Fernande, and by Gertrude Stein reveal that even as a young man Picasso's strong ego caused him to resent playing second fiddle to the considerably older Matisse. At the Stein's Saturday afternoon salons, where they often met, the contrast between the two artists was striking: Picasso, unfamiliar with the language, sardonic, and contemptuous of the failure of others to understand him; Matisse, charming, urbane, and witty. When he appeared without his coterie, Picasso was ill at ease, reticent, and sullen; surrounded by friends, however, he became enthusiastic and confident.

Since only Braque seemed to appreciate the *Demoiselles*, Picasso rolled up the canvas and stored it away. It remained hidden until 1939, when the Museum of Modern Art in New York borrowed it for his retrospective exhibition. Unfinished and executed in two different styles, it is nevertheless a crucial picture in the development of twentieth-century art; it signaled a break with traditional ways of picturing the world and introduced a new vocabulary of pictorial form.

Cubism surely had no direct connection (as is sometimes suggested) with Einstein's special theory of relativity, published in 1905. On one occasion when this comparison was made, Einstein rejected it, explaining that "a multiplicity of systems of coordinates is not needed for the representation of a single, specific case " in science, whereas "this is quite different in the case of Picasso's painting."[3] Nevertheless, while a complete picture could have been developed from any one of the viewpoints indicated in a Cubist painting, Picasso chose to represent multiple points of view. In short, the analogy is not between a Cubist painting and the way a relativist scientist represents reality but, rather, between the painting and the way the scientist perceives reality. At any rate, both relativity and Cubism rejected the notion of absolute space, both indicated the interpenetration of space and matter, and both embraced the idea of structure as emerging from a process of action and reaction rather than according to any a priori plan.

Figure 9. Henri Matisse, French, 1869-1954, *Joie de Vivre*. Oil on canvas, 1905-6, 174 x 238.1 cm. Copyright The Barnes Foundation, Merion, Pennsylvania.

Braque spent the summer of 1909 painting at La Roche-Guyon and Carrières-St. Denis in Normandy, while Picasso spent the summer at Horta de San Juan (also known as Horta de Ebro) in Spain. The two painters returned to Paris in the fall with their summer's production and were surprised at how similar their paintings were. From then until the summer of 1914, these two artists collaborated so closely that it is sometimes difficult to tell their work apart. Braque later remarked: "Closely linked with Picasso in spite of our widely different temperaments we were guided by a common idea . . . . Picasso is Spanish, I am French . . . but we said together during those years things that no one will ever say again . . . things that would be incomprehensible and that have given us so much pleasure . . . . It was rather like being roped mountaineers."[4]

It was an unlikely association, for Braque was one of the youngest and least known of Matisse's followers, whereas Picasso had already achieved notoriety and some success as Matisse's rival. Braque was tall, athletic, good-humored, logical, and possessed impeccable taste. Picasso was short, stocky, unathletic, intuitive, and never hesitated to violate taste in pursuit of invention. In working together for nearly five years, each took the lead at times, and each learned from the other. Like Cézanne before him, Picasso learned to subordinate his ardent temperament to a conscious will to formal order, while Braque learned to be more daring.

In 1907 Daniel-Henry Kahnweiler, a German expatriate, exhibited the works of these two artists in his gallery. In November 1908 he showed a group of Braque's paintings that had been rejected by the Salon d'Automne; in reviewing this show, the art critic Louis Vauxcelles coined the word "cubes" to describe Braque's new works (the word was probably suggested to him by Matisse, who accompanied him on his visit to the exhibition.) The term was not inappropriate. Early Cubist paintings by both Braque and Picasso defined objects in terms of geometrical shapes derived from exterior appearances. Restricting their palettes to earth tones, they rendered their subjects in terms of general, rather than individual, characteristics.

By 1909 both artists were using strong contrasts of value to model forms. Paintings such as Picasso's *Fan, Salt Box, and Melon* (cover and cat. no. 20) clearly suggest three-dimensional objects in space and at the same time reveal the artist's effort to produce a synthesis of the two- and three-dimensional compositions—a problem that Cézanne had struggled with for years. By 1910 Picasso and Braque were fragmenting objects and space into small facets arranged parallel to the painting's surface, and they had adopted Cézanne's device of *passage* (the running together of planes otherwise separated in space). They also expanded Cézanne's practice of combining several typical views of an object in a single, composite image.

Figure 10. Georges Braque, *Le Portugais.* Oil on canvas, 1911, 117 x 81.5 cm. Kunstmuseum Basel, Öffentliche Kunstsammlung.

Picasso and Braque defined space as well as material objects by planes that parallel the picture surface, intersecting and sliding into one another, visually integrating mass and space. By 1911 these small translucent planes—advancing, retreating, and interpenetrating—comprised a kind of thick web across the canvas's surface. In paintings from late 1911 and 1912 these facets nearly obscure the definition of larger objects, making it difficult to perceive these elements as separate from their background: discrete forms in space thus gave way to a comprehensive, pictorial space that incorporated all objects within it.

At the same time, theoretical physicists were developing a model of reality as a universal flux in which solid matter appeared to dissolve into energy. Concepts such as "isolated object" and "material substance" lost their meaning, and reality was pictured as a dynamic web of coherent patterns of energy. Both art and physics thus replaced the image of a world of discrete material forms existing within absolute space with that of a world in which space and matter merge.

The Cubists, like many scientists, retreated from empiricism and created increasingly abstract pictures of the world. Picasso once remarked to Marius de Zayas: "Art is not truth. Art is a lie that makes us realize truth, at least the truth that is given us to understand."[5] A noted mathematician, Morris Kline, comments similarly: "Science is rationalized fiction, rationalized by mathematics."[6]

As early as 1910 the hermeticism of their paintings began to concern Picasso and Braque. They sought to provide the viewer with clues whereby he could orient himself vis-a-vis their subject matter. For example, Braque included trompe-l'oeil nails in at least two of his compositions, and he stenciled letters across a large painting titled *Le Portugais (The Portuguese*; Figure 10) to indicate a stable plane relating the figure to intervening space.

Picasso and Braque had followers, imitators, and supporters. The most important group, formed around the Duchamp brothers (Jacques Villon, Marcel Duchamp, and the sculptor Raymond Duchamp-Villon) created a Cubist theory and program of their own. At various times this group included Albert Gleizes, Jean Metzinger, Juan Gris, Robert Delaunay, Frantisek Kupka, Fernand Léger, and Roger de la Fresnaye. They called their group La Section d'Or, indicating their devotion to mathematical theory, an attitude foreign to Braque and Picasso. Gleizes and Metzinger, the main theorists, published their ideas in the book *Du Cubisme* in 1912. Ironically, this group was probably better known to the general public as Cubists than were the two creators of the style.

The influence of Cubism was also felt outside France. Artists from Germany—Ernst Ludwig Kirchner, Franz Marc, Paul Klee, Vasily Kandinsky, and Lyonel Feininger—visited Paris to meet the Cubists, and some of the Cubists were invited to exhibit in Germany. Robert Delaunay had the greatest influence on foreign artists: his particular brand of Cubism was dubbed "Orphism" by

Apollinaire to indicate its colorful and lyrical character. The combative Italian Futurists adapted the Cubist vocabulary in order to realize their objective of celebrating the dynamic character of the world. (Incidentally, science had postulated four forces—gravity, electromagnetism, a strong nuclear force, and a weak nuclear force—as underlying all phenomena in the universe.) In Holland Piet Mondrian, Theo van Doesburg, and Bart van der Leck evolved a pure, abstract style (Neoplasticism), derived from Cubism. Kasimir Malevich, Mikhail Larionov, Nathalie Gontcharova, El Lissitzky, Naum Gabo, Antoine Pevsner, Vladimir Tatlin, and Alexandre Rodchenko, among other artists in Russia, developed abstract styles such as Rayonism, Suprematism, Non-Objectivism, and Constructivism—all of which were related to Cubism. Americans Morgan Russell and Stanton MacDonald-Wright were in Paris at the time and developed Synchromism, an offshoot of Delaunay's Orphism.

Papiers Collés and Collages, 1912-14

Cubist collages provide a transitional development between the Analytical and Synthetic phases of the movement. In 1912 Picasso created a small, oval composition, *Still Life with Chair Caning*, that incorporates lettering and a piece of oilcloth stamped with the texture of chair caning into its composition. This bit of material from the commercial world opened the door to collages and assemblages. Rather than create an illusion of visible reality, Picasso created an aesthetic object that is as real and independent as the objects to which it obliquely refers. As an added touch of irony, he framed this oval painting with a rope.

Picasso and Braque now began to attach a variety of materials to the surfaces of their paintings and drawings. Shapes cut from wallpaper or newspapers, bottle labels, bits of wood, and other objects were pasted (collaged) to the surfaces of paintings and drawings to become integral elements in the compositions. Fixing such extraneous materials to the picture surface challenged the tradition of brushing colored pigment onto a flat surface so as to indicate natural objects in illusory space. The short, brusque brushstrokes of Analytical Cubism gradually disappeared and images were more clearly defined with large, flat planes. At the same time, the world of visual reality was given up as the point of departure for the work of art. Conception replaced perception as the artist's inspiration.

In their Analytical Cubist paintings Picasso and Braque, like Cézanne, had found it necessary to work from nature in order to articulate their sense of underlying structure. With the collages and *papiers collés* of 1913-14, they shifted their approach from formal analyses of objects and space to the construction of purely aesthetic forms—a shift that led to the final phase of Cubism.

Figure 11. Pablo Picasso, *Three Musicians*. Oil on canvas, 1921, 200.7 x 222.9 cm. Collection, The Museum of Modern Art, New York, Mrs. Simon Guggenheim Fund.

Synthetic Cubism, 1913-25

Theoretically, the creation of a Synthetic Cubist painting consisted of organizing abstract shapes, and then developing these until they suggested natural objects. Juan Gris succinctly explained the process by noting that while Cézanne had turned a bottle into a cylinder, he turned a cylinder into a bottle.[7]

Like traditional art from the Renaissance through Analytical Cubism, classical science started with empirical facts that would then be put into formal (mathematical) terms. The heliocentric theory of the solar system, for example, had been developed in just this way by Copernicus. In a development paralleling Synthetic Cubism, however, scientists now began to derive conclusions about reality from purely formal premises. For example, mathematical considerations alone led James Clerk Maxwell to assert that there are electromagnetic waves that cannot be detected by the senses. In the early twentieth century, scientists such as Einstein, Max Planck, Niels Bohr, Paul Dirac, Louis de Broglie, and Werner Heisenberg all refer to their initial experiences of symmetry from which they derived relevant mathematical equations, and only then sought to find analogies with "reality." In late nineteenth- and early twentieth-century art and science, therefore, empirical and analytical methods surrendered precedence to rational, synthetic procedures. In science this reversal was necessitated by investigations of subatomic existence and of the cosmos, both of which lay beyond the range of human sensory receptors; in art, by the artists' investigations of art itself and their own inner experiences.

Flat, colored, textured, and patterned planes overlap and interlock in Synthetic Cubist compositions. The frequent repetition of certain motifs, such as still lifes with stringed musical instruments, and figures from the Commedia dell'Arte, suggests that the artists actually began with a notion—conscious or unconscious—about the kind of subject that they would end up with. Nevertheless, in an obvious sense, something entirely new was created. Picasso's *Harlequin with a Violin* (cat no. 24), for example, presents a mysterious figure from the Commedia dell'Arte who turns out to be a fusion of the characters Harlequin and Pierrot. Three years later the same two figures appear as separate images, along with a masked and shrouded monk, in two major compositions entitled *Three Musicians* (Figures 11,12). The arcane figure of the monk and the two figures from the Commedia dell'Arte form an enigmatic group defined by hard-edged, brilliantly colored shapes. The shallow space of Analytical Cubism has become flatter and has acquired an air of mystery. In writing about these paintings, Robert Rosenblum refers to "this strange realm of moonlit fantasy."[8]

Figure 12. Pablo Picasso, *Three Musicians.* Oil on canvas, 1921, 203 x 188 cm. Philadelphia Museum of Art, A. E. Gallatin Collection. Photograph by A. J. Wyatt.

Once subjective experience was accorded the primary role in the creative act, the artistic personalities of Picasso and Braque were more easily distinguished through their styles: Picasso's daring inventiveness was evident in bold color combinations, the variety of his compositions, and abrupt transitions of hue, value, and shape; Braque's refined taste expressed itself in elegant composition, restrained colors, and supple transitions. Harmony and grace are characteristic of Braque's style, while Picasso's is often jarringly abrupt and even discordant.

Severely wounded in World War I, Braque did not paint seriously between the summer of 1914 and late 1917. Picasso, who was an alien, and therefore not subject to French military service, continued to work in Paris. In 1917 he moved to the suburb of Montrouge, sharing his long evening walk home from Paris with the composer Erik Satie. This friendship led to Picasso's involvement with the Russian Ballet; he designed sets and costumes for several productions (the first being *Parade*), on which he collaborated with Satie, Sergei Diaghilev, Léonide Massine, and Jean Cocteau. In this connection he also traveled to Italy, where he met a number of Russians, including Igor Stravinsky, Léon Bakst, and a young dancer, Olga Koklova, who became his first wife and the mother of his eldest child, Paulo.

Picasso's work for the Ballet marked a brief return to the romanticism of his Blue and Rose Periods. He also did pencil drawings of Olga, Max Jacob, Apollinaire, Diaghilev, and Stravinsky—all rendered in a sensitive and precise linear style rivaling that of Ingres. These, along with the decorations that he did for the Ballet and certain paintings that he produced in a Neoclassical style, precipitated a rift with some of the more doctrinaire Cubists. Because these dogmatic Cubists remained under attack from the conservative art establishment, they considered themselves revolutionary, and therefore regarded Picasso's new artistic adventures as apostasy. Picasso, however, was much too involved with his investigations to heed their complaints and accusations; indeed, he always rejected the restraints of programs and causes, even those he invented. His Cubism continued to evolve alongside his new styles: like a master juggler, he kept them all going at the same time. As Cocteau wrote: "The work of one who runs faster than beauty will seem ugly, but he will compel beauty to catch up with him."[9]

In 1925 Picasso created a strikingly frenzied composition, *Three Dancers* (Figure 13). The savage intensity of *Les Demoiselles d'Avignon* was revived in this painting, having been suppressed for eighteen years, during which the artist had invented and developed the Cubist vocabulary. This dramatic painting marked the emergence of a new spirit in Picasso's art. The restrained poetry of the Harlequins, Pierrots, and mysterious musicians gave way to the grotesquerie and fury of the dancers. A comment by Rosenblum about Picasso's major works of the early thirties applies

Figure 13. Pablo Picasso, *Three Dancers*. Oil on canvas, 215 x 142 cm. The Tate Gallery, London.

Figure 14. Pablo Picasso, *Glass of Absinthe*. Bronze and plaster, 1914, h. 22.6 cm. Philadelphia Museum of Art, A. E. Gallatin Collection.

equally to this composition: "(They are) the greatest triumph of the Surrealists' efforts to create a pictorial style and imagery appropriate to the exploration of dreams, and to the uncovering of those profound biological roots that link men more firmly to irrational nature than to a technological civilization."[10]

If Picasso had never painted, he would still be accorded a major role in the history of modern art on the basis of his sculpture alone. His earliest works in this medium, such as *Seated Woman* (1901) and *Kneeling Woman Combing Her Hair* (1905-6), reflect the influence of Rodin, but by the time he did *Mask of a Woman* (1908), he was clearly his own artist. *Head of a Woman* (cat. no. 19), done in 1909, represents his first attempt to translate Analytical Cubism into three-dimensional form. Cubist *papiers collés* led Picasso into three-dimensional collages of cardboard and paper, and finally into relief sculptures constructed of sheet metal, wood, wire, and other materials. By 1914 he had carried Synthetic Cubism into sculptural works such as *Glass of Absinthe* (Figure 14).

Picasso was the towering genius of Cubism. Braque was his alter ego, and Fernand Léger and Juan Gris were his major confederates in painting. In sculpture, Jacques Lipchitz and Henri Laurens were his most important early disciples. Lipchitz's *Detachable Figure (Dancer)* (cat. no. 23), executed in ebony and oak in 1915, attests to this sculptor's mastery of the Cubist idiom. He reduced three-dimensional images to basic formal structures, which he then organized architectonically.

1. 1925 is an arbitrary closing date for Cubism. It is the date of *Three Dancers*, a major Synthetic Cubist painting by Picasso that can also be considered as Surrealistic. Cubism, however, is actually open-ended, influencing spatial composition in paintings by later artists such as Jackson Pollock and Robert Motherwell.
2. Despite Picasso's denial, it seems obvious that he had seen African art by this date. An interesting sidelight is Einstein's denial, about the same time, that he was aware of the Michelson-Morley experiment before publishing his special theory of relativity. It is possible, of course, that both Picasso and Einstein were subconsciously aware of these two sources without realizing it.
3. Letter from Albert Einstein to Paul M. Laporte, reproduced in Laporte, "Cubism and Relativity," *Art Journal* XXV/3 (Spring 1966): 246.
4. Roland Penrose, *Picasso: His Life and Work* (New York, Harper and Row, Icon Editions, 1973), p. 173.
5. "Picasso Speaks," *The Arts* 3 (May 1923): 315.
6. Morris Kline, *Mathematics and the Search for Knowledge* (New York: Oxford University Press, 1985), p. 199.
7. Edward Fry, *Cubism* (New York: Oxford University Press, 1966) p. 162.
8. Robert Rosenblum, *Cubism and Twentieth-Century Art* (New York: Harry N. Abrams, 1961), p. 104.
9. Quoted in Pierre Daix, *Picasso* (New York: Praeger, 1965), pp. 113-14.
10. Robert Rosenblum, "Picasso as Surrealist," *Artforum* 5 (special issue on Surrealism, September 1966): 23.

The Move into Abstraction

Impressionism transformed the subject matter of painting into a motif—a touchstone for experiments using color to produce the effects of light and atmosphere. Post-Impressionism replaced the objective attitude of Impressionism with a subjective approach to art and shifted the burden of content from subject to form. The creators of Cubism, Picasso and Braque, nearly lost sight of nature in their Analytical Cubist canvases. They reacted by creating Synthetic Cubism, which clearly pictured the world of exterior reality but began with purely formal compositions—thus preparing the way for abstract art. Once the Cubists went this far, it was only a matter of time until other artists made complete abstractions. The artist who first took this step, however, has still not been clearly identified. Although Vasily Kandinsky is often credited with being the first pure Abstractionist, Frantisek Kupka also has a number of champions.

Abstraction declared that painting and sculpture had a valid existence without representing natural appearances, just as non-Euclidean geometry indicated that mathematics could exist independent of the experience of nature. Mathematics provides the abstract form of the sciences.

The major Abstractionists, other than Kandinsky and Kupka, included: Robert Delaunay in Paris; Piet Mondrian, Bart van der Leck, and Theo Van Doesburg in Holland; and Kasimir Malevich and Eleazer Lissitzky (along with many others) in Russia. Although the artists developed from different stylistic bases and created various kinds of abstract art, they were, without exception, encouraged to take this step by the Cubist experience.

Robert Delaunay (1885-1941)

Delaunay, along with the Czech expatriate Kupka, and Delaunay's future wife, Sonia Terk, formed a group given the name Orphism by Guillaume Apollinaire, who had just completed a series of poems under the title *Cortège d'Orphée (The Retinue of Orpheus)*. In a lecture delivered at Der Sturm Gallery in Berlin in 1912, Apollinaire compared the exploitation of pure color by Delaunay and Kupka with the musical and poetic experiments that he loved to make.

Delaunay's experiments with abstraction were first stimulated by Analytical Cubism. Inspired by Neo-Impressionism and the writings on color by Chevreul, Charles Henry, and other theoreticians of optics, however, he rejected the somber palette of early Cubism. An intuitive artist, Delaunay often joked about the rationalizations of doctrinaire Cubists, such as Albert Gleizes and Jean Metzinger.

Beginning in 1909, Delaunay more or less followed a stylistic development related to Cubism. The interior of the church of St-Séverin and the Eiffel Tower (cat. no. 27) served as his main subjects until, in 1911, he completed an abstract canvas entitled *Window on the City #4*. The buildings in this painting are barely recognizable, since they are nearly obscured by the pattern of short, staccato brushstrokes derived from the Neo-Impressionist technique. Also in 1911, Delaunay came very close to pure abstraction with a canvas titled *Simultaneous Windows*. Only careful study reveals hints of the Eiffel Tower and buildings in the organization of curving and angular shapes of pure, light colors.

In 1912 Delaunay painted *Premier Disque*, a disk that is partitioned into four equal parts by vertical and horizontal divisions with seven concentric circles changing color at the dividing lines. From this painting, Delaunay developed a series of abstract compositions based on complex arrangements of colored disks—*Discs* (1913) and *Circular Forms: Sun, Moon* (1912-13). Others had some recognizable elements: *Homage to Bleriot* (1914) and *The Cardiff Team* (1913).

Orphism developed directly out of Cubism but with an emphasis on high-keyed, lyrical color as a main element in the pictorial structure and suggesting rhythmical movements in nature.

Frantisek Kupka (1871-1957)

Kupka was born in that part of the Austro-Hungarian Empire that later became Czechoslovakia. He studied at the Ecole des Beaux-Arts in Vienna, traveled to London and Scandinavia, returned briefly to Vienna, and finally settled in Paris.

Kupka's reticent and austere nature may explain why it took so long for him to be acclaimed as one of the first artists—if not *the* first—to take the step into abstraction. In 1951 Marcel Duchamp reported:

Almost fifty years ago Kupka gave a memorable New Year's party at his studio at the Rue Caulaincourt and shortly thereafter began to see "abstract" as we call it nowadays. For the word was not yet in the dictionary of that happy time. Apollinaire used the word "Orphism" when he spoke about those things . . . . And now the search for the father is conducted by the father-candidates themselves, who do not believe in any polypaternity of this gigantic child.[1]

Kupka's abstract works can be roughly divided into two main groups: curvilinear, richly colored, romantic compositions, usually with musical titles; and predominantly vertical-horizontal arrangements in restrained greens, grays, and browns, which are architectural in character.

The curvilinear compositions, which came first, were often based upon drawings and paintings (executed between 1908 and 1910) of his stepdaughter playing with a ball. As these compositions became increasingly abstract, Kupka omitted references to the child and ball and assigned them musical titles—for example, *Amorpha, Fugue for Two Colors, II* (cat. no. 28).

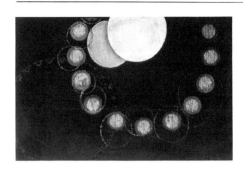

Figure 15. Frantisek Kupka, *The First Step*. Oil on canvas, 1910-13(?) (dated on painting 1909), 83.2 x 129.5 cm. Collection, The Museum of Modern Art, New York, Hillman Periodicals Fund.

At least one of Kupka's paintings, *First Step* (Figure 15; 1909-13?), might predate Kandinsky's and Delaunay's earliest abstract paintings (if the date of 1909 can be accepted). Indeed, there is reason to believe that Apollinaire coined the term Orphism to refer to Kupka's paintings.[2]

Piet Mondrian (1872-1944)

Mondrian was born in Holland, where he qualified to become an art teacher even before attending the Amsterdam Academy. His early paintings were Romantic, and then Impressionist, landscapes. During his first stay in Paris, from 1912 to 1914, he came under the influence of Cubism, but refused to play variations on the Cubist theme, as did artists such as Gleizes and Metzinger. His paintings of this period already revealed a strong, individualistic temperament.

The transition from Mondrian's early landscapes to abstraction is illustrated by a series of drawings and paintings of trees. The earliest works in the series are representational, but they become increasingly abstract. The rhythmical curves of the trunk and branches are first stressed and then modified as the shapes of the interstices between them become increasingly prominent (cat. no. 29). More than just providing a background of space for the representation of the tree, the space itself takes on shape and—because of the thickness of the paint—a palpable character that causes it to be fully integrated with the image of the tree. Thus, in an obvious way, space and material form become one image.

Mondrian returned to Holland just before the outbreak of World War I and remained there throughout the hostilities. During the time that he lived in Laren, on the sea, he painted a series of near-abstractions—one based on the façade of a cathedral and another on the sea, with the waves and a pier creating a horizontal and vertical, linear theme. About the same time, he became friendly with Theo van Doesburg, a painter who was an enthusiastic theoretician; he also met the eccentric painter Bart van der Leck and the theosophist Dr. M. H. J. Schoenmachers, both of whom had great influence on his theories as well as his art.

Through his association with Dr. Schoenmachers, Mondrian's own mystical tendencies were reinforced. For example, he believed that a single, unified form would result from the employment of exact opposites: vertical and horizontal lines, and the three primary colors (red, yellow, and blue) along with the three non-colors (black, white, and gray) (cat. no. 30). Indeed, these are the exact elements from which Mondrian fashioned numerous subtle paintings.

In contrast to Delaunay's approach to abstraction through nature, Mondrian's austere, fully mature canvases resulted from a purely rational and intuitive method. As restrained, geometrical abstractions, they manifest the artist's faith in the power of the mind to intuit the nature of ultimate Reality. For Mondrian—as his paintings indicate—this is a perfectly balanced structure of opposites.

Until the early thirties, Mondrian's art evolved toward ever purer images. Later, his compositions became increasingly complex, culminating in two pictures executed while he was living in New York City during World War II: *Broadway Boogie-Woogie* and his last, unfinished composition from 1944, *Victory Boogie-Woogie.*

Contrary to popular opinion, Mondrian did not arrive at his compositions by mathematical calculations or by using sophisticated tools or instruments (he was, in fact, a poor mathematician). Rather, he developed his delicately balanced arrangements of geometrical shapes intuitively, testing each composition by eye over a long period.

Vasily Kandinsky (1866-1944)

In the early twentieth century, Paris continued to be the main center for avant-garde artistic activity. In Germany there were many centers, including Berlin, Munich, Cologne, Düsseldorf, and Dresden. The most important groups were the Expressionist artists of The Bridge (Die Brücke)—with headquarters first in Dresden, then in Berlin—and a more catholic group of artists from Munich, who called their movement The Blue Rider (Der Blaue Reiter).

The Blue Rider aimed to bring together all manner of experimental art and artists from all over. Members of the group, and artists invited to participate in their exhibitions, included Russians, Americans, Germans, French, Swiss, and Spaniards.

Vasily Kandinsky, the leader of the group, was born in Moscow of a Siberian father. He studied law and political economy before turning to painting at the age of thirty. After several visits to Paris, he moved to Munich, where he discovered German Impressionism, and became a leader of the Phalanx group. From Munich he traveled to Kairouan in Tunisia, to Holland, Italy, and to France, where he lived near Paris for a year.

During this time his palette became rich in color and his brushwork became an important expressive element. In 1909 he founded the New Association of Munich Artists, a group which later became the nucleus of The Blue Rider. He formed close associations with another Russian painter, Alexej Jawlensky; with the German artists Franz Marc and August Macke; as well as with the Swiss-born Paul Klee.

During his stay near Paris he associated with some of the French avant-garde artists, especially Delaunay, who were invited to exhibit with the Munich group. Thus, it was again the influence of Cubism that inspired artists to paint abstractions. Kandinsky is often credited with being the first artist to take this step in 1910, but Delaunay, Kupka, Mondrian, and Malevich, among others, were all moving in the same direction.

Like Mondrian, Kandinsky was influenced by theosophy, but through Madame Blavatsky rather than Dr. Schoenmachers. His early abstractions, like those of Mondrian, Delaunay, and Kupka, were derived from nature: Delaunay's were based on views of Paris; Mondrian's were inspired by a tree, a church façade, and a pier extending into the sea; and Kandinsky's came from the mountainous landscape of Bavaria. Delaunay's and Kupka's styles were sensuous and colorful; Mondrian's, austere and classical; and Kandinsky's, emotional and moody, with deep, resonant colors and loose brushwork.

Kandinsky's paintings done between 1910 and 1920 have dramatic contrasts of colored shapes and vigorous linear motifs suggesting space, atmosphere, and movement (cat. no. 31); even the pure abstractions of this period seem to refer to landscapes. Near the end of this decade Kandinsky spent several years in Russia (following the Revolution) and came under the influence of Malevich's powerful personality, with the result that the space in his paintings became increasingly shallow and the shapes became hard-edged. The loose, painterly character of his earlier abstractions was replaced by precisely painted abstract compositions. Since many of these works still suggest landscapes, however, they remind us that Kandinksy's abstract style developed out of a romantic strain of Expressionism. Indeed, the term ''Abstract Expressionism,'' associated with New York painting around mid-century, was first used to refer to Kandinsky's early abstractions.

In addition to the four major figures of the first wave of abstraction, there were others who were followers or companions of those discussed above. Although artists from many different countries began to create abstractions in various modes, all were influenced by Cubism. They shared a faith that form could by itself convey content.

Constantin Brancusi (1876-1957)

Brancusi defies all stylistic categories. He resisted the analytical approach of early Cubism and the synthetic approach of later Cubism as well as the automatism and dream explorations of Surrealism. After an early period during which he was influenced by Rodin, Brancusi concentrated on his own individual attempt to penetrate to archetypical, essential forms. Images such as *Bird in Space* (Figure 16) or *Fish* bear no resemblance to an actual animal; instead, they bring to mind the Platonic idea of bird and fish.

Born in Romania, Brancusi left his father's farm at eleven to explore the world. In his early twenties he attended the Bucharest Art School on a scholarship, and at twenty-six set off to travel throughout Europe. Two years later, after stays in Munich, Zurich, and Basel, he settled in Paris, where he attended the Ecole des Beaux-Arts and studied under the strict, academic sculptor Antonin Mercié.

Figure 16. Constantin Brancusi, *Bird in Space*. Bronze, unique cast, 1928(?), h. 137.2 cm. Collection, The Museum of Modern Art, New York, given anonymously.

Rodin was sufficiently impressed with Brancusi's work to invite the young artist to work with him, but Brancusi was too independent to accept the offer. He soon gave up whatever influence of Rodin's had affected his work and reacted against Romanticism, Realism, and Impressionism. In giving up all detail, fragmentation, appeals to emotion, and individualization to concentrate on austere, essential forms, Brancusi created a kind of modern classical style as opposed to Neoclassicism. His search for underlying, universal, primordial forms is evident in works such as *Mlle Pogany* (cat. no. 32), the *Sleeping Muse*, and the *Beginning of the World* (in all three, he took the shape of the egg as the basis for the sculpture). *Male Torso* (cat. no. 33), on the other hand, joins three, subtly varied, cylindrical forms.[3]

Brancusi's work was popular in the United States: he exhibited in the Armory Show in 1913, at Alfred Stieglitz's Gallery 291 in 1914, and in the twenties and thirties at the Brummer Gallery in New York. He found his first sales at these exhibitions to the two most important collectors of his work, Walter Arensberg and John Quinn.

1. Quoted in *Kupka*, exh. cat. (New York: Louis Carré Gallery, May-June, 1951), p. 7.
2. Ibid.
3. The date of 1922 has generally been assigned to the wood and brass versions of this image; however, The Cleveland Museum of Art's piece has the artist's signature and 1917 inscribed on the inner right thigh.

The Dada Prelude to Surrealism

In 1916 a group of intellectuals from all over Europe sought refuge from the First World War in Zurich, where they formed an anarchistic movement that they labeled Dada. One of the founders of the movement, Jean Arp, later wrote: "Revolted by the butchery of the 1914 World War . . . . We were seeking an art based on fundamentals, to cure the madness of the age, and a new order of things that would restore the balance between heaven and hell."[1] The mindless fury of the War invited irony and satire, and Dada obliged by mocking bourgeois society and its values and traditions. The bourgeoisie was at first shocked and angered, but eventually it defused Dada's cerebral bombs by embracing them as a new source of amusement and thrills.

Dada artists and poets met and performed in the Cabaret Voltaire in Zurich, where their neighbors included the Russian Bolshevik leader V. I. Lenin and several of his comrades. Although both groups sought the overthrow of existing social and political orders, the Russian revolutionists regarded the Dadaists as dilettantes. Both groups believed that the War would bring an end to bourgeois capitalist society, but the Bolsheviks were prepared with a program for social organization and political control, while the Dadaists preferred a vague anarchism advocating that human nature be allowed to find its own way.

The year before Dada emerged in Zurich, the French artist Marcel Duchamp and certain other expatriate artists along with some Americans formed a Dada-like group in New York. Francis Picabia, Man Ray, and Marcel Duchamp, among others, made their headquarters at the Little Gallery of the Photo-Secession, which Alfred Stieglitz and Edward Steichen had opened in 1913 at 291 Fifth Avenue. Duchamp eventually became a major figure in defining the character of Dada and a "patron saint" of such later developments as Pop Art and Conceptualism.

Following the War, Dada spread across Europe, with centers in Paris, Berlin, Cologne, and Hanover. The Parisian Dadaists included poets such as Paul Eluard, Louis Aragon, Philippe Soupault, and Benjamin Péret as well as the charismatic André Breton and Tristan Tzara who contended for leadership of the group. Berlin Dadaists, such as George Grosz, Richard Huelsenbeck, Johnny Heartfield (Hans Herzfelde), his brother Wieland Herzfelde, and Walter Mehring were actively involved in revolutionary politics. The German painter, collagist, and writer Max Ernst was the leader of the Cologne group. With his friend Johannes Baargeld, he developed close ties with the Paris Dadaists who were less political than the Berlin group. In Hanover, one of the least political figures, Kurt Schwitters, developed a unique kind of Dada that he called Merz; he collected bits of rubbish from the city's streets to use in his own adaptation of the Cubist collage technique.

Dada's attempt to laugh art out of existence failed because the artists could not help creating aesthetic forms; they succeeded only in demonstrating that there are no valid a priori forms of art toward which the artist must strive. Hans Richter called Dada "an artistic revolt against art." It embraced love and laughter, but it also encompassed black humor and nihilism. Ironically, popular success marked its failure as it was embraced by those whom it most scorned, the bourgeoisie.

Jean (Hans) Arp (1887-1966)

Born in Strasbourg, Arp was living in Paris when war broke out. His German citizenship made his presence there uncomfortable, and in 1915 he joined the gathering of disillusioned intellectuals in Zurich and participated in the formation of the Dada movement.

Arp first composed *papiers collés* by dropping torn pieces of paper onto a flat surface and fixing them. Acknowledging that the pieces of paper were consciously adjusted, he nevertheless insisted that this was done "according to the laws of chance" and "without will."[2] He then converted the technique of collage to assemblage by gluing together biomorphic shapes cut out of wood approximately one inch thick. Some of these assembled reliefs were painted (cat. no. 34), but others were left with the raw wood exposed.

Arp spent most of 1919 and 1920 with Ernst and Baargeld in Cologne, where they formed the "Dada Conspiracy of the Rhineland." He collaborated with Ernst on a series of fantastical collages, which they called *Fatagaga*—a name created from the phrase FAbrication de TAbleaux GArantis GAzometriques (Manufacture of Pictures Guaranteed to be Gasometric.)

The birth of the Surrealist movement in 1924 had no discernible effect on Arp's work. He continued to develop a poetic, plastic language using organic forms. "I love nature," he wrote, "but not its substitutes . . . . I do not want to reproduce but to produce . . . like a plant that produces fruit."[3]

Max Ernst (1891-1976)

Ernst left Cologne for Paris in 1921. From then until his death, except for the years spent in the United States during and immediately after the Second World War, he made the French capital his home.

Like Arp, he depended on chance in his creative process, and he adapted the collage method to his own ends. Arp's poetic reflections on the unity that he saw as underlying nature's myriad forms, however, contrast sharply with Ernst's images of demonic and erotic fantasy. Arp's warm wit was also completely different from Ernst's black humor. Nevertheless, these two artists collaborated on a number of works of astonishing imagination and inventiveness. Ernst was later to embrace Surrealism.

Marcel Duchamp (1887-1968)

In New York, Duchamp experimented with "readymades" such as a bicycle wheel mounted upside down on a stool; a bottle-rack; and a urinal, which he titled *Fountain*. By exhibiting these common objects, Duchamp both indicated the important role of selection in the creative act, and implied that the isolation and exhibition of almost any object endows it with a special glamour. By such displays Duchamp demonstrated his rejection of traditional aesthetic values.

A series of works that he called "Stoppages" (lengths of thread let fall at random onto a flat surface and then fixed), like Arp's *papiers collés*, assigned a major role in the creative act to chance.

Beginning in 1915, Duchamp labored for more than eight years on a major work entitled *The Large Glass* or *The Bride Stripped Bare by Her Bachelors, Even* (Figure 17). Satirical representations in lead of imaginary machines symbolizing erotic human figures were fastened to the surface of a large plate glass. The transparent glass permits one to see objects and figures behind the machine-like images, thus involving real life in the composition. He ended his work on this piece in 1923, having brought it to a satisfactory "state of incompletion." Although word went out at this time that he had ceased creating, Duchamp actually continued to work in private on many projects.

Duchamp mocked the romantic image of the bohemian artist and satirized formalism in art. For example, in 1919 he "assisted" a reproduction of the *Mona Lisa* by adding to it a mustache and goatee and giving it the provocative title *L.H.O.O.Q.*; when pronounced rapidly, this becomes *elle a chaude au cul* (roughly translated as "she has a hot bottom"). Paradoxically, this rigorously logical artist became the most convincing champion of the anti-rationalist Dada movement. The Mexican poet Octavio Paz observed:

Perhaps the two painters who have had the greatest influence on our century are Pablo Picasso and Marcel Duchamp. The former by his works; the latter by a single work that is nothing less than the negation of work in the modern sense of the word. The pictures of the former are images; those of the latter are a meditation on the image.[4]

Figure 17. Marcel Duchamp, *The Large Glass*, or *The Bride Stripped Bare by Her Bachelors, Even*. Oil and lead wire on glass, 1915-23, 278.2 x 175.6 cm. Philadelphia Museum of Art, Bequest of Katherine S. Dreier.

1. Jean Arp, *Dadaland*, quoted in Hans Richter, *Dada: Art and Anti-Art* (London: Thames and Hudson, 1965), p. 25.

2. Herbert Read, *The Art of Jean Arp* (New York: Harry N. Abrams, 1968), p. 38.

3. Jean Arp, "Art Is a Fruit," and "Concrete Art," in *On My Way: Poetry and Essays*, Documents of Modern Art Series No. 6 (New York: Wittenborn, Schultz, 1948), pp. 51, 70.

4. Octavio Paz, *Marcel Duchamp's Appearance Stripped Bare*, trans. Rachel Phillips and Donald Gardner (New York: Viking Press, 1978), pp. 1, 3.

**28. Amorpha, Fugue for Two
Colors, II**

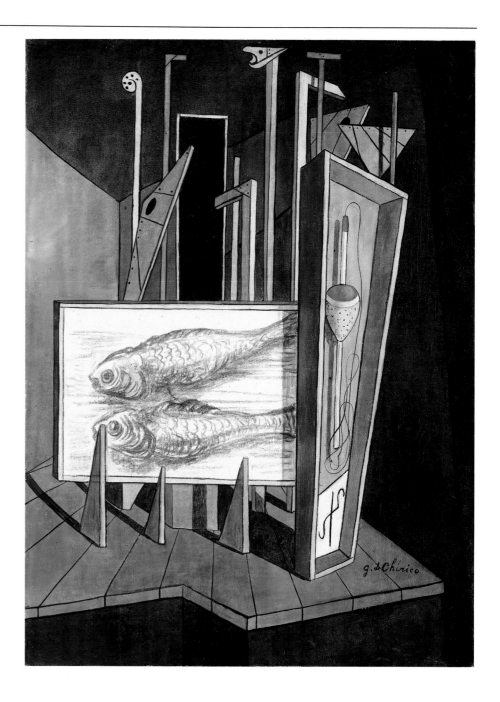

The Surrealist Revolution

Surrealism was not an art style, nor was it primarily a movement of painters and sculptors; it began as a literary movement, deriving from intellectual concepts. The main Surrealist goals were: (1) to discredit conventional views of "reality" based on sensory perceptions and reason; (2) to liberate the primitive nature of man, considered to be the source of all poetic experience; (3) to acquire knowledge of unconscious experience; and (4) to provide a program for life based on the knowledge thus acquired.

In aspiring to a revolution of the human mind by rejecting traditional aesthetic and moral values and acknowledging the unity of objective and subjective experience in an organic universe, Surrealism accorded primary status to the "interior landscape" of the unconscious mind and to automatic methods of exploring it.

André Breton published the *Manifesto of Surrealism* in 1924, revealing his intention to replace the negativism of Dada with a positive, creative policy. His break with Tzara and Dada became unavoidable by 1922, when he wrote: "During recent years I have been able to observe the harm done by a certain intellectual nihilism which in every case raised the most generalized and the most futile question of confidence."[1]

Having visited Sigmund Freud in Vienna in 1921, Breton recognized the significance of psychoanalytical methods for poetic creation. As a consequence, his *Manifesto* elaborated a program based on Freud's theories. Automatism, for example, was an adaptation of Freud's technique of "free association." Breton recommended this method to poets and artists as a means of investigating the unconscious. In the *Manifesto* he defined Surrealism thus:

Surrealism, n. *Psychic automatism in its pure state, by which one proposes to express—verbally, by means of the written word, or in any other manner—the actual functioning of thought. Dictated by thought, in the absence of any control exercised by reason, exempt from any aesthetic or moral concern . . . .*

Encyclopedia. Philosophy. *Surrealism is based on a belief in the superior reality of certain forms of previously neglected associations, in the omnipotence of the dream, in the disinterested play of thought . . . .*[2]

And further:
I believe in the future resolution of these two states, dream and reality, which are seemingly so contradictory, into a kind of absolute reality, a surrealité, if one may so speak . . . .[3]

Some time after the publication of Breton's *Manifesto*, Max Ernst wrote an essay, "Inspiration to Order," in which he stated, "No work which can be called absolutely Surrealist is to be directed consciously by the mind, whether through reason, taste, or the will . . . ."[4] Automatism as a creative principle was clearly central to Surrealism, as was the proposition that objective and subjective experiences are inextricably linked in a single process of perceiving reality.

About the same time Jacques Rivière adroitly pointed to the Surrealist goal with these words:

To grasp our being before it has yielded to consistency; to seize it in its incoherence, or better, in its primitive coherence, before the idea of contradiction has appeared and compelled it to reduce and construct itself; to replace its logical unity, which can only be acquired, by its absurd unity, which alone is innate.[5]

Surrealism thus accepted the proposition that the human personality starts out as a healthy unit that is dissipated as experience is acquired and compartmentalized according to reason. Illogically related images, such as those occurring in dreams, it insisted, provide greater insight into reality than rationally organized concepts.

Surrealism looked to literary precursors such as the Marquis de Sade, Charles Baudelaire, Isadore Ducasse (le Comte de Lautréamont), Arthur Rimbaud, and Alfred Jarry. When painters and sculptors first began to join this movement, the writers protested that Surrealism did not provide a viable program for the visual arts. Breton, however, welcomed the artists. In *Le Surréalisme et la peinture*, published in 1928, he acclaimed the Surrealist nature of works by Picasso, Giorgio de Chirico, Arp, Ernst, André Masson, Joan Miró, and Yves Tanguy, among others. Picasso and de Chirico never actually joined the movement, yet de Chirico's paintings done between 1910 and 1918 are clearly Surrealist in spirit, as are many works produced by Picasso from 1925 on.

Other artists of fantasy and naive imagery, such as Klee and Marc Chagall, were sympathetic to Surrealism and participated in Surrealist exhibitions without actually joining the movement. In retrospect, however, it seems that Chagall's fantastic images derive from his Chassidic background rather than from his unconscious, and reflect his wish to escape reality rather than to penetrate to its core. Picasso, independent as always, epitomized Surrealist subjectivity and was a welcome participant in Surrealist exhibitions and in publications such as *La Révolution Surrealist, Littérature*, and *Minotaure*.

Surrealism and Philosophy

Early in the nineteenth century the German philosopher Immanuel Kant proposed a comprehensive doctrine of experience including both empirical materialism and rational idealism in a complex dualistic system. Kant divided existence into the phenomenal world of sensory experience, and the noumenal world of things as-they-are-in-themselves. Sensory experience is screened and organized according to twelve inborn categories of thought, which are part of the basic structure of the human mind. Kant grouped these under four headings: quantity, quality, relation, and modality. Under each of these are three categories: for example, under quantity, one, many, and totality; under modality, possible, impossible, and contingent. Space and time, of course, were considered to be a priori principles that help structure sensory perceptions.

The noumenal world—the world-as-it-is-in-itself—we can never know directly, Kant argued, but we can know that something exists that excites our senses and that we interpret as colors, sounds, scents, textures, and so on. However, if nothing existed but the physical world, human beings would be mere elements within a universal machine. The concept of free will depends upon the notion of a reality beyond that of matter operating according to the law of cause and effect.

Following Kant, the German philosopher Georg Hegel proposed a dialectical historical process that evolves by means of the constant syntheses of opposites. He used the triad of thesis, antithesis, and synthesis to indicate how concepts generate their opposites, with which they then combine to achieve a higher unity. *Being*, for example, is the broadest, most basic concept of which the mind is capable. Yet, the notion of *being* without any specific thing that *is* being is empty and, thus, is the same as *not being*. To postulate Absolute Being, therefore, is to say at the same time that the Absolute does not exist. The resolution of this contradiction lies in Hegel's notion that the Absolute is *becoming*. That is, the universe is in process of *becoming* Absolute Idea.

Human beings, Hegel argued, attain self-knowledge when they recognize that phenomenal existence cannot be separated from their own experiencing of it. Thus, objective reality is experienced subjectively, and it is subjective experience that determines the nature of the world as apprehended through our senses.

The Surrealist idea of a synthesis of material reality and the dream in a ''sur-reality,'' therefore, finds an approximate analogy in the Hegelian synthesis of subjective and objective experience into Absolute Reality.

Surrealism and the Sciences

Over the centuries, as Auguste Comte first indicated, the sciences have separated themselves from philosophy, each becoming a distinct field of investigation. Assuming that sensory perceptions provide reasonably accurate information about the outer world, especially if mathematically measured and related, each science has based itself on previously accumulated bodies of knowledge.[6]

As the twentieth century began, it was generally believed that the overwhelming success of Western civilization was due to its advanced sciences with their power to explain and control nature. The vision of inevitable progress in human affairs because of scientific advances was exploded, however, by the 1914 World War. Classical science's capability to fully investigate and control the environment for man's benefit was questioned. Surrealists argued that human beings are incapable of separating themselves from the outer world and investigating it objectively. The individual must give up the ambition of objectively studying reality and be content to be integrated within nature.

Surrealism and Psychoanalysis

Sigmund Freud (1856-1939), the founder of psychoanalysis, treated pathological personalities by probing the unconscious levels of their minds. His theory was that all human beings have the same basic urges, drives, and hungers and that these motivate every form of sentient life, even though they are usually disguised in the civilized human being by socially imposed strictures. He further posited that psychic trauma in early life leads to undischarged emotional energy, often causing hysterical behavior, and that efforts to control "sinful" (largely sexual) desires and impulses may well result in neurotic or psychotic behavior.

In the early years of Freud's practice, his patients were encouraged to search for the causes of their feelings and behavior while under hypnosis. (Later he utilized the technique of dream recall and free association.) Once a patient had recalled the events that provoked hysteria, Freud reasoned, catharsis would enable the patient to adjust his behavior, conforming to social norms without undue feelings of guilt.

While serving in the Medical Corps during World War I, Breton had experimented with Freudian techniques in treating battle-damaged personalities, and he later relied upon these ideas and techniques in formulating the theoretical basis of Surrealism. Society itself was psychopathic, he held, and Surrealism would act as its catalyst. He accepted Freud's speculative structure of the human personality: the Id (the impersonal mass of raw, interacting, animalistic urges, drives, and hungers); the Superego (the watchdog of the personality, formed at an early age by the assimilation of what is assumed to be the moral code of one's parents); and the Ego (the sensible part of the personality that is aware of itself and is what we normally mean when we say "I"). The Ego serves as mediator between the primitive, unreasoning demands of the Id and the harsh, often impracticable strictures of the Superego; it tries to satisfy some of the demands of the former without incurring the wrath of the latter.

When the basic drives of the Id are unduly repressed into the unconscious, Freud held that the personality seeks to preserve its equilibrium by allowing such "shameful" desires to find symbolic expression in dreams, and by sublimating them in socially acceptable actions such as the exercise of power or the creation of works of art. When such outlets are unavailable or prove insufficient, the energy of the drive is converted into psychic tensions and conflicts.

In guiding patients into the realms of the unconscious, Freud encouraged them to recall and analyze their dreams, and to allow their thoughts to wander freely, speaking them aloud and uncritically, no matter how evil and shameful they might seem. The Surrealists adapted the same methods for their own explorations of the unconscious, which they viewed as a new source for poetic

imagery. One of their major concerns was the exposition of con-
tradictions inherent in a society that made unrealistic demands on
its members. Rather than bring the individual into conformity with
that society, as Freud aimed to do, the Surrealists hoped to serve
as midwife for a new society without such unreasonable restric-
tions on human behavior. To this end, they first allied themselves
with revolutionary Marxism.

Surrealism and Revolutionary Politics

In 1947 Breton wrote: "There are *three* major goals in Surrealism:
the social liberation of man, his complete moral liberation, and his
intellectual rejuvenation."[7] These goals depended on the repudia-
tion of bourgeois, capitalist society and organized, hierarchical
religion. Thus, Surrealism was in accord with the original Communist goal of an international, classless community that would
theoretically develop out of a proletarian society lacking vested interests and enjoying freedom of thought and speech.

The Bolsheviks put these goals "temporarily" aside during the
civil war that followed the 1917 Revolution and Russia's
withdrawal from the World War. They were indefinitely postponed
with Stalin's triumph over Trotsky and other Bolshevik leaders
following Lenin's death in 1924. Stalin's program originally was
one of national self-containment and the protection of the
Socialist revolution in Russia. The result was a massive bureaucracy
and a state police force responsible to a personal dictator.
Criticism was suppressed, and stubborn old Bolsheviks such as
Zinoviev, Kamenev, Bukharin, and Trotsky were either executed or
assassinated. Socialism in a single state inevitably developed its
own national interests. Patriotic loyalty to the State was man-
datory as Marxist theory was transformed into Stalinist dogma.
Ultimately the Communist Party bureaucracy developed its own
vested interests.

At one point or another, most of the original Surrealists joined
the Communist Party. Some, such as Louis Aragon, vacillated
before remaining in the Party, while others, like Breton, endorsed
Trotsky. Most Surrealists, however, eventually recognized that the
society they had envisioned as essential for the social, moral, and
intellectual liberation of mankind did not exist in the Soviet
Union. When war finally erupted between the Fascist dictatorships
and the Western democracies in alliance with the Soviet Union,
many of the Surrealists fled to the United States to escape the German occupation.

Giorgio de Chirico (1888-1978)

Giorgio de Chirico's metaphysical paintings, done between 1911
and 1917, preceded Surrealism and directly influenced the illu-
sionist Surrealism of René Magritte, Yves Tanguy, Salvador Dali,
and Paul Delvaux. Although he was included in the first Surrealist
exhibition and was highly regarded by the Surrealists, de Chirico

by 1918 had stopped painting the kind of works that they admired. His early metaphysical canvases juxtapose clearly defined but logically unrelated images; they manifest in visual terms Lautréamont's famous simile for beauty: "the chance meeting on a dissecting table of a sewing-machine and an umbrella."[8]

Born in Greece of Italian parents, de Chirico studied in Munich, where he came under the spell of German Romantic painting and the philosophical writings of Friedrich Nietzsche and Arnold Schopenhauer. During 1910 and 1911 he lived in Florence, Milan, Turin, and Paris. In 1911 the poet Guillaume Apollinaire declared him to be the most astonishing painter of his time.

Most of de Chirico's paintings from the early teens join together precise representations of lonely city streets and squares, arcades, walls, trains, chimney stacks, towers, classical sculptures, artichokes, stalks of bananas, shadows of unseen presences, and occasionally, distant human figures. Such eerie settings and images are bathed in late afternoon, autumnal sunlight. De Chirico revealed the source of such imagery in his autobiography (1945) by saying that what interested him most in Nietzsche's writings was "a strange, dark poetry, infinitely mysterious and lonely, based . . . on the atmosphere of an afternoon in autumn when the weather is clear and the shadows are longer than they have been all summer, because the sun stands low in the sky."[9]

Many of these images lend themselves to Freudian interpretations. Unlike Dali's deliberate employment of sexual symbols, however, de Chirico's use of symbols appears to be unintentional—in line with the Surrealists' interest in Freud's theory that repressed urges appear spontaneously in symbolic form in the unconscious.

Interior still lifes and mannequins became the main subjects of de Chirico's painting in 1916 and 1917, when he was living in Ferrara in northern Italy. The still lifes have certain common images: rectangular or trapezoidal boxes containing food, maps, or paintings; various draftsman's tools; and an irregular-shaped, tilted table top on which these objects rest. Space is compressed; thin black lines define the edges of objects; and dark, cast shadows contrast with brightly lit surfaces (cat. no. 35). Indeed, such depictions suggest an ominous dream.

In defense of his vision of a silent, immutable world, de Chirico stated: "We must not forget that a picture must always be the reflection of a profound sensation, that profound signifies strange, and strange signifies not-known or perhaps entirely unknown. A work of art, if it is to be immortal, must go far beyond the limits of man."[10] Again, in words reminiscent of many modern scientists: "Certain aspects of the world, whose existence we completely ignore, suddenly confront us with the revelation of mysteries lying all the time within our reach and which we cannot see because we are too short sighted, and cannot feel because our senses are inadequately developed."[11]

Max Ernst (1891-1976)

Ernst's imagination and inventiveness are evident in his Dada works, in his Surrealist paintings, and especially in his Surrealist novels done in collage: *La Femme 100 Têtes*, which can be read as: The Woman (of) One Hundred (*cent*) Heads, or The Woman without (*sans*) Heads; *Dream of a Young Girl Anxious to Enter a Convent*; and *A Week of Kindness*, or *The Seven Capital Elements*. He constantly invented new techniques for developing images from his unconscious. Buried childhood memories play a major role in determining his subjects: Loplop, Bird Superior, who appears in many of his works, for example, is his personal image that apparently also refers to the death of a pet cockatoo that he adored and the coincidental birth of a sister.

Among the techniques invented by Ernst are frottage (the development of images that his imagination read into textures and patterns made by rubbings of irregular surfaces, such as old floorboards); grattage (the development of images read into surfaces made by scraping down a painting's surface); and novels related by means of images created by collaging sections from printed illustrations.

Ernst described himself as objectively recording his experiences on "journeys of discovery into the unconscious," noting "what one . . . sees, experiences . . . in that border region between the inner and the outer worlds."[12] Indebted to Cubist and Dadaist collages as well as to de Chirico's strange combinations of images, his paintings contain incongruous images that call into question what has been assumed to be real. The combination of unrelated images is familiar in German culture. For example, the eighteenth-century German poet Novalis observed: "When the strangest things come together through a place, a time, a peculiar resemblance, the results are amazing units and curious connections."[13]

Ernst's use of frottage and grattage complemented his automatic process of creation, since they were intended to stimulate the creative process by improvisatory means. Yet, as William Rubin points out, there is an important difference. With automatism, the initial marks derive their impetus from the artist, no matter how unconscious the dictates may be. With frottage and grattage, chance plays the central role: even though the artist selects the surfaces to be rubbed, or does the scraping, the actions are performed randomly, so that he cannot predict the results. Such effects are thus substituted for gestures of the unconscious.[14]

Joan Miró (1893-1983)

Born in Barcelona, the traditional center of avant-garde cultural life in Spain, Miró visited Paris for the first time in 1918; there he met Picasso and saw his work as well as that of Matisse and other leaders of the avant-garde. From 1919 to 1923 he did sharply defined figurative images influenced by Cubism, but in 1923 he developed a looser, semi-abstract, biomorphic style inspired by the

Figure 18. Joan Miró, *Carnival of Harlequin*. Oil on canvas, 1924-25, 66 x 93 cm. Albright-Knox Art Gallery, Buffalo, New York, Room of Contemporary Art Fund, 1940.

art of Jean Arp and Paul Klee. His aesthetic attitude was affected by the writings of Louis Aragon, Paul Eluard, Jacques Prévert, and Ernest Hemingway, as well as Breton's theories.

At the time that Breton was writing the *Manifesto of Surrealism* (1924), Miró was beginning to develop means for exploring his own unconscious. He reported that he was ''not so much trying to escape *from* reality as to escape *into* nature . . . into all of nature, including the imaginary as well as the real . . . .''[15]

In 1925 he began a series of freely painted canvases, such as *Carnival of Harlequin* (Figure 18). Miró attributed this development to hallucinations caused by hunger. At the time, however, he was immersing himself in the writings of Lautréamont, Rimbaud, Jarry, and Novalis. No longer interpretations of subjective experiences, these works were direct translations of inner gestures of the spirit into gestures of the brush. The ground tones in these paintings are thin and translucent and the biomorphic shapes relate— however remotely—to figures and landscapes. In a process similar to that of frottage, Miró would often stare fixedly at old walls, rough floorboards, or clouds, allowing these to suggest images for paintings.

By 1930 Miró had reduced the role of chance in his art, although it always remained important as a means of generating his creative process. In a radio interview with Georges Charbonnier in 1960, he described his working method as follows:

Never, never do I set to work on a canvas in the state it comes from the shop. I provoke accidents—a form, a splotch of color. Any accident is good enough; I let the matière decide. Then I prepare a ground by, for example, wiping my brushes on the canvas. Letting fall some drops of turpentine on it would do just as well . . . . The painter works like the poet; first the word, then the thought.[16]

By the mid-thirties the monstrous forces about to be unleashed in Spain, and then all over Europe, seem to have found appropriate visual metaphors in Miro's pictures. From the fall of 1935 to the spring of 1936 he produced six terrible images in oil on copper, including *Nocturne* (cat. no. 37), and six tempera paintings on masonite. The use of these meticulous, Old-Master techniques made it possible for Miró to better control his definition of the monsters that were forcing their way into his conscious mind.

Four years later, while working at Varengeville in Normandy, Miró unexpectedly began a series of small, lyrical paintings; he called these *Constellations*, one of which is in the Cleveland Museum (cat. no. 38). Women, birds, stars, and moons are the dominant motifs of this astonishing series of twenty-three oil and gouache paintings on paper, ten of which were done under the threat of advancing German armies. He finally fled to his ancestral home at Palma on Majorca and then to Montroig on the Spanish mainland, where he finished the series.

Once the grotesque images of man that haunted his imagination became reality, Miró embraced the sources of love and poetry. He later commented:

At Varengeville-sur-Mer, in 1939, began a new stage in my work . . . . I felt a deep desire to escape. I closed myself within myself purposely. The night, music, and the stars began to play a major role in my paintings. Music had always appealed to me, and now music in this period began to take the role poetry had played in the early twenties . . . .[17]

Miró had a great impact on a group of young American painters who came to prominence during the 1940s and 1950s. While they were motivated by direct contact with Matta, Masson, Ernst, Breton, and other Surrealist refugees from the war, it was the paintings and reproductions of paintings by Picasso and Miró that inspired the Abstract Expressionists. The *Constellations* were the first works from Europe to be seen in the United States after World War II (1945). They have since come to be regarded as a major achievement in Miró's oeuvre.

Paul Klee (1879-1940)

Although Klee, like Picasso, never joined the Surrealist movement, his creative methods had much in common with those espoused by the Surrealists. Klee was concerned with exploring his unconscious and with utilizing automatic methods and chance effects to stimulate the creative process. Unlike the Surrealists, however, he recognized an important role for the intellect and devised a visual language of abstract motifs that he believed could be universally comprehensible. This language was analogous to musical structures in its power to articulate subjective experience by formal means.

Klee was born near Bern, Switzerland, the son of an orchestra conductor. A talented violinist, he was uncertain whether to follow a career in music or painting, but in 1898 chose to attend art school in Munich. After studying painting with Franz von Stuck, he traveled in Italy and then returned to Munich, where he became friendly with Kandinsky and other artists who later formed the Blue Rider group. Even at this early stage, Klee's approach to painting had much in common with a composer's approach to music. He did not set out with a preconception of the finished work; instead, the idea of what the work would be took form as it was being created. Klee said that he created symbols that reassured his mind.

Klee's rejection of traditional techniques and his interest in the art of children, primitive art, and the art of visionaries such as Goya, William Blake, Odilon Redon, and Gustave Doré, paralleled the Surrealists' interests—as did his concern with images from the preconscious and unconscious levels of the mind. In 1902 Klee wrote: ''I want to be as though new-born, knowing nothing, absolutely nothing, about Europe; ignoring poets and fashions, to be almost primitive. Then I want to do something very modest; to work out by myself a tiny, formal motive, one that my pencil will be able to hold without any technique."[18]

Klee expressed belief in a reality beyond that perceived by our limited senses. He indicated that the way to this reality lay through the unconscious and can be discovered by the use of automatic—or nearly automatic—creative methods. Klee's thoughts and actions paralleled those of the Surrealists; the difference between them lay principally in the degree of emphasis each placed on intuition, spontaneity, and chance in the creative act. The Surrealists, for example, raised chance to the highest level, while for Klee there was always the unifying guidance of a single, conscious—or subconscious—intention. In his *Creative Credo* he wrote: "Action may well be the start of everything, *but actions are governed by ideas.*"

1. Quoted in Maurice Nadeau, *The History of Surrealism*, trans. Richard Howard (New York: Macmillan Co., 1965), pp. 101-2, fn. 3.

2. Breton, "Manifesto of Surrealism," reprinted in *Manifestoes of Surrealism*, trans. from the French by Richard Seaver and Helen R. Lane (Ann Arbor: University of Michigan Press, 1969), p. 26.

3. Ibid., p. 14.

4. Max Ernst, "Inspiration to Order," in *Max Ernst: Beyond Painting and Other Writings by the Artist and His Friends*, trans. Dorothea Tanning and Ralph Manheim (New York: Wittenborn, Schultz, 1948), p. 20.

5. Jacques Rivière, quoted in Sam Hunter, *Modern American Painting and Sculpture* (New York: Dell, 1959), p. 159.

6. Thomas Munro, *Toward Science in Aesthetics* (New York: Liberal Arts Press, 1956), p. 89.

7. André Breton, "Comète Surréaliste," in *La Clé des Champs* (Paris: Editions du Sagittaire, 1953), pp. 104-5. Reprinted in Herbert S. Gershman, *The Surrealist Revolution in France* (Ann Arbor: University of Michigan Press, 1974), p. 80.

8. Isadore Ducasse, *Lautréamont's Maldoror*, trans. Alexis Lykiard (New York: Thomas Y. Crowell, 1972), p. 177.

9. Uwe M. Schneede, *Surrealism*, trans. Maria Pelikan (New York: Harry N. Abrams, 1974), p. 17.

10. Jacques Lassaigne, *History of Modern Painting: From Picasso to Surrealism* (Geneva: Albert Skira, 1950), p. 104.

11. Ibid.

12. Schneede, *Surrealism*, p. 64.

13. Ibid., p. 19.

14. The analogy with Rorschach ink blots is obvious.

15. Jacques Dupin, *Joan Miró: Life and Work* (New York: Harry N. Abrams, 1962), p. 141.

16. Jacques Lassaigne, *Miró*, trans. Stuart Gilbert (Geneva: Albert Skira, 1963), pp. 46-48.

17. James Johnson Sweeney, "Joan Miró: Comment and Review," *Partisan Review*, no. 2 (February 1948): 210; quoted in James Thrall Soby, *Joan Miró* (New York: Museum of Modern Art, 1959), p. 100.

18. Quoted in Will Grohmann, *Paul Klee* (London: Lund Humphries, 1954), p. 181.

Innovation in America: Abstract Expressionism

The influx of refugee European intellectuals into the United States is often cited as the main reason for the surge of American art immediately following World War II. André Breton was especially friendly with Arshile Gorky, Wolfgang Paalen and Roberto Matta were close to Robert Motherwell, and André Masson influenced Jackson Pollock. The presence of so many major European artists undoubtedly motivated the Americans, but this was not entirely responsible for the burst of creativity in New York in the late 1940s and the fifties. American artists, after all, had been concerned with avant-garde European art at least since the Armory Show in 1913. Julien Levy, Charles Egan, and Pierre Matisse were showing contemporary European art in New York in the thirties, when artists such as Josef Albers, Hans Hofmann, Salvador Dali, Marcel Duchamp, and Francis Picabia were familiar figures in that city. Furthermore, many American artists had traveled and studied in Europe and then had returned to the United States to work (some on large-scale WPA Federal Arts Projects). Some of them remained European in outlook, while others developed a more typically American point of view. Some were influenced by the Mexican muralists José Clemente Orozco, Diego Rivera, and David Siqueiros. In short, the United States was far from being a cultural desert when the Surrealists began arriving in the early 1940s.

Although the Surrealist expatriate artists were undeniably the catalysts for the Abstract Expressionist movement, they themselves were seldom as innovative as the American artists in the 1940s, and their paintings were not as poetic or authoritative as those by the Americans.

Abstract Expressionist painters were so varied stylistically that at first there seems to be little reason to group them together. Artists as different as Pollock, Rothko, Motherwell, and Franz Kline were all Abstract Expressionists. The word "Imagist" was later applied to paintings by artists such as Rothko, Clyfford Still, and Barnett Newman to differentiate between the abstract images created by their broad fields of color and the energetic gestural paintings of Pollock, Kline, de Kooning, and others. There were significant differences, however, even among the artists of these groups. Of the gestural painters, for example, Kline used a slashing arm motion; de Kooning, the arm or wrist; and Pollock (in his large, fully developed "drip" paintings), not only the hand and arm but the entire body. Other differences were evident in the rococo-like colors and sensuous surfaces of de Kooning, the stark black and white palette of Kline, and the baroque swirls and soft color stains of many of Pollock's mature works.

The Abstract Expressionists were united not by dedication to a particular style, as with the Impressionists or Cubists, but rather by commitment to the idea that the creative act is a process by which the artist defines his inner experiences and his values. The finished work of art was conceived as a form analogous to the artist's inner experience of the world—which included the work being created. This experience is what the painting means, and this meaning is stimulated by the very act of making the painting. In short, the

84

form of the work evolved as the appropriate articulation of an experience that occurred because the work was being made.

The artist normally began his work without a specific idea of how it would come out. During the creative process, artist and work each affected the other, so that as the work took form, its "meaning" emerged. The creative act, therefore, was considered to be an ethical process during which the artist defined himself by means of the actions he took and the decisions he made. (As the Chinese long ago recognized: The art is the man.)

The Abstract Expressionists constantly reinvented the art of painting by relying on spontaneity to stimulate the direct expression of inner experience. Unlike the Surrealists, however, they insisted on a role for conscious choice as the work progressed; they believed that a solution was possible for any compositional problem that occurred during the process of painting.

Rejecting the notion that a work of art is properly the realization in visual form of an already-existing notion about reality, the Abstract Expressionists insisted that any such concept came into being along with the act of creating. The spontaneous generation of the creative act was analogous to a conversation (as opposed to speech making). In this kind of dialogue, as it were, the artist discovered and defined his values through decisions made as he went along.

Coincidentally, during World War II, Jean-Paul Sartre's Existentialist philosophy came into prominence, declaring that mankind is alone in the universe with neither God nor a mechanically structured reality to provide his values and excuses for his actions. Man is free and therefore is responsible for his actions and the invention of his values. Life is nothing until it is lived, according to Sartre, and each individual must make sense of it for himself. Its value is precisely the sense one chooses.

The Abstract Expressionists held that art is nothing until the work of art is being created. An Abstract Expressionist work of art is therefore a psychological self-portrait of the artist as he chooses to be. Existentialism emphasized that anyone who faces his aloneness and has the courage and daring to create himself has acted heroically; in this sense, the Abstract Expressionists are often described as heroic.

A parallel development with Abstract Expressionism was general systems theory, a philosophical-scientific concept that emerged after World War II as an attempt to unify abstract theories such as those dealing with information, communication, control, learning, and artificial intelligence. Of particular concern was the study of behavior in certain abstract systems that are analogous to physically existing systems. By contrast, classical physics dealt with systems that were capable of being isolated and studied objectively by an experimenter without regard for their normal environment. The principle of causality provided the basic rule for establishing laws pertinent to these systems that are considered to be "closed," since all the causes and effects related to the system are known or knowable.

Increased knowledge about subatomic reality, however, led to the discovery of systems that cannot be successfully isolated, and to Werner Heisenberg's uncertainty principle. It was recognized that any study of subatomic systems must inevitably interfere with those systems, since the light used to study them is itself a stream of subatomic particles. The experimenter thus becomes an element in the system he is studying: he both influences it and is influenced by it. Such systems are considered "open."[1]

The difference between the closed and the open system in science appears to be analogous to that between traditional painting processes and the process generally followed by the Abstract Expressionist artist. Like the open scientific system, the Abstract Expressionist work involves an on-going set of relations wherein each part affects all other parts as well as the whole. In both cases there is no stable structure, no objective observer or creator, but only—taking into consideration "feedback"—a constantly changing set of elements, which, as the work nears completion, becomes increasingly stable.

Like creative scientists, the Abstract Expressionist artists followed the leads provided by their work. Comprehension of their work, they insisted, was at least partly the responsibility of the audience. The "open system," consisting of a work of art and its creator, is closed when the artist physically completes the work. That of the work and a perceiver is consummated when the viewer becomes engaged with the work and psychologically completes the experience for himself. Abstract Expressionist art is not intended to entertain or amuse a passive viewer—it relies on the perceiver's participation.

The form of an Abstract Expressionist work of art is part of the behavior pattern of the artist's inner experience itself, just as a cry of anguish or of erotic passion is part of the behavior relevant to those particular experiences.[2] The work of art just has a more elaborate structure.

For all its theoretical emphasis on automatism and pure chance, Surrealism favored an esoteric literary tradition and elegantly made objects, both of which were foreign to the rambunctious pragmatism that dominated American culture. Typically American ideals were often derived from the westward migration across the continent into untamed—often unexplored—territory; myths abound concerning the lonely hero who ventures into virgin territories and creates a new environment. Abstract Expressionism typified this American tendency, which, as Anthony Everitt pointed out, is succinctly captured in an essay by D. H. Lawrence on Walt Whitman:

It is the American heroic message. The soul is not to pile up defenses round herself. She is not to withdraw and seek her heavens inwardly, in mystical ecstasies. She is not to cry to some God beyond, for salvation. She is to go down the open road, as the road opens, into the unknown, keeping company with those whose soul draws them near to her, accomplishing nothing save the journey, and the works incidental to the journey.[3]

86

Abstract Expressionist artists ventured into unknown regions of experience and created works that were indeed "incidental to the journey." The painting and the painter's experience evolved simultaneously in an integrated complex of feeling, doing, choosing, and defining, all in terms of paint. Robert Motherwell remarked that Pollock's "principal problem is to discover what his true subject is. And since painting is his thought's medium, the resolution must grow out of the process of painting itself."[4]

A typical painting by Ernst, Miró, Dali, Magritte, or any other Surrealist artist is an assemblage of images that can be correctly interpreted in terms of Freudian theory. An Abstract Expressionist painting by Pollock, Kline, Rothko or Motherwell, on the other hand, is a single image that functions as a visual metaphor and provides insight into its creator's subjective experience in response to the work of art as it evolved; indeed, it is the central element in an open system that also includes the artist and each perceiver.

Hans Hofmann (1880-1966)

Born in Germany, Hans Hofmann worked in Munich from 1904 to 1907 and in Paris from 1907 to 1914. From 1915 to 1932 he directed his own school in Munich. When he arrived in the United States to stay in 1932, therefore, he was thoroughly familiar with German Expressionism, Fauvism, and Cubism. He had experienced Kandinsky's expressionistic abstract style and he was influenced by Delaunay's Orphist abstractions. He did not paint in a fully abstract style, however, until 1939.

As a teacher, Hofmann taught the expressiveness of color and the significance of formal structure. At first concerned with "the spiritual translation of inner concepts into form," he eventually became interested in purely formal problems. This shift did not mean that he was less concerned with the expressive properties of painting, only that he came to accept the notion that expression was the inevitable result of form making.

A typical abstract painting by Hofmann, *Smaragd, Red, and Germinating Yellow* (cat. no. 41), suggests compensating movements in and out of space—what he referred to as "push and pull." Traditional perspective moves the viewer's eye back into space without an answering movement back out to the surface. Thus, the space in Hofmann's paintings becomes a "breathing" pictorial space.

Color played a central role in Hofmann's carefully integrated, formal constructions. Typically, his paintings are composed of compensating energies. The energy of an area of color provokes reciprocal energy from another area. Equivalent color zones remain, others are modified or eliminated. Transitional areas modulate the intervals between major "force fields" of color until the whole is brought into a balance that depends upon visual tensions.

Because he did not rely on a central style, Hofmann often experienced failure. Each work was a unique effort to solve formal problems and to appropriately express inner experience. He conceived of the creative act as spontaneous, intuitive, constantly in flux, and developing its own rationale as it goes.

Jackson Pollock (1912-1956)

Born in Cody, Wyoming, into a family of sheep ranchers, Jackson Pollock was just under one year old when his family moved to San Diego. They were to move many times around the Southwest before settling in Los Angeles. In 1930 Pollock went to New York, where he studied with Thomas Hart Benton at the Art Students' League. In the mid-thirties he worked for the WPA Federal Arts Project and with David Siqueiros, the Mexican muralist.

An alcoholic, Pollock began psychoanalysis in 1939. The Jungian analyst with whom he worked used Pollock's drawings as a therapeutic aid. Later, a second Jungian analyst used his drawings in the same way.

In 1943 he met Robert Motherwell and began an association during which the two sometimes worked together. About the same time, he met Hans Hofmann, Peggy Guggenheim, and some of the Surrealist emigrés. Miss Guggenheim invited Motherwell and Pollock to exhibit collages in her gallery, and James Thrall Soby of the Museum of Modern Art and the critic Clement Greenberg began to take serious interest in Pollock's art.

In 1947 Pollock gave up representational images and began creating abstractions by dripping paint onto the surfaces of canvases (Figure 19). In taking this step, he extended the automatic painting methods of Surrealists such as Joan Miró and André Masson; indeed, in some ways, Pollock was a Surrealist. Automatism was the essential creative feature of his drip paintings. His brash assault on the canvas was unlike the European Surrealists, however. As Irving Sandler put it, the Surrealists "devised methods to sneak politely around the barriers of reason and inherited culture, Pollock stormed those barriers . . . ."[5]

His method of pouring paint and dripping it from sticks, blunted brushes, and other instruments onto a canvas laid on the floor had precedents: long before, Chinese and Japanese painters had painted on the floor. In fact, they sometimes painted in a state of delirium, especially while drunk, and used an Oriental technique called "flung ink" because of the method of propelling the ink onto the painting surface.

Like these Oriental painters, Pollock made the art of painting into a kind of ritual. He began by splattering and pouring paint onto the canvas, forcing accidental effects, to which he then responded. He developed pure abstractions by turning the act of creation into a kind of dance, during which he dripped and splattered paint onto the canvas. He thus began each painting by deliberately causing chaos, out of which he brought an order that was a record of his creative actions.

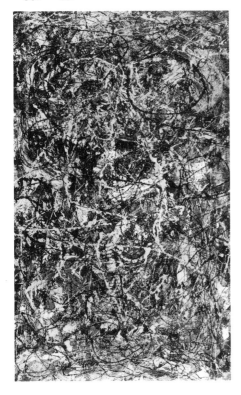

Figure 19. Jackson Pollock, *Full Fathom Five*. Oil on canvas with nails, tacks, buttons, key, coins, cigarettes, and matches, 1947, 129.3 x 76.5 cm. Collection, The Museum of Modern Art, New York, Gift of Peggy Guggenheim.

88

Pollock himself discussed this method:

When I am in my painting, I'm not aware of what I'm doing. It is only after a sort of "get acquainted" period that I see what I have been about. I have no fears about making changes, destroying the image, etc., because the painting has a life of its own. I try to let it come through. It is only when I lose contact with the painting that the result is a mess. Otherwise there is pure harmony, an easy give and take, and the painting comes out well.[6]

Later, in an interview, he denied that he had preconceived images of paintings, but declared: "I do have a general notion of what I'm about and what the result will be."[7]

In his abstract drip paintings after 1947, Pollock was not so much conscious of trying to execute a set task as he was possessed by the act of expression. The evolving work was a direct articulation—in the artist's developing vocabulary of visual form—of his subjective experience. The paintings reveal the kinds of actions he took while making them, and they provide clues for the recognition of his attitudes, moods, and emotions. These spontaneous, innovative compositions, devoid of technical artifice, provide insight into Pollock's blunt, forthright character.

Robert Motherwell (b. 1916)

Born in Aberdeen, Washington, Robert Motherwell has always had a strong interest in French culture. In 1935 he toured France, Germany, and other western European countries. After graduating from Stanford University in 1936 with a major in philosophy, Motherwell returned to Europe to study French Symbolist literature in Paris and at the University of Grenoble. He spent much of 1938 and 1939 traveling, studying, and writing in Europe, and then took a teaching post at the University of Oregon. In 1940 he went to New York to study art history with Meyer Schapiro at Columbia University.

Schapiro, recognizing Motherwell's artistic ability, encouraged him to paint and introduced him to the expatriate Surrealists. Because of his travels, his interest in French literature, and his ability to read and speak French, Motherwell was able to communicate with the Europeans. Indeed, during the next few years he played a central role in putting other young American artists in touch with the Surrealists.

Motherwell studied engraving briefly with Kurt Seligmann and spent time with Roberto Matta and Wolfgang Paalen in Mexico City. In 1942 he contributed, along with the poet and art critic Harold Rosenberg, to the review *VVV*, and he exhibited his work with that of William Baziotes and David Hare in the exhibition *First Papers of Surrealism*. Motherwell, Pollock, and Baziotes along with their wives collaborated on experiments producing "automatic" poems. These three artists were the first Americans to exhibit at Peggy Guggenheim's gallery, Art of This Century, which was usually devoted to exhibitions by the European expatriates.

Like Ernst, Picasso, Braque, and Matisse, Motherwell demonstrated a gift for collage (cat. no. 43); he recognized that the fortuitous association of disparate elements on a single field could generate a creative force the equal of automatism. Both methods force the artist to seek solutions for unexpected relationships among the various elements with which he is working.

Motherwell brought about a synthesis of the forceful American spirit and the more controlled and thoughtful European attitude. While he subscribed to the notion that the creative artist moves into unexplored regions of experience, discovering his responses to unforeseen circumstances, Motherwell also relied upon the intellect to assume control during this process. As with the theoretical scientist, intuition inspired Motherwell's creative act, but discipline and hard work played major roles as well.

Mark Rothko (1903-1970)

Mark Rothko was born in Dvinsk, Russia. When he was ten years old his family emigrated to the United States and settled in Portland, Oregon. He attended Yale University from 1921 to 1923, and then studied painting with Max Weber at the Art Students' League in New York. After years of painting isolated figures in urban settings, Rothko began, in the early 1940s, to experiment with the Surrealist method of automatism. At this point his subjects were hybrid animals, plants, and undersea life forms somewhat like Miró's and Gorky's images. By the mid-1940s he had been affected by the ideas and methods of the expatriate Surrealists, and by 1947 he became a member of the group known as Abstract Expressionists and was developing compositions based on soft-edged, irregular shapes (later he reduced these to a few horizontal rectangles on a vertical ground). Reluctant to paint pure abstractions, Rothko always remained intensely concerned with meaning in his art.

His deceptively simple compositions consist of several horizontal rectangles mounted one above the other on a vertical ground (cat. no. 44). His method of applying paint, in multiple, thin glazes and scumbles,[8] was derived from a technique of working transparent watercolor, which he favored in the mid-1940s. The thinly painted, soft-edged rectangles floating on a translucent ground produce the effect of a luminous atmosphere devoid of material substance. Within each color area, subtle variations of hue and value provoke the sensation of pulsations and, thus, of life. The broad veils of color dematerialize the flat surfaces, producing the illusion of a vast, indefinite space in which the brooding mists of color appear to advance and recede. All that exists here is colored light and space.

Robert P. Crease and Charles C. Marin, in discussing a theory of unified forces by Howard Giorgi and Sheldon Glashow, noted that according to these authors, when a quark emits a certain very heavy particle (nicknamed "ponderon" by Glashaw) the quark turns into a lepton. They go on to explain:

If the quark is part of a proton, the proton will fall apart. The pieces of the proton will, in turn, decay into electrons and positrons, which will eventually meet each other to form photons—light. This light will ultimately traverse an utterly empty plenum. Because protons are a nonrenewable resource, the Universe will end as it began, with light.[9]

Whether this notion is correct is unimportant here. It is significant, however, that Rothko's paintings can be experienced as metaphors for a similar vision. The scientists articulated their picture in logical verbal terms, and Rothko formulated his in paint.

Franz Kline (1910-1962)

Kline emerged as a major Abstract Expressionist painter around 1950. He was born in Wilkes-Barre, Pennsylvania, and grew up in Philadelphia. After studying at Boston University and spending a year in London studying at Heatherly's Art School, Kline settled in New York. During the late 1930s and the 1940s he lived precariously doing caricatures and humorous drawings, especially of life in a tavern in Greenwich Village. In 1950 he turned his attention to black-and-white abstract paintings. The story of his conversion to abstraction is well known: he projected one of his drawings onto his studio wall and was so impressed by the vigor of this stark image that he immediately began to do large black-and-white abstractions.

Although Kline is commonly thought of as the major painter of black-and-white canvases, he was not the only, or even the first, post-World-War-II artist to so restrict his palette. Hofmann, Pollock, Motherwell, and de Kooning in the United States, and Hans Hartung and Pierre Soulages in France all did similar abstractions before Kline. However, none of these artists restricted their palettes as severely, and only Pollock and de Kooning were as vigorously gestural. Kline made the black-and-white gestural painting his primary instrument of expression.

No other painter produced works with the blunt dynamism and drama of Kline's canvases. They carry no suggestions of atmosphere, light, or mystery—only energy. The bold thrusts and counter-thrusts of the stark blacks and whites in paintings such as *New York* (Figure 20) establish visual tensions that result in an over-all balance as delicate as a piece of complex engineering. Indicating Kline's sense of free spirit and raw power, these large canvases also reveal his unequivocal toughness and courage.

Figure 20. Franz Kline, *New York*. Oil on canvas, signed, 1953, 200.6 x 128.3 cm. Albright-Knox Art Gallery, Buffalo, New York, Gift of Seymour H. Knox, 1956.

David Smith (1906-1965)

Smith was born in Indiana into a family whose ancestors included pioneers and stern Calvinists. His father worked for a telephone company and was an inventor. As a young man working as a riveter in an automobile factory, Smith developed great respect for labor (eventually he called his studio at Bolton Landing in upper New York State The Terminal Iron Works).

Although Smith studied painting at the Art Students' League in New York, gradually—via collages, painted reliefs, and relief sculptures—he became a sculptor.

Smith was of the same general age as the Abstract-Expressionist painters and counted most of them as friends—especially Motherwell and Rothko. The paintings of Pollock and Kline, however, seem closest in spirit to Smith's sculpture, which expresses, above all, a big, expansive spirit, a kind of daring and toughness that can be inferred both from the simple, commercial materials and the way in which Smith used them. A direct, courageous—almost reckless—approach to the creative act is shared by these artists, as is their integration of space within the form of their works.

Like the Cubist and Dada artists, Smith used "found" materials in his sculptures. He preferred objects or parts from objects that had been useful—that had done work—like tractors, plows, tanks, and boilers (cat. no. 46). He also used great sheets and bars of iron and steel, stating that "The material called iron or steel . . . possesses little art history. What associations it possesses are those of this century: power, structure, movement, progress, suspension, destruction, brutality."[10]

Smith dispensed with the preliminary drawings traditionally used by sculptors to develop their concepts. His drawings often were done while he was actually working on the sculpture, sometimes in chalk on the floor. Although this kind of spontaneous approach can lead to a relatively high rate of failure among the finished works, it is the method by which the artist can come to grips with the basic problems of his art and can learn most through his attempts to solve them. Furthermore, the works themselves achieve a vigorous character that is unobtainable by other means.

Isamu Noguchi (b. 1904)

In contrast to David Smith's rough, welded metal pieces, Noguchi's use of stone, wood, and bronze is refined. Born in Los Angeles to a Japanese father and a mother of Scottish descent, Noguchi spent his early years in Japan, first at a Japanese school and later at an English one. He returned to the United States in his early teens to study at a private school. The school failed and he got a job tutoring the son of Gutzon Borglum, the creator of the Mt. Rushmore portraits.

Discouraged, after a brief period of studying sculpture with Borglum, he turned to the study of medicine. However, he soon returned to sculpture and attended several art schools in New

York. In 1927 he received a Guggenheim scholarship for study in India but went to Paris instead and for the next two years worked as an assistant to Constantin Brancusi. While in Paris he met Alberto Giacometti and Alexander Calder, who introduced him to Surrealism. It was Brancusi, however, who had the deepest and most lasting effect on Noguchi.

He also studied drawing techniques with the master Ch'i Pai-shih in China, and then, in Japan, he worked with a potter. He later spent time in London and Mexico before returning to the United States. During the years of World War II, when Abstract Expressionism burst upon the scene, Noguchi was in an internment camp, where he had volunteered to go in order to teach the Japanese-Americans detained there how to make their living environment more attractive. Since the early 1950s, Noguchi has divided his time between Japan, where he has a home and studio, and the United States, where he has a studio in New York.

Although Noguchi was not around as Abstract Expressionism was emerging in New York, he nevertheless has always been friendly with artists such as Rothko and Motherwell, and he has shared the spirit of Abstract Expressionism. From Brancusi he learned to regard the creative act as a search for "basic forms" in a process of exploring materials. Like the Abstract Expressionists, Noguchi has always been concerned with creating forms that provide insights into inner experiences. This is not allegory, beloved of Neoclassical artists and certain Symbolists; rather, it is what has here been called "visual metaphor."

There are two distinct tendencies in Noguchi's art: early Greek and early Japanese. His marbles, such as *Woman with Child* (cat. no. 47), usually embody the chaste spirit and subtle refinements of archaic Greek sculpture, whereas the wooden pieces and bronzes often refer to the simplicity and asperity of Japanese Haniwa figures. The purist strains in both cultures are reinforced by the influence of Brancusi.

1. For a full discussion of general systems theory see *Views on General Systems Theory*, Proceedings of the Second Systems Symposium at Case Institute of Technology, ed., Mihajlo D. Mesarović (New York, London, Sydney: John Wiley and Sons, 1964).

2. For a discussion of this point see: Sherman E. Lee and Edward B. Henning, "Works of Art, Ideas of Art, and Museums of Art," *On Understanding Art Museums*, ed. Sherman E. Lee (Englewood Cliffs, New Jersey: Prentice-Hall, 1975), p. 29.

3. Anthony Everitt, *Abstract Expressionism* (Woodbury, New York: Barrons, 1978), pp. 15-16.

4. Quoted in Francis V. O'Connor, *Jackson Pollock* (New York: Museum of Modern Art, 1967), p. 31.

5. Irving Sandler, *The Triumph of American Painting: A History of Abstract Expressionism* (New York and Washington: Praeger, 1970), p. 107.

6. Ibid., p. 102.

7. Ibid., p. 81.

8. A glaze is a thin, transparent or translucent layer of a darker color applied over a lighter one. A scumble is a thin application of a lighter tone worked over, or into, a darker area.

9. Robert P. Crease and Charles C. Mann, *The Second Creation: Makers of the Revolution in 20th-Century Physics* (New York: Macmillan Co., 1986), p. 402.

10. Quoted in Fairfield Porter, "David Smith," *ArtNews* 56 (September 1957): 41.

Catalogue

Catalogue entries have been prepared by several authors, whose initials appear at the end of their texts.

Susan Davis	SD
Edward B. Henning	EBH
Geraldine Wojno Kiefer	GWK
William H. Robinson	WHR

Claude Monet
French, 1840-1926
1. Spring Flowers

Claude Monet
2. La Capeline Rouge (The Red Hood)—Madame Monet

Oil on canvas, signed, dated 1864, 116.8 x 90.5 cm.
The Cleveland Museum of Art, Gift of the Hanna Fund 53.155

Collections: Léon Monet, Rouen; (Wildenstein and Company, New York).

The Atlantic coast near Monet's home, a haven for *plein-air* painters in the 1860s, seems to have nurtured Monet's early passion for still life. As he wrote to his friend and fellow flower-painter Frédéric Bazille in 1864: "There at the moment in Honfleur . . . Boudin and Jongkind are here; we get on marvellously . . . . There's lots to be learned and nature begins to grow beautiful . . . I shall tell you I'm sending a flower piece to the exhibition at Rouen; there are very beautiful flowers at present."[1] More significant, however, was the influence of Gustave Courbet. Monet may well have seen some of Courbet's flower pieces in January of 1863, when, with Henri Fantin-Latour, Courbet staged an exhibit at the Hôtel de Ville in Paris.

This work and Courbet's *Woman with Flower* (or *The Trellis*) and *Magnolias* are empirically developed works; that is, they reveal a typical attitude of mid-nineteenth-century scientists, novelists, and philosophers that sensory data rather than the mystery of metaphysics should provide the basis for art. "The wind blows in the direction of science," declared Emile Zola at the 1866 Paris Salon. "Despite ourselves, we are pushed towards the exact study of facts and things."[2]

Spring Flowers derives much of its freshness and immediacy from its composition, which spills downward and outward from the pots of geraniums at the rear through the potted hydrangeas in the middle ground to the fully mature, plucked peonies in the foreground. Brushwork

engenders striking energies. Within the foreground, for example, curvilinear strokes define the form of individual peonies while also directing the eye along the diagonal line of blossoms. In the middle ground, square, rectangular, and circular patches detail the hydrangeas and basketed lilacs, thus forming a second diagonal that parallels the one formed by the peonies. Indeed, Monet's composition is organized by brushwork, not by plant specimen or even by color. As such, it is a construct of sensation.

The imagery of the work points to another aspect of Monet's maturing sensation. While the title suggests a panoply of spring growth, the plucked peonies and tulips—with petals opened at the apogee of life—suggest the passing of spring to early summer. No intimations of death or *vanitas*, a traditional flower-painting theme, are present. Like Monet's *Terrace at Sainte-Adresse* and his paintings from Bougival, with their associations of youth and courtship, *Spring Flowers* also represents the emergent summer of Monet's art. GWK

1. Henry S. Francis, "'Spring Flowers' by Claude Monet," *Bulletin of The Cleveland Museum of Art* 41 (February 1954):24.

2. Quoted in Linda Nochlin, *Realism* (New York: Penguin Books, 1971), p. 41.

Oil on canvas, ca. 1870, 110.4 x 80 cm.
The Cleveland Museum of Art, Bequest of Leonard C. Hanna, Jr. 58.39

Collections: Michel Monet, Giverny; Captain Edward Molyneux, Paris; (Carrol Carstairs Gallery, New York); Leonard C. Hanna, Jr., Cleveland.

Although scholars are unable to assign a precise date to this work, most associate its technique and domestic subject matter with the artist's early Impressionist paintings of the late 1860s. The image has few precedents in the history of art: the viewer is located inside a room, looking through a French window at a figure walking outside in the snow. The woman in the hood has been identified as Monet's first wife, Camille, who died in 1879, probably from malnutrition. Perhaps her presence explains why this is one of the few paintings from that period of early, classic Impressionism that the artist refused to part with; it remained in his possession until his death in 1926.

Monet broke with conventional painting methods in *The Red Hood* by transferring "the aesthetics of the sketch into a finished painting."[1] Contours are broken and forms dissolved with rapid, sketchy brushwork. Modeling with half-tones and other devices for creating an illusion of three-dimensional form are replaced by abruptly juxtaposed patches of strong, unmodulated color. The abbreviated and blurred features of the woman convey sensations of movement, so the image does not seem fixed or static as would a more conventional or "studied" composition. Instead, Monet offers a new way of seeing that more closely resembles the act of casual glancing or rapid visual scanning, and such fleeting glimpses or "slices" of

life give the painting an immediacy and a wholeness possible only by isolating instantaneous moments of existence.

Monet's particular interest in recording unusual optical effects is evident here in the intense reflected light that floods the room from the snow-covered landscape outside, flattening objects and obliterating details—an effect that the artist achieved by heavily overpainting certain areas (for example, the walls flanking the window). A secondary effect is that the walls are reduced to a series of large, flat planes that parallel the grid-shape of the window, thus emphasizing the two-dimensionality of the picture surface. At the same time, the optical interaction of certain hues creates powerful spatial movement; for example, the strategic placement of intense red (the hood) in the center of a field of cold blues, silver whites, and greens forces the flat planes forward and backward in space simultaneously. Ultimately, Monet opposes the decorative patterns relating to the picture surface with these optical movements of forms in space, resulting in dynamic tensions that animate the composition.

Paintings like this one did not look "composed" to Monet's contemporaries because they offered a radically new type of composition in which the artist shifted emphasis from narrative to purely optical effects—effects that form the basis of an unconventional, distinctly modern way of looking at the world. WHR

1. Kermit Champa, *Studies in Early Impressionism* (New Haven: Yale University Press, 1973), p. 23.

Oil on canvas, signed, 1888, 64.2 x 91.5 cm.
The Cleveland Museum of Art, Gift of Mr. and Mrs. J.H. Wade 16.1044

Collections: (Boussod and Valadon Galerie, Paris); (Durand-Ruel Galerie, Paris); Mr. and Mrs. J.H. Wade, Cleveland.

After 1886 Monet's works became more relaxed and lyrical. In the winter of 1888 he journeyed to Antibes, where under the Mediterranean sun his colors became lighter and his brushwork more refined. He wrote to Alice Hoschedé from Antibes: "What I bring back from here will be sweetness itself, white, pink and blue, all enveloped in a magical air."[1]

In this painting, one of several titled *Antibes*, sparkling sunlight is suggested by high-keyed colors applied with Monet's typical short, patchy brushstrokes. These form a rich and uniform surface, indicating that what we are looking at is not so much a cottage, foliage, sea, and sky as it is shimmering light reflected from their surfaces. While painting on the Côte d'Azure, the artist's palette consisted largely of light pinks, blues, violets, and greens.

The surface of the painting is rich and luxurious. No longer striving to develop his skills, Monet in this work exhibits his great facility as master of a method. EBH

1. *Impressionist and Post-Impressionist Masterpieces: The Courtauld Collection* (New Haven: Yale University Press, 1987), entry 13.

Oil on canvas, signed, ca. 1919-22,
200.6 x 425.3 cm.
The Cleveland Museum of Art, John L.
Severance Fund 60.81

Collections: Monet family, Giverny; (M.
Knoedler and Company, New York).

Shortly after his second trip to Antibes in
1888, Monet worked on several series of
paintings that included haystacks, poplar
trees, the façade of Rouen Cathedral, the
Thames River in London, and his garden at
Giverny. This last subject occupied him for
nearly thirty years, until his death in 1926.
With most of Monet's serial paintings,
because the subject—light—changed constantly, the artist painted the motif over
and over again.

   In a series of large paintings of his water
garden, including *Water Lilies*,[1] Monet indicated his subjective response to the subject while carrying the Impressionist

tendency to render surface effects to its
farthest extreme. By concentrating on the
surface of the pond, he eliminated the
horizon and any indications of movement
back into space. The motif includes lilies
floating on the water, reflections from that
surface, and fronds of water plants dimly
seen beneath the water's surface.

   Monet thus narrowed his vision to concentrate on a single realm, which, at the
same time, permitted great latitude for the
interpretation of his inner sensations. Here,
the result is a canvas of gloriously rich col-
or and over-all brushwork that in many
ways predicts the abstractions painted by
artists such as Jackson Pollock and Phillip
Guston some twenty-five to thirty years
later. EBH

1. The Cleveland canvas is one of a set of
three that was originally intended to be exhibited together as a triptych. The other
two are in the Saint Louis Art Museum
and the Nelson-Atkins Museum of Art in
Kansas City, Missouri. All three canvases
have been exhibited together four times in
recent years.

Edgar Degas
French, 1834-1917
5. Race Horses

Pastel on cardboard, ca. 1873-75, 57.5 x 65.5 cm.
The Cleveland Museum of Art, Bequest of Leonard C. Hanna, Jr. 58.27

Collections: Henri Lerolle, Paris; Hector Brame, Paris; Cesar de Hauke, New York; (Jacques Seligmann and Company, New York); Leonard C. Hanna, Jr., Cleveland.

It is evident that Degas, whose fame resides primarily in his ballet pictures, was interested in physicality—specifically animal locomotion. Indeed, horses appear in his paintings long before ballet dancers.

Degas developed his knowledge of equine anatomy both in the field and by studying other artists' works. In the sixties he visited his friend Paul Valpinçon's estate in Normandy, where he modeled horses in wax and also studied English hunting and racing prints.

Denys Sutton may have been describing Cleveland's pastel when he wrote:

Degas's attitude to the race was characteristically individual: he never depicted it at that moment when attention is concentrated on the jockeys and their horses striving to win; on the contrary he preferred to depict the tense minutes before the race, or when a horse was pulled up, or when jockeys were training in the early morning. For Degas the fascination of such scenes lay in the chance they provided of painting a series of brilliant juxtaposed colours—colours hard to find elsewhere, unless in female costumes or at the theatre, and in suggesting the movement in terms of line, as befitted a descendant of the classicists for whom Ingres was God.[1]

Race Horses is executed in quick, nervous, Impressionistic strokes. Cropped like a snapshot or a print by the eighteenth-century Japanese artist Hiroshige (Degas had a long-standing interest in photography and Japanese prints), it characteristically includes two horse-and-rider groupings at rest and two incipiently violent (rearing) positions. Spontaneity is implicit through careful and studied juxtapositions of form and direction. Alfred Werner called the work an asymmetrical composition of "premeditated instantenousness" that creates an illusion of naturalness.[2]

But Degas was interested in more than perceptually based effects. Like Monet, he was intent upon constructing compositional energies. Febrile force fields animate *Race Horses*, bending trees and exercising horses and jockeys to a choreographed pattern in flexible space.

"Instantaneity is photography, nothing more," Degas wrote in a letter of November 1872. In the mid-eighties he elaborated, "It is essential to do the same subject over and over again, ten times, a hundred times. Nothing in art must seem to be accidental, not even movement.[3] Degas' attitude toward the horse and jockey was the same toward the ballet dancer. The movements of both were disciplined; both required repeated and empathetic study to be fully understood. Neither a professional rider nor a dancer, Degas nevertheless understood choreography. Following a visit to Degas' studio in 1874, Edmond de Goncourt reported, "The painter shows you his pictures, from time to time adding to his explanation by mimicking a choreographic development, by imitating, in the language of the dancers, one of their arabesques."[4]

The French poet and art critic Paul Valéry has observed that, "No animal is closer to a *première danseuse*, a star of the corps de ballet, than a perfectly balanced thoroughbred, as it seems to pause in flight under the hand of its rider, and then trips forward in the bright sunshine. GWK

1. Denys Sutton, "Degas: Master of the Horse," *Apollo* 119 (April 1984): 290, 294.

2. Alfred Werner, *Degas Pastels* (New York: Watson-Guptill, 1980), p. 60.

3. Keith Roberts, *Degas* (Oxford: Phaidon Press, 1976), p. 14.

4. John Rewald, *The History of Impressionism* (New York: Museum of Modern Art, 1961), p. 278.

Oil on canvas, signed, ca. 1883, 70 x 200.6 cm.
The Cleveland Museum of Art, Gift of the Hanna Fund 46.83

Collections: Paul Durand-Ruel, Paris; Max Liebermann, Berlin; Dr. and Mrs. K. Rietzler, Berlin; (Paul Rosenberg and Company, New York).

Painted by Edgar Degas around 1883, *Frieze of Dancers* has neither the complex psychological implications of his portraits—for example, *The Duchess of Montejasi-Cicerale*—nor the compositional originality of *Ballet Girls* (cat. no. 7). It shares with many of his paintings a certain detachment from the subject. The multiple image conveys much about the hard-working ballet "rats" that this artist delighted in drawing or painting, but it tells us nothing about the individual portrayed.

Degas' arrangement of four different views of the same figure is theoretically related to later Cubist practices: applying the same principle, Picasso and Braque combined various views into a single image.

Unlike Monet, Degas was not at all concerned with rendering the effects of sunlight reflected from the surfaces of nature. Instead, he was intrigued with ordinary, urban subjects caught unaware in unposed moments—as in this work. His ability as a draftsman to record such subjects with exquisite precision is clearly discernible. His palette is far from the typical Impressionist one of light, prismatic tones suggestive of reflected sunlight; indeed, no light source can be inferred in this picture. Furthermore, his use of orange for the hair and acid green for the shadows must have seemed unusual even to the Impressionists.

Degas' natural affinity for free-standing sculpture can be adduced from the four views of the ballerina: each is so interesting visually that the artist must have been constantly thinking of the figure in the round. EBH

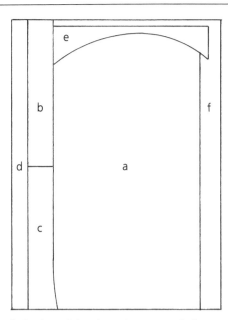

Pastel on paper pasted on cardboard, signed, ca. 1897, 55.2 x 41.1 cm.
The Cleveland Museum of Art, Gift of Mr. and Mrs. J.H. Wade 16.1043

Collections: Paul Durand-Ruel, Paris; Mr. and Mrs. J.H. Wade, Cleveland.

Degas is reported to have created around 1,500 paintings, prints, pastels, and sculptures employing the subject of the ballet.[1] This work does not, however, depict the more glamorous aspects of a ballet performance. Instead, we are brought backstage to witness a more mundane event: off center-stage and unaware of the viewer's presence, three dancers execute a series of routine stretching and warm-up exercises.[2] The image is thus characteristic of the way Degas habitually depicted his subjects at unexpected and revealing moments.

Painted in thick layers, *Ballet Girls* has the rough, deeply pitted surface that characterizes the artist's late pastels. Since pastel consists of powdered pigment lacking a strong binding agent, it can be extremely difficult to handle; in most cases, reworking only smears or muddies the color. Degas, however, invented special techniques and fixatives that allowed him to build up layer upon layer of color exhibiting various degrees of transparency and opacity, comparable to glazing and scumbling techniques in oil. The richly worked surfaces and the intense, vibrating hues in *Ballet Girls* are the result of such innovative methods.[3] Moreover, the vigorous hatching of hot oranges over strong greens creates a sense of space and volume, mainly through the optical "push/pull" effect of contrasting warm/cool colors.

The pose of the dancer with the raised arm in *Ballet Girls* can be traced to an earlier pastel by Degas, *The Rehearsal of a*

Ballet (1872).[4] In fact, the poses of all three dancers in *Ballet Girls* were used repeatedly by Degas in paintings and pastels dating from at least 1872 to 1900.[5] In two other late pastels similar to *Ballet Girls*, Degas included a fourth dancer on the right.[6]

The three dancers in the present work are arranged in an asymmetrical pattern, reflecting the influence of Japanese prints. The most prominent dancer—the one seen from behind, in the right foreground—is in shadow, her right elbow sliced off by the picture edge. The torsos of the other two are bisected by both a vertical bar on one side and by the left picture edge on the other. Employing radically new compositional devices—asymmetrical designs, extremely high or low viewing angles, bold foreshortenings, and unusual framing devices that crop figures at the picture edge—Degas gave his images a deceptively informal appearance, as if they had been captured instantaneously, like a snapshot.

Ballet Girls actually consists of six separate sheets of tracing paper (indicated by letters A-F in the diagram included here) attached to cream-colored paper, mounted on cardboard. The initial design was executed in charcoal on the center section (A), which extends to the vertical bar on the left, forms a circular arch near the top of the picture, and ends 3.8 centimeters from the right edge. The artist then added two strips of paper (B and C) that form the support of the vertical bar on the left; a third vertical strip of paper (D) was added on the extreme left so that the artist could extend the body of the dancer on that side. A small, arched strip of paper (E) was also added directly above the central section, and an inverted "L"-shaped strip (F) was added above this to form most of the top and the right

edges of the picture. The handling of pastel varies from section to section: while the center area is vigorously worked, the technique for the vertical strips on the far right and extreme left is distinctly softer and more delicate.

Degas' use of tracing paper enabled him to appropriate figures from various works that could then be re-combined to form new compositions. The art dealer Ambroise Vollard commented: "Because of the many tracings that Degas did of his drawings, the public accused him of recreating himself, but his passion for perfection was responsible for his continual research."[7] Historian George T.M. Schackelford, however, sees another motive behind the artist's method: "The point of Degas' repetition was not, of course, the correction of old mistakes but the exploration of new, uncharted fields of possibility."[8] WHR

1. George T.M. Schackelford, *Degas: The Dancers* (Washington, D.C.: National Gallery of Art, 1984), p. 16.

2. Schackelford notes that upperclass gentlemen of the ballet audience were frequently permitted backstage to observe and visit with the young dancers (Ibid., p. 38).

3. It is interesting to note that while the first layer is fixed, the second is not.

4. Collection of the Metropolitan Museum of Art, New York.

5. The pose of the dancer with the raised arm in *Ballet Girls* is also very similar to that of a dancer in a photographic negative of uncertain authorship, now in the collection of the Cabinet des Estamps, Bibliothèque Nationale, Paris. These photographic negatives are reproduced and discussed in Schackelford, *Degas*, p. 114.

6. The two pastels, both titled *Danseuse*, are listed as numbers 1247 and 1248, and dated ca. 1896, in P.A. Lemoisne, *Degas et son Oeuvre*, vol. 3 (Paris: Arts et Métiers Graphiques, 1946).

7. Ambroise Vollard, *Degas, An Intimate Portrait*, trans. Randolph T. Weaver (New York: Crown Publishers, 1937), pp. 62-63.

8. Schackelford, *Degas*, p. 125.

Bronze, ca. 1896-97, h. 45.7 cm.
The Cleveland Museum of Art, Hinman B.
Hurlbut Collection 2028.47

Collections: (Buchholz Gallery, New York);
Hinman B. Hurlbut, Cleveland.

Precisely when Degas began making
sculpture is not known. None of his wax
or clay models were cast in bronze during
his lifetime, and he saw only one of his
sculptures exhibited.[1]

When Degas died (1917), the dealer Paul
Durand-Ruel discovered around one hundred and fifty sculptures in his studio.
Most were in such poor condition, due
largely to the artist's experimental techniques and unconventional working
methods, that only seventy-three could be
saved. With the exception of *Little Dancer
of Fourteen Years* (Figure 1), the seventy-
three salvageable works were assigned
numbers from 1 through 72. Each original
was then cast in bronze by the foundry of
A.A. Hébrard. Twenty-three sets were
made of each original, and the individual
sets were distinguished by letters from A
through T.[2] This explains the stamp on the
base of the Cleveland bronze: CIRE PERDUE
A.A. HEBRARD 67/B. The "67" corresponds to
the original of the work and the "B" refers
to the second set of casts.

The rough, tactile surface, lacking the
finish of an early Degas sculpture like *Little
Dancer of Fourteen Years* of 1880-81,
clearly indicates that this is a late work. Art
historian Charles Millard has dated it about
1900 to 1910, based partly upon comparison with several related works that the
artist is known to have executed during
that period, and partly upon recorded
statements by one of Degas' models.[3] Yet,
Millard cautioned: "Stylistically it would
seem to have been modelled somewhat
earlier, perhaps around 1890."[4]

Like the bold, patchy brushwork in
Degas' late paintings, the heavily
manipulated surface of *Dancer Looking at
the Sole of Her Right Foot* defies academic
standards of finish and concern for detail.
Similarly, the omission of the dancer's left
hand can be compared with such innovative compositional devices as the cut-off
forms and the incomplete figures in Degas'
paintings. The rough, spontaneously
modeled surfaces provide direct evidence
of the physical process of the object's
making, and thus anticipate future
developments in modern sculpture. Formally, the broken surface functions to capture
light, animate the figure, and provide
directional movement to the rotation of
volumes through space.

Degas posed the figure of the dancer in
a most difficult position because it offered
a series of daring foreshortenings and
unusual views. Since it is physically impossible for anyone to hold such an unconventional pose for more than a moment, the sculpture conveys the same
sense of instantaneity—of precarious but
exact balance—that characterizes Degas'
paintings. Millard commented:

*To realize his poses of disequilibrium,
Degas' subjects had to be dancers, for only
they could (hold) a rapid succession of
balanced movements sufficiently ritualized
that he could observe them repeatedly. His
observation was so intense that he was
eventually able to suggest successive motion in a static object.*[5]

Degas was not afraid to alter or distort
natural forms to enhance the formal composition of his sculptures. In this work, for
example, the curvature of the limbs and
small anatomical distortions, such as the
protrusion of the right hip, animate the
figure and give it an explosive vitality.

Degas created four variations on the
theme of *Dancer Looking at the Sole of
Her Right Foot*, which Millard believes may
have been inspired by the Classical bronze
statue *Spinario*.[6] In the Cleveland bronze,
however, Degas stripped the figure of
details, finish, facial features, and narrative,
replacing these with a distinctly modern
concern for abstract form. As the viewer
walks around the dancer, a series of startling and constantly changing silhouettes
unfold. Every angle reveals how carefully
and completely Degas conceived the integration of figure and space, mass and
void, open and closed form—concerns that
anticipate the later sculpture of such
masters as Pablo Picasso and Henry Moore.
WHR

1. Degas' sculpture *Little Dancer of Fourteen Years* was exhibited in 1881.

2. The twenty-third set (intended for the
heirs of Degas) was marked "HER" rather
than with a single letter.

3. Charles W. Millard, *The Sculptures of
Edgar Degas* (Princeton, New Jersey:
Princeton University Press, 1976), pp.
18-19.

4. Ibid.

5. Ibid., p. 105.

6. In the Palazzo dei Conservatori, Rome;
see Millard, *Sculptures*, p. 69.

James Abbott McNeill Whistler
American, 1834-1903
9. Nocturne in Black and Gold: Entrance to Southampton Water

Auguste Rodin
French, 1849-1917
10. The Age of Bronze

Oil on canvas, ca. 1872-74, 50.8 x 76.2 cm.
The Art Institute of Chicago, The Stickney Fund. Copyright 1987 The Art Institute of Chicago. All rights reserved.

In his "Ten O'Clock Lecture" of 1885, Whistler urged the elimination of narrative or story-telling in art; he was thus among the first to establish a theoretical basis for abstract painting. "As music is the poetry of sound," Whistler wrote, "so is painting the poetry of sight, and the subject-matter has nothing to do with harmony of sound or of colour."[1] These ideas were visually manifested in a series of paintings called Nocturnes, in which Whistler omitted details, radically simplified forms, and reduced his palette to a few close-valued hues.[2] In *Nocturne in Black and Gold: Entrance to Southampton Water*, for example, only a few faint, shadowy forms are suggested; these are bathed in a misty atmospheric envelope that blurs the natural boundaries between objects, obscures depth perception, and unifies the entire scene in a continuous veil of soft, floating color.

Whistler employed extremely delicate relationships of form and color in this painting, not to define a specific landscape, but to create an evocative mood of poetic reverie. This attempt to evoke various emotional states through fugitive color sensations has literary parallels in the Symbolist poetry of Paul Verlaine and Stephane Mallarmé.

To emphasize the formal or decorative aspects of his art, Whistler employed musical titles, often calling his paintings "Symphonies," "Arrangements," and "Harmonies." The picture popularly referred as to *Whistler's Mother*, for example, is actually titled *Arrangement in Black*

and Gray: The Artist's Mother. The Nocturnes also bear musical connotations, although Whistler first called these works "Moonlights"—suggesting associations with the piano sonatas of Ludwig von Beethoven.[3]

Whistler's aim in the Nocturnes was to create a totally harmonious, decorative design in which the meaning of an image would be conveyed purely through the arrangement of shape and color, as opposed to any representational element. Concern with subject matter was thus replaced by an "art-for-art's-sake" aesthetic. "Art," Whistler said, "should be independent of all clap-trap—should stand alone, and appeal to the artistic sense of eye or ear, without confounding this with emotions entirely foreign to it, as devotion, pity, love, patriotism, and the like."[4] WHR

1. James Abbott McNeill Whistler, *The Gentle Art of Making Enemies* (London: W. Heinemann, 1890), p. 127.

2. The earliest Nocturnes date from the mid-1860s.

3. See Denys Sutton, *Nocturne: The Art of James McNeill Whistler* (London: Country Life Limited, 1963), p. 64.

4. Whistler, *Making Enemies*, pp. 127-28.

Bronze, signed, 1876, h. 180.8 cm.
The Cleveland Museum of Art, Gift of Mr. and Mrs. Ralph King 18.328

Collections: Mr. and Mrs. Ralph King, Cleveland (ordered from Rodin before his death).

The subject of intense debate among its contemporary critics, *The Age of Bronze* was Rodin's first life-size sculpture to be exhibited. The model for the figure was Auguste Neyt, a young Belgian soldier who was stationed at a barracks near Rodin's home in Brussels. Neyt, who had to obtain special permission from his commanding officer to pose for Rodin, later described the arduous and exacting process of working with the great sculptor:

I had to go through all kinds of poses every day in order to get the muscles right.

102

Rodin did not want any exaggerated muscle, he wanted naturalness. I worked two, three, even four hours a day and sometimes for an hour at a stretch. Rodin was very pleased and would encourage me by saying: just a little longer.[1]

To make the long hours of posing more bearable, Rodin let Neyt rest his left arm on a stick, which became a spear in the final composition (it was removed, however, before the work was completed).

Rodin's working method involved examining his model from all sides and angles in order to maintain absolute fidelity to nature; he even "procured one of those ladders painters use for their big canvases . . . and climbed up and did what I could to make my model and my clay agree in foreshortening, and I looked at the contours from above."[2] According to Judith Cladel, Rodin's friend and biographer, *The Age of Bronze* was completed in December 1876, eighteen months after its inception in June 1875.[3]

The plaster cast of the sculpture, which Rodin initially titled *The Vanquished*, was immediately controversial upon its January 1877 unveiling at the Cercle Artistique in Brussels. Critics called the work "very beautiful and extraordinarily original"[4] and praised it for its startling lifelike qualities demonstrating "a realism that comes directly from the Greeks,"[5] but they suggested that the naturalism Rodin had labored eighteen months to achieve was the result of casting the figure from life.

The unidealized nude male figure—a drastic departure from the traditional academic sculpture of the day—was the subject of disbelief from fellow artists: a review of the 1877 Paris Salon, where the plaster cast traveled next, warned that "Rodin should be cautious, because the artists are suspicious; perhaps they are even a little jealous . . . (because) sometimes people who make casts are given the qualification of sculptor."[6] Rodin, incensed at the idea that his work was not an original creation, immediately complained to Eugène Guillaume, the president of the Salon sculpture jury and director of the Ecole des Beaux-Arts, who suggested that he make plaster casts from the model and submit comparative photographs as well. Rodin complied, but when he requested "the result of the examination, they gave me back my photographs, and . . . the seals of the envelope in which all of this was enclosed had not even been broken."[7] The controversy was finally resolved when a group of artists wrote a letter to the French Department of Fine Arts attesting to Rodin's talent.

The French government purchased the plaster cast of *The Age of Bronze*, which was cast in bronze in 1880, and eventually the work became so popular that it was issued in reduced versions.[8] SD

1. Quoted in John L. Tancock, *The Sculpture of Auguste Rodin* (Philadelphia: Philadelphia Museum of Art, 1976), p. 349.

2. Ibid., p. 342.

3. Judith Cladel, *Rodin* (New York: Harcourt, Brace and Company, 1937), p. 48.

4. Ruth Butler, ed., *Rodin in Perspective* (Englewood Cliffs, New Jersey: Prentice-Hall, 1980), p. 33.

5. Ibid.

6. Ibid., pp. 34-35.

7. Tancock, *Sculpture*, p. 347.

8. A complete list of the extant casts of *The Age of Bronze* is available in Athena Tacha Spear, *Rodin Sculpture in The Cleveland Museum of Art* (Cleveland, 1967), pp. 94-95.

Bronze, signed, 1883, h. 41.9 cm.
The Cleveland Museum of Art, Bequest of James Parmelee 40.581

Collections: William E. Henley; Henry Symons; (Knoedler Galleries, New York); James Parmelee, Washington.

Rodin's greatest early critical success was in response to his work in portrait-sculpture. In an article published in the *Magazine of Art* in 1888, an enthusiastic English critic wrote that Rodin "accentuates in the human face rather what is characteristic and individual than what is harmonious and of plastic effect, and thus succeeds chiefly with types which unite energetic characterization with subtlety of expression."[1]

William E. Henley, a particularly fine example of Rodin's virtuosity as a portraitist, ably supports this critic's summation. Modeled from life, the bust has both particularized and generalized qualities that combine to produce a forceful, dynamic likeness. The careful facial modeling, evident in details such as the painstaking treatment of the flaccid eye tissue, reveals the underlying bone structure of the sitter's head without sacrificing the sense of living flesh. Eyes, ears, nose, and mouth are also carefully rendered in detail. In contrast, however, the hair appears to have been more rapidly worked. The areas around the crown and the back of the head seem to have been purposefully left in an unmodeled state, and the sideburns are articulated with only a few sharp strokes of a pointed sculpting tool.

Paul Cézanne
French, 1839-1906
12. The Pigeon Tower at Bellevue

Rodin met William E. Henley (1849-1903), the English poet and critic, when he visited England in 1881 at the invitation of Alphonse Legros, a mutual friend of the two men. From 1882 to 1886 Henley was editor of the influential *Magazine of Art*, and because of his enthusiastic articles about Rodin's work, the sculptor became popular in England while still remaining relatively unknown in his native country. SD

1. Claude Phillips, "Auguste Rodin," *Magazine of Art* XI (1888): 144.

Oil on canvas, 1894-96, 64.2 x 80 cm. The Cleveland Museum of Art, The James W. Corrigan Memorial 36.19

Collections: (Ambroise Vollard, Paris); Ralph Coe, Cleveland.

Cézanne's sense of an underlying structure in nature as contrasted with the Impressionist concern for an all-encompassing atmosphere and light is clear in *The Pigeon Tower*. The composition is divided roughly into three horizontal zones: predominantly salmon orange across the bottom fourth of the canvas, blue across the upper half, and a primarily green area between these two. There are, however, some greens and blues in the lower region; some greens, salmons, and pinks in the upper section; and a great deal of blue and salmon as well as yellowish white in the middle, or green, range.

These three areas are also to be read as foreground, background, and middle distance. The middle, green section is a transitional area where dominant key shifts occur, going from warm to cool, lower to upper, and close up to far distance. It is where most of the visual activity takes place as the bulky foliage swirls around the columnar pigeon tower to be stabilized by the vertical poplars on the right-hand side, which form right angles with the horizontals of the ground area.

The palpable blue of the sky curtains off visual penetration of deep space. The tower serves as an axis around which the other forms in the middle distance revolve. It tilts slightly to our left, and the roof is seen from a higher viewpoint than the rest of the building.

Cézanne's broad, blocky brushstroke indicates a constructive attitude rather than an analytical attitude. The entire composition finally achieves a state of balance dependent upon reciprocal visual tensions. EBH

Oil on canvas, 1894-1900, 71.5 x 92.1 cm. The Cleveland Museum of Art, Bequest of Leonard C. Hanna, Jr. 58.21

Collections: (Ambroise Vollard, Paris); Schweitzer, Berlin; Auguste Pellerin, Paris; Alphonse Kahn, Paris; (Galerie Barbazanges, Paris); (Reinhardt Galleries, New York); (Valentine Gallery, New York).

Cézanne painted the Sainte-Victoire mountain many times. While Monet painted a motif repeatedly because the subject changed whenever the light changed, Cézanne painted a motif again and again because he kept finding better solutions for indicating an underlying structure in nature. Furthermore, he wanted to paint the mountain from varying viewpoints.

Here the mountain looms up on the canvas but is held back in space by the trees in the middle distance that overlap it, and by the road in the foreground that winds back towards it. The foreground, middle ground, and distance are painted, as we noted in *The Pigeon Tower*, in salmons, greens, and blues. The green middle distance again serves as a modulating area of great visual activity between the salmon tones of the foreground and the rich blues of the sky and distant mountain.

The full-foliaged limb extending out from the upper left-hand side parallels the long contour of the mountain, thus establishing a strong visual tie between middle distance and background. The low-lying foliage in the middle ground spreads out and down into the foreground, thus connecting these two areas.

Even more clearly than in *The Pigeon Tower*, Cézanne's broad brushstroke creates a uniform pattern across the surface of the canvas without differentiating between distances or textures. If, in our imagination, we remove the contour line defining the ridge of the mountain, for example, its rocky bulk would merge with the sky.

In reality, this ''mountain'' is little more than a large, rocky hill, but it dominates the landscape around Aix-en-Provence. Its looming, domineering presence is what Cézanne emphasized, not its actual size.

The plastic character of Cézanne's painting can be realized if we imagine that we can reach into the painting and lift out the scene that is depicted: it would surely come out as a cohesive form, like a sculpture or a complex architectural unit. EBH

Vincent van Gogh
Dutch (French School), 1853-1890
**14. The Road Menders at
Saint-Rémy**

Oil on canvas, 1889, 73.7 x 92.1 cm.
The Cleveland Museum of Art, Gift of the
Hanna Fund 47.209

Collections: Leclerc; G. Fayet, Igny; (Paul
Rosenberg, Paris); Gilbert E. Fuller.

In May of 1889, after suffering several
mental attacks accompanied by visual and
auditory hallucinations, van Gogh left Arles
and voluntarily committed himself to an
asylum in the small town of Saint-Rémy.
Since he remained perfectly lucid between
these attacks, he continued to paint; in
fact, he created some of his greatest
works during his period of convalescence
at the Saint-Rémy asylum, including *Starry
Night* and *Wheat Field with Cypress Trees*,
both executed during the summer of
1889.[1]

It can be determined from the artist's
letters that *The Road Menders at
Saint-Rémy* was painted in late 1889. On
November 20 of that year, Vincent asked
his brother Theo to send some canvas
from Paris. Sixteen days later, on December 7, Vincent wrote again to thank Theo
for the recent arrival of ten meters of canvas and mentioned—for the first time—a
painting that undoubtedly is *The Road
Menders at Saint-Rémy:*

*In spite of the cold, I have gone on work-
ing outside till now, and I think it is doing
me good and the work too. The last study
I have done is a view of the village, where
they were working—under enormous
plane trees—repairing the pavement. So
there are piles of sand, stones, and gigantic trunks—the leaves yellowing, and here
and there you get a glimpse of a house
and small figure.[2]*

On January 7, 1890, Vincent informed
Theo that he had painted a copy of this
picture, and he distinguished the two by
describing the first work as a "study from
nature" and the copy, now known as *The
Road Menders* (Phillips Collection, Washington, D.C.), as "perhaps more finished."[3]
The artist's brushwork in the Cleveland
painting is certainly more spontaneous and
hurried than the controlled, "finished" version in the Phillips Collection. And the palette of the Phillips Collection painting is
both more complex and more subdued—
containing dull ochres, grays, aqua blues,
and olive greens—than the pure, intense
yellows, whites, and emerald greens of the
Cleveland version. Two additional elements
distinguish the first version from the copy:
the Cleveland painting curiously lacks a
ground layer, and it was painted not on a
traditional artist's canvas but on a commercial fabric (probably a tablecloth) with
a pattern of small red diamonds that is
clearly visible in the many unpainted areas
of the design layer. The unusual commercial fabric support may be interpreted as
evidence that van Gogh painted this picture between November 20 and December
7, or after he had requested more canvas
from Theo but before the new shipment
arrived from Paris. The absence of a
ground, on the other hand, suggests that
van Gogh worked quickly to record these
"yellowing leaves" and autumnal effects,
perhaps hurried by the cold weather.

It is not difficult to understand why van
Gogh, who loved the simple, honest lab-
orers depicted in the paintings of Jean
François Millet, found this scene so compelling. Here, Provençal villagers are
depicted walking along a street, engaged
in daily activities, while on the far right
men toil beneath a canopy of plane trees,
whose massive anthropomorphic trunks

reach upward in great heroic gestures. Van
Gogh even enhanced the expressive
shapes of the trees by exaggerating their
contours with long, powerful, flowing
brushstrokes. The paving stones and rocks,
on the other hand, were rendered as simple, strong, boxlike or circular shapes.

Throughout the painting details have
been ignored, colors heightened, and
forms exaggerated or distorted with nervous, impulsive brushwork applied in both
short hatchings and long, continuous
strokes. Not just an objective or descriptive
representation, the painting suggests the
intense emotional excitement that the artist must have experienced in the presence
of this magnificent autumnal scene. WHR

1. The precise nature of van Gogh's illness
has never been determined. Historians
speculate that he may have suffered from
epilepsy, schizophrenia, syphilis, or a combination of physical and mental disorders,
exacerbated by poor diet and excessive
drinking of absinthe.

2. Vincent van Gogh, *Further Letters of
Vincent van Gogh to His Brother, 1886-
1889* (New York: Houghton-Mifflin Co.,
1929), no. 618

3. Ibid., no. 621.

Oil on canvas, 1890, 50.2 x 50.2 cm.
The Cleveland Museum of Art, Bequest of
Leonard C. Hanna, Jr. 58.31

Collections: (Bernheim-Jeune & Cie, Paris);
Katherine Dreier, New York; Mrs. Cornelius
J. Sullivan; (Parke-Bernet); Leonard C.
Hanna, Jr., Cleveland.

In May of 1890 van Gogh left Saint-Rémy
and went to live in Auvers, situated only a
few miles to the north of Paris. Although
placed under the care of Dr. Paul Gachet,
van Gogh rented a room at the inn of
Arthur Gustav Ravoux. A month after his
arrival, van Gogh painted three portraits of
Ravoux's daughter Adeline, including the
one in the Cleveland Museum collection.
The other two portraits, both in private
collections, depict Mlle Ravoux in complete
profile, from the knees up, seated in a
chair, and placed before a dark blue
background. In a letter to his brother
Theo, dated June 24, van Gogh mentioned
two of these paintings: "This week I made
a portrait of a girl of about sixteen, in blue
against a blue background, the daughter
of the people with whom I am staying.
I have given her this portrait, but I have
made a variant of it for you, a size 15
canvas.[1]

Historian J.-B. de la Faille believes that
the "variant" refers to the three-quarter
view now in Cleveland, and he considers it
of "higher quality" than the original.[2] The
third portrait of Mlle Ravoux is a copy of
the profile view.

While van Gogh is remembered mostly
for his landscapes and still lifes (especially
his flower paintings), it should be noted
that the artist placed an equally high value
on his portraits. "What excites me most in
my profession," he stated in a letter dated
June 1890 to his sister Wilhelmina, "much,
much more than anything else, is portraiture, modern portraiture."[3] In this same
letter, he commented:

*I should like to paint portraits which a
hundred years from now will seem to the
people of those days like apparitions. Thus
I do not attempt to achieve this through
photographic resemblance, but through
our impassioned aspects, using our science
and our modern taste for color as a means
of expression and of exaltation of
character.*[4]

Although he found portrait painting extremely stimulating, van Gogh had great
difficulty finding sitters, no doubt because
he defied conventional modes of portraiture. By boldly exaggerating the essential features of his sitters, he turned his
portraits into subjective interpretations of a
sitter's inner, spiritual self. Moreover, color
and line, in their pure or "musical" state,
were often used to convey symbolic meaning. The white flowers in *Mademoiselle
Ravoux*, for example, may be interpreted
as a symbol of youth, hope, or innocence,
and the dark blue background may represent eternity.

Van Gogh considered yellow an especially beautiful color and associated it with
divinity. Here, he has covered Mlle Ravoux's
face with intense, radiant yellows, similar
to the brilliant celestial bodies set against a

nocturnal sky in *Starry Night* of 1889. "In
a picture," van Gogh wrote to artist Emile
Bernard, "I want to say something as com-
forting as music. I should like to paint men
and women with that certain something of
the eternal which the halo used to symbolize and which we seek to achieve by
the actual radiance and vibration of our
modern colorings."[5] In this light, we can
offer a symbolic interpretation of
Mademoiselle Ravoux: Van Gogh may have
seen this attractive sixteen-year-old girl as a
modern Madonna or Venus, a symbol of
the eternal woman, set against the infinite
blue night like a radiant star, promising
hope and life through her youth and innocence. WHR

1. Jan Hulsker, *The Complete van Gogh:
Paintings, Drawings, Sketches* (New York:
Harry N. Abrams, 1980), p. 468

2. See J.-B. de la Faille, *The Works of Vincent van Gogh: His Paintings and Drawings*
(Amsterdam: Meulenhoff International,
1970), no. F:786.

3. John Rewald, *Post-Impressionism: From
Van Gogh to Gauguin* (New York:
Museum of Modern Art, 1956), p. 394.

4. Ibid.

5. Ibid.

Paul Gauguin
French, 1848-1903
16. Woman in the Waves (Ondine)

Oil on canvas, signed, dated 1889, 92 x 72 cm.
The Cleveland Museum of Art, Gift of Mr. and Mrs. William Powell Jones 78.63

Collections: (Vente Gauguin, Paris, 23 February 1891); M. Jeanson; Gustav Fayet; Wilhelm Hansen, Denmark; (Leicester Galleries, London); Mr. and Mrs. Frank Ginn, Cleveland; Mr. and Mrs. William Powell Jones, Cleveland.

Paul Gauguin's *Ondine* is steeped in Impressionist technique and theory. Its light, aerated texturing, buoyancy, supple pose, and fine sense of contour relate it to Edgar Degas' pastels, one of which formed part of Gauguin's collection. Its outdoor setting—Le Pouldu in Brittany, where it may well have been painted— reflects Impressionist attention to locale. Its indebtedness to Japanese prints, and above all, its vibrant complementary color scheme, show that Gauguin's concerns of the late 1880s, like those of Vincent van Gogh, Georges Seurat, and Henri de Toulouse-Lautrec, were revisionist rather than radical.

At this time the effectiveness and affectiveness of color contrast were prime topics for theoretical speculation in Paris. Following M.-E. Chevreul's *Loi du Contraste Simultané des Couleurs* (1839) and Ogden N. Rood's *Modern Chromatics* (New York, 1879), both of which were "color primers" for the avant-garde, David Sutter published a series of articles, *Les Phenomènes de la Vision*, in 1880, and Emile Zola published his novel *L'Oeuvre* in 1885 and 1886.

In the Zola work, the protagonist, painter Claude Lantier, utilized complementary color theories in an empirical fashion. So Zola wrote, "Thus science entered into painting; a method was created for logical observation."[1] Yet he did not "interpret the scientific speculations on colour as a continuation and enrichment of the methods of the impressionists, but as a condition for the creation of a transcendental, idealist picture—in other words a symbolic painting."[2]

Working out the symbolic qualities of color—that is, developing a color harmony or contrast geared to establish correspondences with emotion—was not an Impressionist trait, but a Symbolist one. Seurat, leader of the Neo-Impressionist, "scientific" school of painting, considered painting not a demonstration, but a harmony. Like Zola and Seurat, some of whose theoretical sources he shared, Gauguin moved in the eighties from Impressionism to Symbolism. "Art is an abstraction," he wrote in 1888, "derive this abstraction from nature while dreaming before it."[3]

The red-haired *Ondine*'s flesh varies from bluish to orange tints. Her right hand raised to her mouth in a gesture of horror (Gauguin consulted his own paintings and works by Degas and Odilon Redon for the pose), she hurls herself into a wave-crested green sea. Rather than express the physicality of penetrating the water, as Seurat had done in his very different and still-Impressionist *Une Baignade Asnières*, of 1883-84, Gauguin separated the nude from her fluid surround by a heavy contour. In adopting Cloisonnisme (the technique introduced to him by his young artist friend Emile Bernard) for this image, Gauguin intimated metaphor and stasis rather than action. Having brought his viewers intuitively to the brink of enjoyment, he cut the figure out of the picture, as it were, to present it as an icon of a new sensibility.

Ostensibly a femme fatale, the Ondine, popularized in a fin-de-siècle legend (first published in Germany in 1811), was a water nymph who could win a soul only by marrying a mortal and mothering his child. She wooed a knight, who married her only to later abandon her for a human love; on his wedding day she emerged from the depths and killed him with a kiss. For Gauguin, as Wojtech Jirat-Wasiutynski has pointed out, the fatal woman was an index of the low state of civilization wherein true and free love—a state intensely desired by Gauguin—was perverted. She also, according to Wayne Andersen, represented a personal death wish. For Gauguin saw himself as the primitive of a new epoch, an androgynous child born of the new Eve (the Virgin Mary), who could emerge only when the old Eve (the sexually tainted Ondine), had been terminated.[4]

Working multiple illusions and metaphors into works of art, thereby creating dense images that could be understood only with textual commentary, Gauguin aligned himself with the Symbolist generation who, echoing Stephane Mallarmé, painted not things, but the effects the things produced, and, following Gustave Kahn, objectified the subjective. He also linked himself to subjective psychological theory, not only that of Charles Henry and David Sutter (who were concerned with lines, emotive linear directions, and colors) but also that of the preeminent evolutionary psychologists Herbert Spencer and Hippolyte Taine, and the perceptualist Hermann von Helmholtz. These men all agreed that in both humanity and the world at large a hidden, internal significance governed. Accessible in part through scientific research (for example, the irradiation or contrast of colors), this reality ultimately eluded scientific inquiry. As the critic G.-Albert Aurier wrote, of Gauguin and quite possibly of *Ondine* in 1891, what mattered was ideist, symbolist, synthetic, and subjective.[5] GWK

1. Sven Lövgren, *The Genesis of Modernism* (Stockholm: Almquist and Wiksell, 1959), p. 38. Translation mine.

2. Ibid., p. 40.

3. Herschel B. Chipp, *Theories of Modern Art* (Berkeley and Los Angeles: University of California Press), 1971, p. 60.

4. Wojtech Jirat-Wasiutynski, *Paul Gauguin in the Context of Symbolism* (New York: Garland Publishing, 1978), and Wayne Andersen, *Gauguin's Paradise Lost* (New York: Viking Press, 1971).

5. Chipp, *Theories*, p. 92.

Oil on canvas, 1901, 130.2 x 90.2 cm. The Cleveland Museum of Art, Gift of the Hanna Fund with an additional gift from Leonard C. Hanna, Jr. 43.392

Collections: (Ambroise Vollard, Paris); Baron Wolf Kohner, Budapest.

When Gauguin left Tahiti for the Marquesas Islands in 1901, he was in full control of an idiom based upon "aristocratic" primitivism and decoration. Beginning with early Tahitian paintings such as *We Hail Thee, Mary* (1891) and concluding with the monumental *Where Do We Come From? What Are We? Where Are We Going?* (1897), Gauguin had developed a repertoire of poses, stances, proportions, and figural groupings derived in part from his models and in part from prototypes that he felt signified the aristocratic and mythically complex Tahitian civilization. The prototypes included sculpture and reliefs from Java, Egypt, and Peru (most of which he was familiar with in his Paris years), while his models were the Island women, whose aristocratic characteristics he admired and sought to capture in his paintings. Gauguin had observed that "what distinguishes the Maori woman from all other women, and often makes one mistake her for a man, is the proportions of the body. A Diana of the chase, with large shoulders and narrow hips . . . ."[1]

A decorative aesthetic—that is, treating the canvas as an illusionistically unpuncturable plane or wall onto which objects disport themselves according to the logic of the bounding edges—had been seen by Gauguin, G.-Albert Aurier, and their followers as an essential bridge to feeling. Inspired by the compatriot and muralist Puvis de Chavannes, they wished to move art beyond "noisy" bourgeois narrative to silent, non-narrative evocation (like Puvis's

The Child St. Genevieve at Prayer, 1876-77). Decorative work, wrote Aurier, was ideist, symbolist, and synthetic by definition. For Gauguin in *The Spirit of the Dead Watching*, for example, not only the pose of his recumbent Tahitian model but also the color and fabric of her bedcovers communicate the mood of quiet, pensive, and haunting foreboding that he desired.

The Call is one of several 1902 canvases that Jehanne Teilhet-Fisk has described as "themes which question in a softer, abstract fashion the mysteries of life and death. These often seem to be the works of a new, mellower Gauguin—the ruthless domineering warrior who had at least temporarily hung up his shield."[2] Within a river-bisected landscape structured in part upon the principles of Cézanne and in part upon an arbitrary, disjunctive color harmony first adumbrated in Gauguin's 1888 *Vision after the Sermon*, two rhythmically counterposed Marquesan women occupy center stage. One gestures to the viewer; the other, to an unseen personage outside the picture. Given the title and the fact that the seated bather looks in the same direction as the woman to the right, the "caller" is probably fate, destiny, heaven, or a tropical Nirvana (the white lily in the foreground, a symbol of purity, indicates that the path the two standing women follow is hallowed ground).

The Call incorporates a number of poses typical of Gauguin. For example, the bare-breasted standing woman derives from *Scene from Tahitian Life* (1896); the crouching bather, from *Tahitians on the Beach. The Invocation* (1903), one of Gauguin's last works, requotes the two standing women. Compelling in *The Call* are the quietude and rightness engendered by the horizontal, vertical, and curvilinear relationships that meander across and up the picture plane.

In the Marquesas, his fourth and last stop in a fifteen-year flight from civilization, Gauguin found new sources for his primitivism. On the island of Hiva Oa he sketched a statue of Takaii, the most barbaric of the remaining large Marquesan stone sculptures known. Yet in certain paintings, among which *The Call* assumes major stature for its poetic, dreamlike content, planar structure, facture, and coloristic complexity, he subsumed primitivism in decoration, and thus renewed his long-standing dialogue with European Symbolism. GWK

1. Jehanne Teilhet-Fisk, *Paradise Reviewed, An Interpretation of Gauguin's Tahitian Symbolism* (Ann Arbor: University of Michigan Research Press, 1983), pp. 156-57.

2. Ibid., p. 156.

Henri Rousseau
French, 1844-1910
18. The Jungle

Oil on canvas, 1908, 172.1 x 191.5 cm.
The Cleveland Museum of Art, Gift of the
Hanna Fund 49.186

Collections: Joseph Brummer; John Quinn;
(Valentine Gallery); Mrs. John Alden
Carpenter; Mrs. Patrick J. Hill; (Pierre
Matisse Gallery, New York).

Rousseau, a self-taught painter who at the
age of forty-one quit his job in the Paris
Municipal Toll Service to devote himself
entirely to art, has had a considerable influence on modern art. He became the
doyen of the Parisian avant-garde in the
opening years of the twentieth century, to
the extent that in 1908 Picasso turned his
studio in the *bateau lavoir* over to a ban-
quet in his honor.

In *The Jungle* each specimen of flora
and fauna is present as a discrete and
forceful entity, a weighted form in shallow
space. Rousseau knew and frequented the
hothouses of the Paris Jardin des Plantes,
and he considered himself an academic in
the tradition of masters such as Jean-Léon
Gérôme. Thus it is not surprising that, like
Gérôme and his colleagues, Rousseau
relied upon pre-existent images for his
work—specifically M. Boitard's 1845 book
on the Jardin, and the album *Wild Beasts*,
a special publication of Les Grands
Magasins "Aux Galeries Lafayettes" at the
end of the century. For the fight in *The
Jungle* Rousseau went back to an etching
by Eugène Pirodon, which he enlarged, using a pantograph.

Far from reworking his prototypes into
paintings where documentary accuracy
was the measure of success, as Gérôme
would do, Rousseau personalized and in-
tensified his imagery, so that each plant
and weighted fruit might be considered
the image of an experience. "One day
when I was painting a fantastic subject I

had to open the window because fear
seized me," Rousseau said.[1] Indeed, intensity of feeling, condensed in each object
and object-group, convinces the viewer
that, despite major inaccuracies (the
bananas are growing upside down), the
painting is a true "jungle scene."

For Rousseau, color was as important as
it was for his contemporaries, the Impressionists. Like them, he did not mix his
pigments with black, but unlike them, he
used pure black—for example, in the buffalo's coat and the tiger's stripes. There is
a certain amalgam of freshness and still-
ness in *The Jungle* engendered by broad
areas of slightly changing intensity that
pulsate evenly across the picture plane.
The Jungle reflects a rhythmic repetition
and variation within a labyrinthine texture,
similar to a tapestry or a carpet.

Rousseau's purposes, unconsciously aesthetic, were quite consciously symbolic. In
his painting he relied upon faith in the ef-
ficacy of the images, and a dream uncon-
ditioned by peculiarities of personality. He
shared these traits not only with folk artists but also with extremely sophisticated
artists, such as Vasily Kandinsky, who considered him the father of the new realism.
Rousseau had a formative influence on the
entire Blue Rider group in Munich, who
were not as concerned as the French with
rational formalism, but who looked for
empathy as the tool of artistic communication. For these painters, Rousseau had a
direct line to the "mysterious center of
thought." As Franz Marc wrote in a letter
to Robert Delaunay, "The douanier
Rousseau is the only one whose art often
haunts me. I constantly attempt to understand how he painted his marvelous pictures. I try to identify myself with the inner
state of this venerable painter, that is to
say, with a state of great love."[2]

In his 1910 article "The Fourth Dimension from a Plastic Point of View," the
American painter Max Weber, who arranged the first United States showing of
Rousseau's work, may have been thinking
of the power of works such as *The Jungle*
when he wrote:

*The ideal or visionary is impossible without
form; even angels come down to earth. By
walking upon earth and looking up at the
heavens, and in no other way, can there
be an equilibrium. The greatest dream or
vision is that which is regiven plastically
through observation of things in nature.*[3]
GWK

1. Robert Goldwater, *Primitivism in
Modern Art* (Cambridge: Harvard University
Press, Belknap Press, 1986), p. 183.

2. Peter Selz, *German Expressionist Paintings* (Berkeley and Los Angeles: University
of California Press, 1957), p. 210.

3. Linda D. Henderson, *The Fourth Dimen-
sion and Non-Euclidean Geometry in
Modern Art* (Princeton, New Jersey:
Princeton University Press, 1983), p. 168.

Bronze, 1909, h. 41.2 cm.
Collection of the Fort Worth (Texas) Art Museum, Acquired with a Donation from Mr. and Mrs. J. Lee Johnson

What is sculpture? What is painting? Everyone clings to old-fashioned ideas and outworn definitions as if it were not precisely the role of the artist to provide new ones. Pablo Picasso[1]

Picasso's *Head of a Woman* is comparable in its effect upon the development of sculpture to his 1907 *Les Demoiselles d'Avignon*, which forever changed painting. Earlier, portrait-sculptors had begun with an ovoid mass that they articulated in a lifelike fashion. While Picasso maintained a solid core, he developed it into a surging, seething sea of shapes and forms that coalesce in a singular expression. The post-1909 sculptures of Roger de la Fresnaye, Raymond Duchamp-Villon, Alexander Archipenko, Juan Gris, Henri Laurens, Jacques Lipchitz, and particularity Umberto Boccioni are indebted to this dashing feat of bravado, the sole Cubist portrait-sculpture.[2]

The *Head* touches upon a major issue in early Cubism: simultaneity. As in his figure paintings of 1909, Picasso incorporated and exaggerated the profile view within the three-quarter view—that is, suggested the turning of the head. Simultaneity for Picasso was a means of making the perceived image more dynamic, more penetrable, more absolute in total realization. Moreover, it was a conceptual problem involving space, time, tactile and motor sensations, and scientific abstractions that Picasso understood and wished to formulate concretely. In the *Head* Picasso exaggerated the vertical median within an alternatively convex and concave "landscape" of form. The central ridges, of

which the nose is the most prominent, read like the arises of volcanically formed mountains. Albert Elsen has observed, "The nose seems to serve as a keel to stabilize the face in its rough sea of heaving forms."[3]

Elsen and Werner Spies have also implied another dimension of simultaneity in the *Head*: the accentuation of both the eye cavity and the "artistic muscle" in the hair, the back and side of the head, and the neck. "The contrast between the flaccid, guttate units which constitute the hair and the upward-thrusting ridges which characterize the twisted neck set up an autonomous rhythm: the heavy, symmetrically arranged hair meets the dynamic thrust of the ridges that run counter to it."[4]

Picasso's solution, albeit his own, did not emerge without precedent. The Cubist *Head* derives directly from primitive, specifically African, sculpture, which Picasso exploited to angularize the planes of the face and accentuate resulting ridges and valleys, and to inculcate a sense of presence. In 1905, soon after meeting her, Picasso had modeled a bust of Fernande Olivier in an Impressionistic, almost Romantic fashion. Soon thereafter, passing quickly through an Iberian sculpture stage that culminated in the painted portrait of Gertrude Stein, Picasso severed all connections to Impressionism and Realism. In 1907, 1908, and early 1909 he executed a series of sharply geometric, African-mask-inspired sculptures and paintings of female heads, for which Fernande was the primary model—as indeed she was for the present work. The Cubist sculpture of Fernande cannot justifiably be considered apart from the paintings, sculptures, and studies that preceded it, however. Comparable to the *Head* in rhythmic structure are two superb

Fernande portrait-paintings, the *Bust of Fernande* and *Woman with Pears*, executed in Horta de Ebro in the summer of 1909.

Picasso rightly cited the formal strengths of early Cubism and the *Head* when he said that he was "searching again for an architectonic basis in the composition, trying to make an order of it . . . we felt the temptation, the hope, of an anonymous art, not in its expression but in its point of departure."[5] However, the power of the bust emanates equally, if not more, from its psychological intensity, the force behind Picasso's "will to primitivize." Unlike the paintings that preceded it, the 1909 sculpture is pensive, reticent, and inward-turning. Whereas Fernande's cheeks in the paintings may be read as either concave or convex (depending upon how one structures the planar relationships), in the sculpture they ripple from concave to convex to concave, there to pool and distill a quiet emotion. Moreover, Fernande's sculpted hair mounts upward like a still life of ripe pears or melons, swelling and palpable. Since Picasso had transformed Fernande into a pear-filled fruit dish early in 1909 (his metamorphosis of *Carnaval au bistrot* into *Bread and Fruitdish on a Table*,[6] it is not inconceivable that he changed the fruit back to Fernande in his sculpture later that year. Not just a model, Fernande was also Picasso's lover and a major source of the reorientation of his art from instability and insecurity (the Blue Period) to robustness and virility (the Rose Period and Cubism to 1911). GWK

1. Albert Elsen, ''The Many Faces of Picasso's Sculpture,'' *Art International* 13 (Summer 1969): 26.

2. Picasso's *Glass of Absinthe* of 1914 is a metaphorical portrait of an absinthe drinker, but not a bust per se.

3. Elsen, ''Many Faces,'' p. 26.

4. Werner Spies, *Sculpture by Picasso* (New York: Harry N. Abrams, 1971), p. 27.

5. Elsen, ''Many Faces,'' p. 26.

6. William S. Rubin, ''From Narrative to 'Iconic' in Picasso: The Buried Allegory in *Bread and Fruitdish on a Table* and the Role of *Les Demoiselles d'Avignon*,'' *Art Bulletin* 65 (December 1983): 615-49.

Oil on canvas, 1909, 81.3 x 64.8 cm. The Cleveland Museum of Art, Leonard C. Hanna, Jr., Fund 69.22

Collections: Dr. G.F. Reber, Lausanne; Edward van Saher, Amsterdam; The Hyde Collections, Glens Falls, New York; (M. Knoedler and Company, New York).

Picasso and Georges Braque, both moved by the great Cézanne exhibition of 1906, attempted to carry Cézanne's main developments beyond where he had left them. In 1907, while Braque was still a minor member of the Fauvist movement, Picasso completed his early, proto-Cubist masterwork *Les Demoiselles d'Avignon* (Figure 8). Braque, who was more concerned with pictorial structure than most other Fauve artists, responded positively to Picasso's canvas. In their first Cubist paintings done in 1908, Picasso and Braque moved, instinctively, very close to one another. In 1909 they began one of the closest collaborations in the history of art.

Both artists rejected the Impressionist concerns with immediate perceptions of light and the fortuitous effects of nature. They restricted their palettes to umbers, earth greens, ochres, grays, black, and white. They defined objects and figures in terms of general rather than individual characteristics. Above all, they followed Cézanne in suggesting three-dimensional forms and space while still respecting the flat surface of the painting. To achieve this unification of two- and three-dimensional composition, they developed devices such as: tilting or turning planes—which would normally seem to recede into space—so that they become parallel to the picture surface; organizing colors to create an even pattern of tones over the painting's surface; and distributing lights and darks so as to define individual planes rather than developing lighting as if emanating from a single source.

During 1909 Picasso's paintings reflected a severe, angular character through his use of sharp edges and strong contrasts of tone. The vigor and clarity of these works indicate the strength of Picasso's emotional impulses. Like Cézanne, Picasso subjected himself to a rigorous effort to control his volatile nature and organize logical structures. The elan that stimulated the production of a work such as *Fan, Salt Box, and Melon* is conveyed by the strong and vigorous formal structure of the work. EBH

Oil on canvas, 1912, 72.4 x 54 cm.
The Cleveland Museum of Art, Leonard C.
Hanna, Jr., Fund 72.8

Collections: Carlo Frua dei Angeli, Milan;
Bank Gut, Streiff A.G., Zurich; (Galerie
Beyeler, Basel).

Executed by Picasso in the spring of 1912,
this painting exemplifies Analytical Cubism
at its peak. The larger planes of early
Cubism had been reduced in size and were
overlapped and integrated. Not only were
the three-dimensional elements in the
composition analyzed structurally in terms
of planes, space was also articulated in
such terms. Futhermore, the planes defining material objects and space were
merged.

The objects in *Bottle, Glass, and Fork* are
not as obvious as those in *Fan, Salt Box,
Melon*, but they can, for the most part, be
discerned. The bottle, the glass, and the
fork of the title are clear enough, as is a
knife just above the center on the right-
hand side of the composition. A second
bottle near the center of the composition,
a hard roll (or perhaps a potato) with a
curved knife inserted in it, a table, a rope
nailed to the wall from which a clay pipe is
hanging, and a few other details can also
be detected. Clearly, Picasso had no intention of abandoning nature; but he had
given up the mimetic representation of
surface appearances in order to investigate
and analyze the structures and structural
interrelationships of objects and space. The
artist himself said:

*It was really the manifestation of a vague
desire on the part of those of us who participated in it to get back to some kind of
order . . . . We were trying to move in a
direction opposite to Impressionism. That
was the reason we abandoned color, emotion, sensation, and everything that had
been introduced by the Impressionists, to
search again for an architectonic basis in
the composition, trying to make an order
of it . . . .*[1]

Objects and space in *Bottle, Glass, and
Fork*—defined by planes parallel to the
canvas's surface—are merged to create a
shallow, palpable, "breathing" space. A
thick web of flickering planes engulfs
discrete forms and integrates these within
a shallow space.

During the years when Picasso and
Braque were developing Cubism, physical
scientists were theorizing that the ancient
notion of an absolute, empty space in-
habited by discrete material objects was no
longer tenable. Reality, it was now proposed, could be conceived of as an integrated
network of fields around pockets of
energy. EBH

1. Paul Waldo Schwartz, *Cubism* (New
York: Praeger, 1971); quoted from
Françoise Gilot and Carlton Lake, *Life with
Picasso* (New York: McGraw-Hill, 1964).
Schwartz notes that Gilot's association
with Picasso began in 1943 and, therefore,
"a quotation of this length, recounted
after a passage of years, cannot be accurate . . . only the sense of Picasso's
words has been preserved."

Georges Braque
French, 1882-1963
22. Still Life with Violoncello

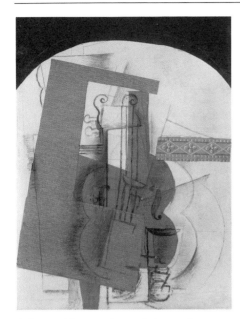

Collage with gouache and charcoal on chipboard, ca. 1912-13, 71.7 x 51.8 cm. The Cleveland Museum of Art, Leonard C. Hanna, Jr., Fund 68.196

Collection: Jean Paulhan.

In 1910 Braque painted tromp-l'oeil nails in three of his works in an effort to provide the viewer with visual clues relating the near abstractions to the natural world. In 1911 he began stenciling letters and numbers onto surfaces of paintings; these introduced a new decorative element and also referred to mundane reality. In 1912 Picasso pasted a piece of oilcloth, patterned like chair caning, onto the surface of an oval picture and wrapped a rope around the edge of the painting to serve as a frame. Later that same year, Braque created his first *papier collé*. From 1912 to 1914 Braque and Picasso created a group of collages notable for their uniformly high aesthetic level.

Beginning as an attempt to introduce elements from the exterior world into Analytical Cubist paintings that had become so abstract they were difficult to "read," the *papiers collés* ended by posing the most serious challenge yet to the traditional concept of a painting. Picasso and Braque used the most ordinary materials to create elegant works of art: wallpaper, newspaper, bottle labels, and other such materials became integral elements in their compositions. Their innovation changed the course of Western painting from the reproduction or analysis of sections of nature to the creation of autonomous aesthetic objects. Where Analytical Cubist paintings are tied directly to specific objects in the real world, the *papiers collés*

are independent of exterior reality. The artist's motifs—musical instruments, fruit, dishes, bottles, and figures—evolved out of the process of manipulating the formal elements, thus reversing the traditional creative process and leading to Synthetic Cubism.

The format of *Still Life with Violoncello* daringly uses a half-round top. Although Braque and Picasso frequently composed within oval or circular shapes, this appears to be the only half-round shape in their combined oeuvre. The materials include newspaper, wallpaper, paper with simulated wood graining, dark brown construction paper, gouache, and charcoal. Braque probably began by adjusting these elements—cutting and trimming them, and drawing until the image took shape. The main thematic elements—the double curve and the right angle—are repeated and varied like musical themes. The violin shape only vaguely resembles a musical instrument, and its various parts are represented from different points of view. These have been assembled primarily to conform to the demands of the composition rather than to closely resemble the instrument.

Traditional devices for representing deep space on a flat surface—linear and aerial perspective—have been given up. The surface of the picture is no longer a plane to be visually penetrated; instead, it is a plane from which the artist built out by means of a series of overlapping and interacting shapes and contours.

Braque was concerned with space suggested by overlapping planes and also with visual paradoxes that occur when the abstract shapes are considered along with the images. Logical spatial relations are often violated and even reversed. A section of wallpaper border, for example, which, in life, would be above and behind the other objects, actually overlaps them. The large section of wallpaper (perhaps representing a tablecloth) overlaps the musical instrument, which, in reality, would be lying on top of the table. Such logical displacements are disturbing only if one expects to "read" the work in terms of traditional spatial relations as developed according to a single perspective. Instead of a mimetic representation of the subject, Braque invented a synoptic view of it. EBH

114

Ebony and oak, 1915, h. 98.2 cm.
The Cleveland Museum of Art, Gift of Mrs. Aye Simon 72.367

Collections: Mrs. Aye Simon, New York.

Lipchitz was one of the first artists to solve the difficult problem of translating the aesthetics of Cubism into fully realized, three-dimensional sculpture. He began producing modernist sculpture influenced by Picasso in 1913, yet he considered his works of 1913-14 "proto-Cubist" rather than true Cubist sculpture.[1] Not until 1915, when he began concentrating almost exclusively on formal issues, did Lipchitz create his first mature Cubist works. Composed of carved oak and ebony blocks fastened together with screws, *Detachable Figure (Dancer)* is one of the finest sculptures from that seminal year in the artist's career. Other "detachable," or constructed, figures were created in 1915, but the artist cast most of these in bronze, fearing that the delicate wood sculptures would not survive.

Lipchitz considered his sculptures of 1915 more fully realized than the earlier works because he was "finally building up the figure from abstract forms, not merely simplifying and geometrizing a realistic figure."[2] *Detachable Figure*, for example, was constructed by assembling a series of abstract geometric shapes into a vertical composition. The artist also noted that this was one of the first attempts at "constructed sculpture, an idea then extremely new and very important for the subsequent history of sculpture."[3] While the artist acknowledged that the assemblage technique and geometric shapes of *Detachable Figure* refer to "machinery" and "machine forms," the selection of wood as a material implies associations with primitive and folk art.[4] The artist perceived other analogies as well: "The *Detachable Figure*," he once said, "reminds me of certain ancient devices I have collected, such as a part of a Chinese crossbow from the Han period."[5]

From the left side of this work one can distinguish the raised arm of the dancer (light oak block in the upper left), her head facing left (triangular ebony piece with incised features and projecting nose), a long torso, two protruding buttocks, and a pair of arched legs. When viewed from the front, two slender ebony blocks in the upper center form a second, more abstract face resembling an African mask: the upper block flares outward at the bottom like a nose, the lower block suggests a mouth, perhaps seen from above. The light oak block beneath the two ebony ones may be part of the face or it may represent a second arm. Most likely, it represents both simultaneously. As one walks around the sculpture, other multiple and simultaneous images emerge, but all are carefully integrated within a complex composition of interlocking, abstract shapes.

The oak and ebony blocks, which can be interpreted as patterns of light and shadow referring to a system of interpenetrating voids and solids, contribute a significant element to the viewer's spatial experience of *Detachable Figure* absent in the bronze casts. Lipchitz in 1913 noted that: "I suddenly discovered that volume in sculpture is created by light and shadow . . . . When the forms of the sculpture are angular, when the surface is broken by deep interpenetrations and contrasts, light can work to bring out the truly sculptural qualities."[6]

As in Cubist paintings, however, the alternating patterns of light and dark in *Detachable Figure* do not correspond with the way natural light from a single source would fall upon the object. Instead, the disparately colored blocks were arbitrarily arranged into an invented or "synthetic" composition in which constantly changing tonal patterns generate internal rhythmic energy. This is not the motion of a figure turning in space, however, as these implied movements remain contained within the system of interlocking, interpenetrating volumes. Lipchitz himself commented:

The most significant change between the 1915 and 1916 sculptures and the proto-cubist works is that the former are no longer composed around a pivoting axis. Works like Sailor with Guitar *(1914) or the* Dancer *(1913) revolve and create their sense of three-dimensional space by the pivoting of the figure around its axis. This is actually the manner in which later Greek sculptors and sculptors of the High Renaissance tended to create a sense of existence in space.*[7]

Spatial movement is therefore implied in *Detachable Figure* by means entirely different from that of Renaissance and Baroque sculpture. Even though the dancer's powerful, springing legs produce a kinesthetic feeling of tremendous explosive energy, as in African sculpture, these dynamic tensions remain contained within the rigorous verticality and angular, blocklike planes of the composition. WHR

1. Jacques Lipchitz, *My Life in Sculpture* (New York: Viking Press, 1972), pp. 24-25.

2. Ibid., p. 18.

3. Ibid., p. 26.

4. Ibid.

5. Ibid.

6. Ibid., p. 17.

7. Ibid.

Oil on canvas, signed, 1918, 142.2 x 100.3 cm.
The Cleveland Museum of Art, Leonard C. Hanna, Jr., Fund 75.2

Collections: (Paul Rosenberg, Paris); John Quinn; Paul Rosenberg, New York; Alexandre P. Rosenberg, New York.

The Analytical phase of Cubism had ended in 1912, and from that year through 1914 Picasso and Braque had developed the technique of *papier collé* before moving into the next phase of Cubism, called Synthetic. *Harlequin with Violin* is one of the major works from this period.

Painted in 1918, this picture clearly demonstrates the autobiographical character of Picasso's work. Picasso began this painting just after returning from Rome, where he had designed the sets and costumes for the ballet *Parade*. While there, he had worked with Jean Cocteau, who wrote the story for the ballet; with Erik Satie, who composed the music; and Sergei Diaghilev, Léonide Massine, and Léon Bakst of the Ballet Russe. He also met Igor Stravinsky and Manuel de Falla. This brief stay in Italy, as well as the circus theme of the ballet, reawakened his interest in characters from the Commedia dell'Arte that had appeared earlier in his Rose Period pictures.

Picasso returned to Paris with Olga Koklova, one of the young dancers from the ballet. This painting was done about the time of Picasso's marriage to Olga and the death from a war wound of his close friend, the poet Guillaume Apollinaire.

Picasso frequently portrayed himself in the guise of the gay sprite, juggler, and magician Harlequin. In the late teens and early twenties he did a series of drawings and gouaches of Harlequin and the melancholy poet Pierrot. *Harlequin with Violin*

appears to combine these two images. The wraithlike Pierrot can be detected only by a gray silhouette behind the image of Harlequin and by part of his high-crowned white hat on the right side of the figure's head. This ghostlike form may have been Picasso's homage to Apollinaire.

The round black eye and broad, blunt nose seen through the mask indicate that Picasso has again put himself in the role of Harlequin. The sheet of music with the song title "Si Tu Veux" may be Picasso's reply to Olga, who was pressing for marriage at the time.[1] Both Diaghilev and Bakst warned Picasso that he would have to marry Olga, but Picasso thought they were joking.[2]

Portions of this painting (in the black area of the ruff; to the left of the head; and to the right of the lower jaw, neck, and shoulder) reveal evidence of changes that were made during the course of painting. Such pentimenti occur only in paintings that Picasso seems to have considered important enough to rework. Normally, he would do another canvas incorporating the desired changes.

Although Picasso and Braque tended not to work directly from nature during the period of Synthetic Cubism, Robert Rosenblum has remarked that, "this presumed independence of nature is often more of degree than of kind."[3] Picasso's many Synthetic Cubist paintings of Commedia dell'Arte figures and still lifes with common elements suggest that these subjects were derived from a priori concepts rather than being fortuitously suggested by his manipulation of purely formal elements. EBH

1. "Tu veux?" is also a common way of propositioning someone on the street.

2. Jean-Paul Crespelle, *Picasso and His Women* (New York: Coward-McCann, 1969), p. 121.

3. Robert Rosenblum, *Cubism and Twentieth-Century Art* (New York: Harry N. Abrams, 1961), p. 71.

Oil and sand on canvas, signed, dated 1924, 81.3 x 101 cm.
The Cleveland Museum of Art, Leonard C. Hanna, Jr., Fund 78.45

Collections: (Paul Rosenberg, Paris).

Painted in 1924 at Juan-les-Pins on the French Côte d'Azure, this work belongs to a series of large Synthetic Cubist still lifes created by Picasso in the mid-twenties. Its high-keyed palette and playful mood correspond to a relatively tranquil period in the artist's personal life—specifically, during the years after the birth (1921) of his son Paulo and before his relationship with his first wife Olga began to deteriorate. At that time Picasso was painting in several styles simultaneously, often mixing elements of Cubism, Realism, and Neoclassicism. In Synthetic Cubist paintings like *Still Life with Biscuits*, abstract forms were invented and arbitrarily arranged according to the formal requirements of a composition; however, since relatively large, simple planes were used to create forms suggesting objects in the natural world, the subject matter tends to be highly recognizable. In this work, for example, one can easily discern a tall blue bottle on the left; an oval bowl with three fruits in the center; a glass on the right; a plate with biscuits, a knife, and a partly peeled fruit; all arranged in an elliptical pattern on the top of a table.

Picasso characteristically focused more attention on the primary motif of a painting than on the background, especially when he had some emotional attachment to the subject. In *Still Life with Biscuits*, however, he labored to an unusual degree over peripheral areas, adjusting and repainting the various colored planes of the background many times to create a completely unified "decorative" design.

These planes and their associated colors and other decorative elements were variously arranged to animate the composition through a series of balanced tensions; for example, the swinging movements of the circular table top and the lively, decorative foliage patterns of the tablecloth are balanced by the more severe geometry of the large, rectangular planes directly behind the table. These flat, rectangular planes also function to prevent recession, thus allowing the artist to work within a continuous "Cubist" space of tightly integrated, interpenetrating planes tied closely to the picture surface.

For *Still Life with Biscuits* Picasso invented a complex, highly imaginative pictorial space in which certain objects function simultaneously as both positive and negative shapes. The red shape (perhaps a chair) in the upper left, for example, reads as a positive shape around the exterior but as a negative shape on the interior. Similarly, the three olive-green fruits in the center of the composition appear at times to hover above the picture surface, while at other times they seem to form negative holes in the blue-gray octagonal shape above the oval bowl. The spatial complexity of the composition becomes most apparent when one is forced to decide whether the black shape at the top of the painting recedes or advances in space. The extreme right side of this shape is joined to both a blue plane (abutting the right picture edge) situated *behind* the still life and to a gray-violet plane connected to the *middle* of the table. On the left, the black shape is joined to both a pink plane that intersects the *back* of the table and to a gray plane running parallel to the picture surface along the left edge until it joins the *front* of the table at the bottom of the picture. Such intriguing spatial ambiguities

are largely responsible for the playful mood of the painting.

Still Life with Biscuits is also full of surprising textural effects. In certain areas, such as the tan shape on the tablecloth and the blue-gray octagonal form in the center of the table, paint was mixed with sand to create rough, granular surfaces, while a palette knife was used to create the contrasting smooth surfaces of the white oval bowl and the cream-colored biscuits. In overpainting certain areas (the red shape, for example, contains at least four separate levels of paint), Picasso often applied a painterly impasto over smooth, glossy paint surfaces. Over time, this has produced the extensive traction crackle that covers much of the surface—the result of different levels and textures of paint expanding and contracting at different rates. Now stable, the traction crackle provides a fascinating opportunity to view early paint levels and to speculate on why Picasso made certain changes in the composition.

The sensuous palette and the complex spatial construction of *Still Life with Biscuits* are characteristic of late Synthetic Cubism. By this time, Picasso had solved the formal problems of the style to the extent that he was free to explore issues of decorative design. He thus gave more attention to the background and peripheral areas of this painting than is typical of his early Cubist paintings. WHR

Oil on canvas, dated 1939, 59.2 x 91.6 cm. The Cleveland Museum of Art, Leonard C. Hanna, Jr., Fund 85.57

Collections: Walter Bareiss, Greenwich; (Eugene V. Thaw, New York).

Bull's Skull, Fruit, Pitcher, dated January 29, 1939, was painted during an especially difficult period in Picasso's life. For much of that winter he had been bedridden with painful attacks of sciatica. On January 13, the artist's mother died in Barcelona; seven days later, Barcelona fell to Franco, climaxing a series of Fascist victories that signaled the beginning of the end of the Spanish Republic (the previous year Picasso had sent his monumental painting *Guernica* on a world tour to enlist support for the Republic). "The fall of Barcelona," recalled Picasso's close friend Roland Penrose, "and the defeat of the last faint hopes of the Republicans filled us with an intense depression."[1]

The subject of this painting derives from the traditional memento-mori theme reminding us of the inevitability of death. During the late 1930s and early 1940s Picasso returned to this theme obsessively, depicting countless human skulls and decaying animal heads—perhaps as a pessimistic comment about the fate of Western Civilization.

Picasso's presentation of this theme is especially cruel and horrifying in the present work. A bull's skull covered with rotting yellow flesh is placed upon a table; its powerful jaws and protruding teeth, on one hand, seem to mock death, and, on the other hand, to cry out in anguish like the wounded horse in *Guernica* (the sharp, pointed shapes inside the bull's mouth are especially reminiscent of the spiked tongue of the screaming horse in *Guernica*). The skull is punctuated by three circular holes,

each of which can be interpreted as an empty eye socket. As one examines this strange, hallucinatory skull, it metamorphoses into several different, contradictory heads. This is characteristic of the way Picasso and certain Surrealists used extreme spatial dislocations and confused sensory perceptions to create an ambiance of emotional trauma and severe psychic stress.

Other elements in *Bull's Skull, Fruit, Pitcher* augment the disquieting effect of the skull: an apple in the lower center of the painting is painfully pierced by a nail; the shape of the intensely colored pitcher on the right—whose curvaceous shape Picasso often associated with female anatomy—is twisted and contorted like a figure writhing in agony. Behind the still life are indications of a distant landscape; but the barlike forms directly behind the table separate us from that vista, and we thus become imprisoned with the skull in the foreground, as if to suggest that death is our constant, unavoidable companion.

The composition is dominated by sharp, angular, piercing shapes that meet near the center of the painting to form an "X," similar to a skull-and-crossbones motif. From the very heart of this X, and from the nose-tip of the bull's skull, there sprouts a flowering tree, reminiscent of the cross poised above the skull at Golgotha: surely this tree represents a symbol of hope and rebirth.

Employing an essentially Cubist formal vocabulary in *Bull's Skull, Fruit, Pitcher*, Picasso transformed a simple still life into a compelling image of great emotional power, something comparable to a modern Crucifixion, offering hope for the future regeneration of civilization and the redemption of man in spite of the unbridled barbarism and chaos about to unfold in the winter of 1939. WHR

1. Roland Penrose, *Picasso: His Life and Work*, rev. ed. (New York: Harper and Row, 1973), p. 332.

Robert Delaunay
French, 1885-1941
27. Eiffel Tower with Trees

Photograph by Robert E. Mates

Oil on canvas, 1910, 124.4 x 91.9 cm.
Solomon R. Guggenheim Museum, New
York

Robert Delaunay's name has become
synonymous with the exaltation of moder-
nity and a technological utopia in early
twentieth-century Europe. The dirigible,
propeller, airplane, and Eiffel Tower
motivated his search for visual equivalents
of invisible force fields, which reached
their most poignant distillations in his
abstract disks of 1912 and 1913. However,
the Tower best exemplifies Delaunay's
researches, and this work, one of his first
"fractured" compositions, exemplifies his
discovery of simultaneity.

The term "simultaneity" occurred first in
literature, in the writings of Henri Bergson,
Jules Romains, and Henri-Martin Barzun.
Central to the doctrine of Unanimism, it
held that the forces of life were urban
forces that joined in space and time—
unanimously—to soar to the universe. In
Romain's words:

*The city is going to move this morning.
It is going to break away from the earth,
Root up its foundations
Disentangle them from the greasy clay . . .* [1]

Simultaneity was what the Eiffel Tower
was all about. Erected in 1889 as a monu-
ment to the industrial accomplishments of
modern France, by the first decade of the
twentieth century it had become an illu-
minating beacon, a meteorological station,
and a laboratory for the study of aerody-
namics. For less technologically inclined
but perceptually intense observers, it was a
vehicle for new sight. The poet Blaise Cen-
drars wrote of his and Delaunay's
experiences:

*None of the known techniques of art can
claim to have solved the pictorial problems
of the Eiffel Tower. Realism diminishes it;
the ancient laws of Italian perspective at-
tenuate it. The Tower rises above Paris,
slim as a hat pin. When we moved away
from it, it dominated Paris, stiff and per-
pendicular; when we approached it, it tilted and leaned over us. Seen from the first
platform, it spiraled upward; seen from the
top, it sank into itself with straddling legs
and indrawn neck. Delaunay wanted to
show Paris simultaneously, to incorporate
the Tower into its surroundings.* [2]

And Delaunay himself, thinking about the
Tower and the city, penned his 1912 essay
"Light" around the thought "Simultaneity
in light is *the harmony, the rhythm of colors* which creates *Men's Sight.*" [3]

What the Eiffel Tower did to Delaunay's
sight is clearly apparent in the Guggenheim Museum's version with trees. In
order to capture it as a singular yet
energy-emanating entity, Delaunay appears
to have circumnavigated it from base to
top, then moved in upon telling views. He
combined and interpenetrated several perspectives: a view close to the base; a head-
on view from a distance, presumably from
a park; and (for the summit) another close-
in view. He rendered the effects of stream-
ing sunlight by bombarding the tower
with disks, spheres, rays, and fractured
planes—all derived from the vocabulary of
early Analytic Cubism. His ultimate sources
were Cézanne's Provençal landscapes, constructed of diagonally stroked, broken, and
interpenetrating color planes.

By framing the light-struck tower with
trees, Delaunay anchored his soaring and
plummeting verticals and diagonals while
maintaining a semblance of flux. Equally
important, he forged a link of technology

with nature that was to become part and
parcel of his mature philosophy: "Modern
inventions were products of the forces that
govern people and nature alike, and therefore should be incorporated into a structure conceived in nature." [4] Delaunay
shared this philosophy with Henri
Rousseau, who had also painted the Eiffel
Tower and whose schematized leaves and
branches reappear in Delaunay's *Eiffel
Tower with Trees.*

Even in this early, pre-abstract work,
Delaunay provokes, strains, and manipu-
lates our eyes so that we become acutely
conscious of the process and activity of vision. The painting provides a perceptual
and psychological experience, and it shares
with late nineteenth-century philosophy an
avant-garde concern for abstract representations. GWK

1. Sherry Buckberrough, *Robert Delaunay,
The Discovery of Simultaneity* (Ann Arbor:
University of Michigan Research Press,
1982), p. 54.

2. Gustav Vriesen, "Robert Delaunay's Life
and Work from the Beginning to Orphism," in Vriesen and Imdahl, *Robert
Delaunay, Light and Color* (New York:
Harry N. Abrams, 1969), p. 28.

3. Robert Delaunay, "Light," in Vriesen
and Imdahl, *Delaunay,* p. 9.

4. Buckberrough, *Simultaneity,* p. 36.

Frantisek Kupka
Czechoslovakian, 1871-1957
**28. Amorpha, Fugue for Two
Colors, II**

Oil on canvas, 1909-12, 111.8 x 68.5 cm.
Contemporary Collection of The Cleveland
Museum of Art 69.51

Collection: Alexander Liberman, New York.

Frantisek Kupka was a Bohemian painter
as well as a medium. He operated on the
premise that matter had dissolved into
pure spiritual energy and that the vibrations of music and color, along with the
natural process of growth, expansion, dila-
tion, and rotation, were aspects of that
energy. These were forces so powerful and
pervasive that they caused corresponding
vibrations in the soul.

Upon leaving Central Europe for Paris,
Kupka resolved "to get out of the
transcendental labyrinth, and to limit
myself to my sense organs . . . . I am men-
tally intoxicated by the Parisian air which
forces one to be very pragmatic and leads
one away from introspection . . . ."[1]
However, in Paris Kupka found that his
powerful vibrations aligned him with a
group of artists and writers who thought
along similar lines—his neighbors and
friends the Puteaux Cubists. Psychic
research, spiritualism, and romance with
the ether and the atom concerned these
intellectual artists, including Jacques Villon,
Raymond Duchamp-Villon, Marcel
Duchamp, Francis Picabia, and Guillaume
Apollinaire.

Despite the fact that much of the
pseudo-scientific jargon of this group
reflected outdated theories, it made sense
for these artist-mystics who, living in the
generation of Michael Faraday's "lines of
force," Guglielmo Marconi's wireless
telegraphy, and Alexander Graham Bell's
telephone, wished to make sensation
simultaneous with science. Kupka worked
on the *Amorpha, Fugue for Two Colors*
theme from 1909 to 1912, at the height
of these discussions. The final work,
shown in the 1912 Salon d'Automne in
Paris, may well have prompted Apollinaire
to coin the term "Orphic," designating
those Cubists who painted "new structures
with elements which have not been borrowed from visual reality, but have been
entirely created by the artist."[2]

The Cleveland painting has "ethereal"
qualities that link it to Puteaux concepts. A
figure presses from right to left, while its
aura metamorphoses from a quiet pink
oval (at the right) to a charged green oval
(at the upper left). The green oval activates
pink parabolas, trajectories of an invisible
body. These culminate in a "ring of fire"
that swoops down to the figure's knees.

Kupka's technique ultimately helped to
revive and transform the Neo-Impressionist
"brick" or "stitch" stroke, which also
structured the Italian Futurists' exploration
of lines of force, electricity, and solar
energy. Like Giovanni Segantini's sun,

Giacomo Balla's streetlight, and Umberto
Boccioni's charging horse, Kupka's small
stepdaughter Andrée (playing nude outdoors with a ball) serves as the leitmotif.
Kupka rigorously worked to abstract this
motif to a whorl of energy and light, but
unlike his Italian contemporaries, whose
theories he would assuredly have known,
he abrogated psychological expressionism
(those Futurist states of mind that hurled
the spectator to the center of the picture)
to place the spectator outside the picture.
He made the picture a curtain, however,
or rather several translucent curtains
through which the girl passes, and having
passed, deforms. Like Joris-Karl Huysman's
Symbolist hero des Esseintes, Kupka
created "*essences.*"

Kupka's metaphysics were not purely
ethereal, however. The trajectories and
afterimages in *Amorpha, Fugue for Two
Colors, II*, reflect keen interest in the
chronophotographs of Etienne-Jules Marey,
a pioneer of motion photography. The
subject moved before Marey's camera, as
before Kupka's eye and memory; through
multiple exposures, both captured com-
pound images moving through space and
time. Marey liked to point out that his process neutralized all possible positions of
the subject to virtual presences; Kupka
said, "Movement is no more than a series
of different positions in space . . . . If we
capture these positions rhythmically, they
may become a kind of dance."[3]

Kupka was not so much an innovator as
a synthesizer. His force fields in this painting limit themselves to screens parallel to
the picture plane; unlike Boccioni's, they
do not surge diagonally into space to suggest a continual flux of matter and energy.
Unlike Mondrian's, his building blocks are
not pure geometric form, but post-Neo-
Impressionist blocks of colors suggesting
light. Nonetheless, his vision and his painting are cosmic, rhythmically beautiful in
color and form and potentially released
from material reality. Kupka, along with
Kandinsky, Mondrian, and Malevich, explored visions of cosmic structure that
eventually sustained a completely abstract
art.[4] GWK

1. Margit Rowell, "Frantisek Kupka: A
Metaphysics of Abstraction," in *Frantisek
Kupka, 1871-1957, A Retrospective* (New
York: Solomon R. Guggenheim Museum,
1975), p. 48.

2. Virginia Spate, *Orphism* (Oxford: Clarendon Press), 1979, p. 37.

3. Rowell, *Kupka*, p. 58, and Rowell,
"Kupka, Duchamp and Marey," *Studio International* 189 (January-February 1975): 49.

4. Bruce Boice, "Problems from Early
Kupka," *Artforum* 14 (January 1976): 36.

Oil on canvas, 1911, 75.2 x 11.6 cm.
Collection of Munson-Williams-Proctor
Institute, Museum of Art, Utica, New York

Horizontal Tree retrospectively summarizes
Mondrian's naturalism modified by his introduction to modernism. Its cool and
warm, near-complementary color contrasts
cap his three-year study of Neo-
Impressionist color theory. The work
recalls, now diversified and in combination,
the hues of *Red Tree* and *Blue Willow*
(both 1908). Coiled and tentacular,
Horizontal Tree also focuses attention
upon itself as a symbol, quite possibly of
growth and tenacity through adversity. The
slightly bowed, domelike welter of branches extends to the framing edges on both
sides, suggesting an identification of the
tree with the otherwise unstated horizon,
thus with the life-giving earth. Both a vertical *and* a horizontal element, the tree
begins to suggest that the growths and
nurturing forces of nature not only might
be symbolized in a singular image but also
be reduced to an abstract equivalent: the
intersection of a vertical and a horizontal
line.

In this sense, *Horizontal Tree* also takes
its place alongside Mondrian's pre-Cubist
windmills, house façades, and wooded
landscapes as an incipiently abstractable
vertical force in an eminently horizontal,
flat world—the reclaimed territory of the
Netherlands. Had Mondrian not shifted his
focus to France and specifically to the
discoveries of Picasso, however, he probably would not have discovered the
aesthetic matrix that was to carry his
forces to non-objectivity, the Cubist grid.

Horizontal Tree, painted in the winter of
1911, soon after Mondrian moved to Paris
(he was to stay there until the outbreak of
war in 1914), shows a mature grasp of the
space-defining and space-enclosing possibilities of Cubist lines and translucent
planes. In over-all conception, it recalls
Picasso's *Portrait of D. H. Kahnweiler*
(1910). In its oval-generated movements
(the "crown" of thin branches surrounding
the central mass), it recalls Picasso's oval
canvas *Point of the Ile de la Cité, Paris*
(1911), which may also have influenced
Mondrian's early Cubist *Still Life with
Ginger Pot* (1911). In its tendency to concentrate form and plasticity in the center
and bleed it into atmosphere at the
periphery, it recalls contemporary work of
both Picasso and Braque.

When considered in the light of Mondrian's achievements of 1912 and 1913,
Horizontal Tree becomes transitional: still
within the confines of the tree motif, the
artist reduced color to grays and whites,
placed parallel pairs of verticals in opposition to parallel pairs of horizontals, and
reinforced the sense of uninterrupted horizontal expansion. These experiments culminated in Mondrian's first strictly conceived linear configuration, *Composition in
Line* (1917).

Nevertheless, *Horizontal Tree* is a pivotal
work because of its revelation of Mondrian's increasingly complex constructive
processes. His pre-Cubist tree paintings
and studies hew to factual, observable
phenomena (for example, the connections
between an arching trunk and secondary
branches, and the deformation of a tree
by the continual force of wind). But
Horizontal Tree is an abstractly realized
conception. Its pictorial energies are as
logical geometrically as they are naturalisti-
cally. Mondrian's aim with this subject was

the investigation not of observable facts,
but vertical and horizontal forces that were
confirmed in observable facts. In effect, he
was paralleling in painting the abstract
conceptualizing of two contemporary
French scientists: the physicist Pierre
Duhem, who in a 1906 text claimed to
replace "the laws which experimental
method furnishes directly with a system of
mathematical propositions representing
those laws;"[1] and the mathematician Henri
Poincaré, whose models for work were intuition and mathematical creativity. GWK

1. Pierre Duhem, *The Aim and Structure of
Physical Theory*, trans. Philip P. Wiener
(Princeton, New Jersey: Princeton University
Press, 1954), p. 21.

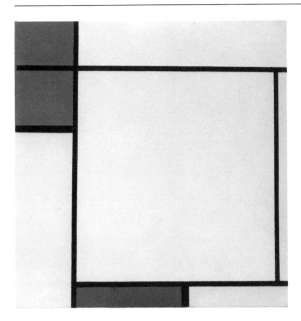

Oil on canvas, dated 1927, 51.1 x 51.1 cm.
Contemporary Collection of The Cleveland Museum of Art 67.215

Collection: J. J. P. Oud, Wassenaar.

Natural (external) things become more and more automatic, and we observe that our vital attention fastens more and more on internal things. The life of the truly modern man is neither purely materialistic nor purely emotional. It manifests itself rather as a more autonomous life of the human mind becoming conscious of itself.

The new plastic idea cannot, therefore, take the form of a natural or concrete representation, although the latter does always indicate the universal to a degree, or at least conceals it within. This new plastic idea will ignore the particulars of appearance, that is to say, natural form and color . . . . Once the solution was discovered, there followed the exact representation of relations alone, that is to say, of the essential and fundamental element in any plastic emotion of the beautiful.[1]

Composition with Red, Yellow, and Blue quintessentially realizes the reductive complexity of Mondrian's ideas of the 1920s. Having progressed by way of a thorough immersion in landscape in his early years to a methodical study of trees, architecture, and oceanfront piers in the mid-teens, Mondrian by the late teens was ready to release himself from nature and compose according to the constructions of his mind. He initiated a rigorous dialogue between framing edge and internal content with a series of lozenge paintings (1919) that are based upon a division of the pictorial surface into regularly spaced lines upon which heavily outlined rectangles are superimposed. From 1921 to 1923

Mondrian concentrated upon the conventional rectangle, evolving therewith a fluid system of relationships between the actual frame, an internal frame composed of colored and white rectangles outlined in black, and an internally framed white square. In these works, according to Kermit Champa, "the entire geometrical layout has become a complex pictorial proposition wherein pictured inside motif and pictured inside frame are made so mutually reliant, responsive and reactive that overall painting shape seems to originate naturally from the inside motif itself and overall field from just outside it."[2] Immediately after doing this series, Mondrian returned to the lozenge, and thence to the enframed square, which he reinvigorated with implied diagonal movements. This last stage, beginning in 1925, includes Cleveland's *Composition with Red, Yellow, and Blue.*

The Cleveland work is animated not only by implied diagonal energies, moving within the enclosed square both from upper left to lower right and from lower right to upper left, but by relational tensions set up between the enclosed square and its enframement. It looks ahead to Mondrian's works of the late 1920s and early thirties in the prominence and centrifugal force afforded the cruciform shape and contiguous, colored rectangle at the upper left. Not only is the red rectangle defined and divided by two black horizontals, it is also set into a pulsating and floating tension with them, as the horizontals are truncated before they reach its left edge (the left edge of the canvas as well). This truncation, a legacy from Mondrian's oval-within-a-rectangle compositions of the mid-teens, serves here actively to dramatize a simultaneous interpenetration and juxtaposition of cross and red plane.

Mondrian had written earlier of the importance of "internal things." For him, the cross—the intersection of horizontal and vertical forces—was a sign of internal harmonies and a recognition of absolute spirit. Mondrian was well acquainted with the writings of Dr. M. H. J. Schoenmachers, a Dutch theosophist who taught a comprehensive religion and world view that encompassed Eastern and Western philosophies and emphasized the predominance of spirit over matter. He also read theosophical works by Rudolf Steiner, who referred to "ethereal" color manifestations, and Madame Blavatsky, the founder of Theosophy, who posited the cross as the union of the male and female principles (for her, it expressed a single mystical concept of regeneration and immortality).

For Mondrian and Theo van Doesburg, the principal artists of the Dutch de Stijl movement, dialectic processes of reasoning were comparable to pure mathematics. Their works comprised not absolutes, but constructed and alterable relations that they believed could be made visible in exact mathematical figures. Similar ideas, paralleling speculation in science, were known to other members of the postwar avant-garde.

That Mondrian's 1927 return to the cross signals his decision to grapple with a formal issue that he had not researched in depth since his lozenges of 1919 is only part of his story. He returned to it because the cross and its potential for relationships—within itself and with color planes—had profound philosophical meaning for him. The cross in *Composition with Red, Yellow, and Blue* generates multiple, interpenetrating forces, and signals a new, evolutionary stage in Mondrian's art. GWK

1. Piet Mondrian, "Natural Reality and Plastic Reality," in Herschel B. Chipp, *Theories of Modern Art* (Berkeley and Los Angeles: University of California Press, 1971), pp. 321, 322.

2. Kermit Champa, "Piet Mondrian's 'Painting Number II—Composition with Grey and Black,'" *Arts* 52 (January 1978): 87.

Vasily Kandinsky
Russian, 1866-1944
**31. Improvisation 28
(Second Version)**

Photograph by Robert E. Mates

Oil on canvas, 1912, 111.4 x 162.1 cm. Solomon R. Guggenheim Museum, New York, Gift, Solomon R. Guggenheim, 1937

Russian-born painter and theorist Vasily Kandinsky was a pioneer in the development of abstraction. In his seminal treatise *Concerning the Spiritual in Art*, published in 1912, he categorized his works in musical terms: Impressions, Improvisations, and Compositions. Although Kandinsky considered the Compositions to be the most studied and worked out of his paintings, his Improvisations were no less considered; by 1914 he had executed thirty-five of them, many of which (including *Improvisation 28*) were preceded by sketches.

The painting is organized on long, sweeping diagonals and open, curvilinear grids that intersect them. Swirling arabesques anchor the otherwise fluid energies at the bottom right and left corners. At the upper left and right are outlines of a mountain range and the sun, respectively. Such compositional diagramming links the work to Kandinsky's later, hard-edged abstractions. By 1922, when he accepted a teaching position at the recently formed Bauhaus in Weimar, Germany, Kandinsky had consolidated his geometric tendencies and introduced schematic constructions. However, in his earlier Munich period, from which *Improvisation 28* derives, Kandinsky's thinking centered on constructive principles. In *Concerning the Spiritual* he wrote: "The more abstract is form, the more clear and direct is its appeal. In any composition the material side may be more or less omitted in proportion as the forms used are more or less marginal, and for them substituted pure abstractions, or largely dematerialized objects. The more an artist uses these abstracted forms, the

deeper and more confidently will he advance into the kingdom of the abstract."[1]

The meaning of *Improvisation 28* emerges from the configurations hidden within its textures. Kandinsky thought in terms of coherent formal structures, visualizing them in his mind's eye and translating them to his canvases. The pyramidal forms throughout relate indirectly to Kandinsky's principle: that his place (along with other artists and scientists) was at the summit of an ascending spiritual pyramid. More specific symbols, no doubt equally important to the painter, remain obscure.

Rose-Carol Washton Long has pointed out that Kandinsky's veiled and condensed imagery—for example, the medieval, towered city on the mountain at the upper right and the reclining, embracing couple below it—is indicative of the complexity and depth of his spiritualism. These are images of hope and fulfillment in opposition to those of cataclysmic explosions and premonitions of deluge (the wave and serpent's tail on the mountain range at the upper left).[2] Indeed, Kandinsky and his artistic and literary circle in Munich were obsessed with eschatology in the immediate prewar years, believing that the world must virtually come to an end before a new civilization, the "epoch of the great spiritual" and the "third revelation," might be born. Kandinsky and his friend Franz Marc designed their important prewar manifesto-anthology, *Blaue Reiter Almanac*, as "a kind of 'medicine book'—an agent of healing, even of exorcism and salvation, prescribed to restore a society diseased with the multiple ills of materialism and decadence."[3]

In this context *Improvisation 28* takes on great significance. If the mountains and pyramids pictured therein were to house both artists and scientists, these thinkers would be spiritualists, even mystics. For Kandinsky and his intellectual circle, the most profound discovery of the age was that the atom was *not* the fundamental unit of the universe. This opened the way for Kandinsky to embrace the idea of the spirit as the most essential form of the universe.

Thus, Kandinsky's painting emerges not as a hermetic assemblage of lines and colors, but as a highly communicative, symbolic device meant to sever the old world from the new. In relying upon the psychological and symbolic power of image complexes, he aligned himself with European avant-garde thinking in applied science, spiritualism, and literature.

And so at different points along the road are the different arts, saying what they are best able to say, and in the language which is peculiarly their own. Despite, or perhaps thanks to, the differences between them, there has never been a time when the arts approached each other more nearly than they do today, in this later phase of spiritual development.[4]
GWK

1. Wassily Kandinsky, *Concerning the Spiritual in Art*, trans. M. T. Sadler (New York: Dover Publications, 1977), p. 32.

2. Rose-Carol Washton Long, "Kandinsky's Vision of Utopia as a Garden of Love," *Art Journal* 43 (Spring 1983): 52; and Washton Long, *Kandinsky, The Development of an Abstract Style* (Oxford: Clarendon Press, 1980), pp. 131-32.

3. Peg Weiss, "Kandinsky and the Symbolist Heritage," *Art Journal* 45 (Summer 1985): 142-43.

4. Kandinsky, *Concerning the Spiritual Art*, p. 19.

Constantin Brancusi
French (b. Romania), 1876-1957
32. Mlle Pogany

Bronze, 1913, h. 44.5 cm.
The J.B. Speed Art Museum, Louisville, Kentucky 54.16

Margit Pogany, the inspiration for this bronze, was a young Hungarian painter who lived at the Parisian boarding house where Brancusi ate his meals. In 1910 the sculptor invited her to his studio under the pretense of showing her his new work; actually, he wanted to see her reaction to a recently completed marble portrait of her that he had carved from memory. Margit Pogany later wrote that upon seeing the bust, which Brancusi exhibited as *Danaide*, "I felt that it was me, although it had none of my features. It was all eyes."[1] Impressed with the sculpture, she asked Brancusi if she could sit for another portrait, and he enthusiastically agreed:

I sat for him several times. Each time he began and finished a new bust (in clay). Each of these was beautiful and a wonderful likeness, and each time I begged him to keep it and use it for the definitive bust—but he only laughed and threw it back into the boxful of clay that stood in the corner of the studio—to my great disappointment. Once I had to sit for my hands but the pose was quite different than that of the present bust, but he only wanted to learn them by heart as he already knew my head by heart.[2]

Brancusi finished a marble version of *Mlle Pogany* in 1912, and in 1913 a plaster cast of the sculpture was exhibited at the New York Armory Show, where it caused an uproar. One critic called it "a hardboiled egg balanced on a cup of sugar,"[3] and a New York newspaper printed a poem entitled "Lines to a Lady Egg":

*Ladies builded like a bottle
Carrot beet or sweet potato—
Quaint designs that Aristotle
Idly drew to tickle Plato—
Ladies sculptured thus, I beg
You will save your tense emotion
I am constant in devotion,
Oh my egg!*[4]

The J.B. Speed Museum version of *Mlle Pogany* is one of four polished bronzes that Brancusi cast in 1913. Except for the medium and the black patina applied to the hair area, the bronze *Mlle Pogany* differs little from the original marble bust. In both sculptures the curved placement of the arms against the side of the face draws the viewer's eye upward in a spiraling motion, which compels a study of the portrait from a variety of angles. Brancusi radically simplified Miss Pogany's appearance while emphasizing her most salient features: large eyes, tiny mouth, and the bun she customarily wore at the base of the neck. The artist later commented that "the hands were modeled quite definitely, the hair was bound at the back of the head, but the face has been generalized almost to the obliteration of the features, except for the eyes and the arching sweep of the eyebrows."[5]

The great degree of abstraction does not obscure the bust's function as a portrait; stopping short of caricature, it still retains an uncanny resemblance to the sitter. Brancusi remained fascinated with this subject and continued the process of radical simplification even further in several other marble and bronze versions of *Mlle Pogany*. SD

1. Quoted in Sidney Geist, *Brancusi: A Study of the Sculpture* (New York: Grossman Publishers, 1968), p. 190.

2. Ibid., p. 191.

3. Milton W. Brown, *The Story of the Armory Show* (New York: Joseph H. Hirshhorn Foundation, 1963), p. 112.

4. Ibid., p. 113.

5. Ionel Jianou, *Brancusi* (New York: Tudor, 1963), p. 7.

Polished brass, signed, dated 1917,
h. 46.8 cm.
The Cleveland Museum of Art, Hinman B.
Hurlbut Collection 3205.37

Collection: Joseph Brummer.

One of the great pioneers of modern
sculpture, Brancusi brought to the avant-
garde an appreciation for the purity and
simplicity of both primitive and folk art
(first encountered during his youth in rural
Romania). He played an equally pivotal role
in advancing certain modernist principles,
such as the use of new materials and techniques, the elimination of narrative and
allegory from art, and a belief in the
capacity of abstract form to convey meaning.

Male Torso, which incorporates many of
these ideas, is a deceptively simple sculpture. At first glance, it may appear completely symmetrical, as if based upon a
purely intellectual or mathematical formula; however, the torso is actually replete
with subtle irregularities that confer a
sense of life upon these chaste, geometric
shapes. The sculpture consists of three
cylindrical segments joined at angles of approximately 120 degrees; the lower two
rise from the pedestal at a subtle incline
(see side view) that deviates slightly from a
perfect 90-degree vertical; both "legs" are
delicately tapered along the back, as if to
define buttocks; the uppermost segment
culminates in an elliptical plane that slants
downward on the right, thus breaking the
symmetry of the front view; a slight swelling at the base of this central segment
seems to suggest a genital area. The omission of overt genitalia paradoxically draws
attention to the sculpture's over-all phallic
appearance, while giving the torso an androgynous character that allows us to interpret it as a symbolic union of male and
female principles.

Brancusi characteristically exploited the
propensity of various materials and techniques to confer metaphorical and symbolic meanings upon his sculptures. Here,
the polished brass surface[1] tends to
dissolve the sense of weight and mass normally exhibited by nineteenth-century
metal sculpture, such as Rodin's *Age of
Bronze* (cat. no. 10). Moreover, the highly
reflective surface appears to glow with a
radiant, golden light. Light and perfect
form (sometimes expressed through symmetrical design) have traditionally been
associated with spirituality as well as with
divinity. Thus, the near-perfect shapes and
the smooth, textureless, light-reflective surface of Brancusi's torso tend to emphasize
its spiritual, symbolic meaning rather than
its temporal or physical presence.[2]

By reducing the torso to basic geometric
shapes, Brancusi emphasized its universality.
He has expressed the male-torso concept
in terms of a simple, integral form that
transcends the particular and seeks the
plane of timeless, universal meaning. Such
extreme simplicity offers the possibility for
many different interpretations; for example, the singular, upright form brings to
mind associations with prehistoric mono-
liths and ritual objects. The essential
"meaning" of the torso, however, resides
directly in the language of abstract or absolute form.

Male Torso derives in part from Rodin's
formal innovation of the partial figure. Yet,
this sculpture is not really a "fragment" of
a larger, more complete work: rather, it
can be more accurately described as a universal symbol created by distilling the idea
of a male torso to its most essential level.

In this way, Brancusi replaced traditional
allegory and rhetoric with abstract, symbolic form as the fundamental language of
sculpture. Such works, he insisted, have a
greater capacity to represent "reality" than
do sculptures that merely imitate the surface appearance of nature: "They are im-
beciles who call my work abstract; that
which they call abstract is the most realist,
because what is real is not the exterior
form but the *idea*, the essence of things."[3]
WHR

1. Brass is an alloy made by mixing copper
with zinc. Bronze, on the other hand, consists of copper mixed with tin. *Male Torso*
is made of an unusual combination of all
three metals—copper, zinc, and tin—but
because there is a larger amount of zinc
than tin, the medium is listed here as
brass.

2. The small scratches on the front are not
part of the original surface; they were
created several years ago when a museum
visitor accidently knocked over the work.

3. Herschel B. Chipp, *Theories of Modern
Art* (Berkeley and Los Angeles: University
of California Press, 1968), p. 365.

Jean (Hans) Arp
French (Alsatian), 1887-1966
34. Forest

Giorgio de Chirico
Italian (b. Greece), 1888-1978
35. Metaphysical Interior

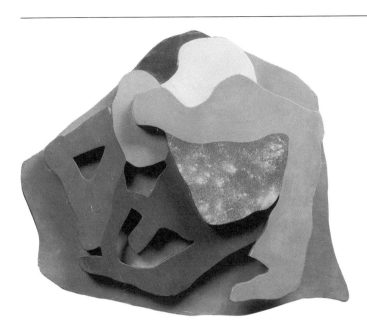

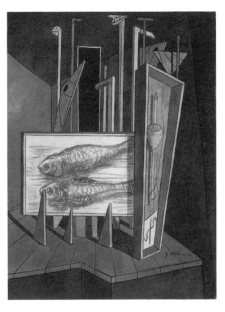

Painted wood, ca. 1916, w. 50.8 cm. Contemporary Collection of the Cleveland Museum of Art 70.52

Collections: Paul Eluard, Paris; Sir Roland Penrose, London; (Eugene V. Thaw, New York).

Arp left wartime Paris in 1915 to join his family in Weggis, Switzerland. When Hugo Ball invited him to join a group of artists, poets, and other intellectuals who were gathering in Zurich, he hastened to accept, and so participated in the formation of the Dada movement.

In Zurich Arp made rectilinear *papiers collés* by tearing pieces of paper, allowing them to fall "according to the laws of chance," and fixing them. In 1916 he transformed the process of collage into assemblage by gluing together pieces of wood, about one inch thick, that he had cut into biomorphic shapes. Some of these reliefs, such as *Forest*, were then painted; others were not. The elements constituting the present work were inspired by branches, foliage, and pebbles around Lake Maggiore in Ascona.

Like Paul Klee, Arp believed that a work of art was produced by the artist as gratuitously as "a fruit is by a tree." His biomorphic designs from late 1916 are indebted to Vasily Kandinsky's early abstract works and, to a lesser extent, to Art Nouveau.

Along with his colleagues in Zurich, Arp was a prime mover of the Dada movement, born of disillusionment, sorrow, and anger over the cataclysmic events of World War I. Arp explained the movement's origins thus:

Revolted by the butchery of the 1914 World War, we in Zurich devoted ourselves to the arts. While the guns rumbled in the distance, we sang, painted, made collages and wrote poems with all our might. We were seeking an art based upon fundamentals, to cure the madness of the age, and a new order of things that would restore the balance between heaven and hell.[1]

Although Dada was far from monolithic, the dominant attitude was anarchistic and the prevailing mood, pessimistic. Arp shared Dada's revulsion of the War, yet his art remained life-embracing—even joyful. One of the true artists of the group, he is one of only a few Dadaists to achieve stature as a major figure in modern art. EBH

1. Quoted in Hans Richter, *Dada: Art and Anti-Art* (London: Thames and Hudson, 1965), p. 25.

Oil on canvas, 1917, 71.7 x 52.7 cm. The Cleveland Museum of Art, John L. Severance Fund 81.51

Collections: Paul Eluard, Paris; Bernard Poissonier, Brussels.

Guillaume Apollinaire, in 1914, declared de Chirico to be the most astonishing painter of his time. There appears to be no direct ancestry for his clear representations of lonely city streets and squares, arcades, clocks, towers, walls, trains, stalks of bananas, artichokes, Classical sculptures, menacing shadows, and distant figures in silhouette. De Chirico and his bizarre canvases appeared in Paris in 1911, when Analytical Cubism was at its peak.

Cubism dealt with formal analysis, whereas de Chirico emphasized subject matter. His eerie landscapes and still lifes, however, suggest a world of interior reality—perhaps a dream world—rather than that of ordinary sense perceptions. (It is interesting to note that de Chirico began painting these so-called metaphysical canvases some fourteen, years before the publication of André Breton's Surrealist manifesto, which clearly makes him a precursor of Surrealist art.) Where Cubism produced a shallow, ambiguous space in which material forms and space were integrated, de Chirico created the illusion of absolute space in which discrete objects are illuminated by the clear, flat light of a late afternoon sun. Cubism paralleled, in some ways, the world being described by early twentieth-century physics; de Chirico's art seems to refer to a Freudian dream world.

Collage, 1929, 24.5 x 20 cm.
The Cleveland Museum of Art, John L.
Severance Fund 82.39

Collections: Arturo Schwarz, Milan;
G. Plouvier, Antwerp.

Cubism shared with de Chirico's art only unusual combinations of objects not normally associated with one another. De Chirico wrote: "A picture must always be the reflection of a profound sensation . . . profound signifies strange, and strange signifies not-known or perhaps entirely unknown. A work of art, if it is to be immortal, must go beyond the limits of man. Good sense and logic have no place in it. That is the way in which a painting can approximate to a dream-like or child-like state of mind."[1]

The two fish in *Metaphysical Interior* constitute a rare motif in de Chirico's painting.[2] The interior still life and the thinly painted surface is typical, however, of many of the works done in Ferrara in 1916 and early 1917.[3] Ironically, it was some ten years after de Chirico renounced this kind of "metaphysical" painting, which had great influence on Surrealists such as Max Ernst, René Magritte, Yves Tanguy, and Salvador Dali, that André Breton referred to him as one of two "fixed points" by which the Surrealists could determine "the straight line ahead . . . ."[4]

De Chirico had earlier written: "Certain aspects of the world, whose existence we completely ignore, suddenly confront us with the revelation of mysteries lying all the time within our reach and which we cannot see because we are too shortsighted, and cannot feel because our senses are inadequately developed. Their dead voices speak to us from nearby, but they sound like voices from another planet."[5] De Chirico thus declared his belief that much exists outside the limited range of our senses—a position that the physical sciences also took and that is commonly accepted today. EBH

1. Jacques Lassaigne, *History of Modern Painting: From Picasso to Surrealism* (Geneva: Albert Skira, 1950), p. 104.

2. Maurizio Fagiolo, a prominent de Chirico scholar, has written that for him the image of a fish *normally* signifies a painting by Carlo Carrà. However, fish appear in de Chirico's *The Sacred Fish* (1919) and *The Dream of Tobias* (1917). Furthermore, the appearance of *Metaphysical Interior* and its history make it clear that this is a painting by de Chirico.

3. James Thrall Soby dated this painting 1917, while William Rubin dates it 1916. Dating de Chirico's canvases is especially difficult due to his practice of later repeating themes that he painted between 1911 and 1918 and putting the early dates on the later paintings.

4. André Breton, *Surrealism and Painting*, trans. Simon Watson Taylor (New York: Harper and Row, 1972), p. 13.

5. Lassaigne, *Modern Painting*, p. 104.

One of the most creative artists of the twentieth century, the Surrealist Max Ernst invented a multitude of new artistic processes. He originated the techniques of *frottage* and *grattage*, and adapted the medium of collage—first employed by the Cubists as a formal device for restructuring space—into a means of bringing distant realities into unexpected and often illogical relationships, thereby liberating the mind from the control of reason.[1] Most importantly, Ernst discovered that this method offered a vehicle for revealing hidden meanings latent in the unconscious. Rather than being concerned with producing an "aesthetic object," Ernst's creative activities were primarily directed toward exploring ideas, mysterious affinities between objects, and what Breton referred to in *The First Manifesto of Surrealism* as "the very process of thought."

By the late 1920s Ernst had begun making "decoupages-collages," such as *Jeanne Hachette et Charles le Téméraire*, in which collage elements are attached to an already-completed image (in this case, a nineteenth-century engraving). Ernst also employed this technique to create the illustrations for the three Surrealist novels he executed between 1929 and 1934.

The subject of this work, created in 1929 as part of an unrealized collage-novel titled *Morceaux choisis de l'histoire de France* (Minor Events Selected from the History of France), derives from an obscure

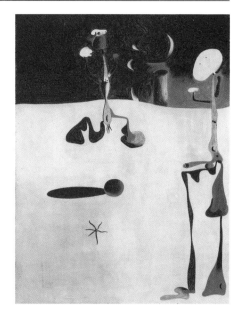

incident in French history involving Charles the Bold (1433-1477), the last duke of Burgundy, and a woman known as Jeanne Hachette, or Jean Hatchet.[2] After invading France in order to reclaim the provinces of Alsace and Lorraine, Charles the Bold laid seige to the city of Beauvais. On June 24, 1472, just as the Burgundians were about to overwhelm the French defenders of Beauvais, a young woman (Jeanne Hachette) appeared on the ramparts brandishing an axe. She hurled a Burgundian soldier to his death and ripped down the enemy flag. Her actions so inspired the French that they rallied to defeat the Burgundians. The event is still celebrated in Beauvais.

Ernst created the collage by attaching various cut-out elements to a nineteenth-century engraving that depicts a young prince leaping out of a bucket, with a castle and a moonlit sky in the background. He attached several new elements to the illustration: 1) a picture of a woman was cut out from some other source and carefully inserted into the engraving by slicing apart the upper rim of the bucket; 2) the prince was given a strange bird- or dolphinlike head; and 3) a beetle was added in the lower left to cover the signature of the original illustrator (Ernst cleverly used several letters of that artist's name to form the insect's legs and antennae). Examination of the collage through an infrared viewer reveals that the signature beneath the beetle reads "Montégut," which certainly refers to Louis Montegut, a nineteenth-century illustrator who worked for *La Chronique Parisienne*. After covering that artist's name with the beetle, Ernst signed the collage himself in the lower right.

As a result of these alterations, Ernst transformed a banal engraving into a fantastic dream image that eludes logical analysis or finite interpretation. The exact nature of the prince's head, for example, cannot be identified with any certainty: it may represent a monstrous bird's head and would thus refer to Ernst's childhood obsession with his pet bird "Loplop" who died suddenly and coincidently on the same day that his sister was born; or, if the head represents a dolphin, it may have been intended as a pun on "dauphin." By bringing such disparate elements and contradictory elements into sharp juxtaposition, Ernst effaced the original meaning of each, thereby creating a totally new reality—or a "surreality"—in which the everyday world and the dream world collide. WHR

1. *Frottage* is the method of making rubbings over a textured surface. This method produces unexpected, random images that can be used to stimulate the artist's imagination and, through automatic suggestion, to explore the unconscious. *Grattage* is a technique in which paint is scraped away from a surface.

2. Among the other collage-illustrations from this unrealized novel are: *L'esprit de Locarno, Nostradamus, Blanche de Castille et le petit Saint-Louis,* and *L'autel de la patrie* (all 1929).

Oil on copper, signed, dated 1935, 41.9 x 29.2 cm.
The Cleveland Museum of Art, Mr. and Mrs. William H. Marlatt Fund 78.61

Collection: Sir Roland Penrose, London.

By the mid-1930s premonitions of the terrible events soon to occur in his native Spain, and then in the rest of Europe, found their way into the imagery of Miró's art. Between October 23, 1935, and May 22, 1936, he produced six paintings in oil on copper and six in tempera on masonite panels. *Nocturne* is one of the paintings on copper. The non-absorbent plate caused the oil to dry slowly, allowing the artist time to rework the dreadful images now finding their way into his painting.

Two violently distorted humanoid forms meet in a barren landscape. Acerbic colors suggest an infernal glowing light beneath a lurid sky. The sex of the monsters is indicated by their genitalia. The female writhes toward the waiting male, whose eyes stare blankly from a large, tilted, mushroomlike head.

Behind these two figures, a phallic column rises from the horizon beneath a crescent moon. Beside it, a snakelike shape undulates upward like a palpable ribbon of smoke. Below the female figure a spherical shape casts a long shadow—harking back to paintings by de Chirico—and a strange starfish lies on the desert surface.

Miró's own words seem appropriate for this eerie painting: "Empty spaces, empty horizons, empty plains, everything that is bare and empty always impresses me . . . ."[1] EBH

1. Jacques Dupin, *Miró* (New York: Harry N. Abrams, 1962), p. 21.

**38. Constellation: Woman with
Blond Armpit Combing Her Hair
by the Light of Stars**

Gouache and oil on paper, 1940,
38.1 x 46 cm.
Contemporary Collection of The Cleveland
Museum of Art 65.2

Collection: Mrs. S. S. White, Ardmore,
Pennsylvania.

In the mid-thirties Miró's imagery was
dominated by demons deriving from his
despair over the terrible forces about to be
loosed on the world. In 1940, however,
while working at Varengeville on the
Channel Coast in Normandy, he unexpectedly began a series of small, lyrical
paintings called by the generic term "Constellations." Women and birds under starry
night skies is the dominant theme of these
twenty-three paintings. He later reported:
"At Varengeville-sur-Mer, in 1939, began a
new stage in my work . . . . I felt a deep
desire to escape. I closed myself within
myself purposely. The night, music, and
the stars began to play a major role in suggesting my paintings . . . music in this
period began to take the role poetry had
played in the early twenties . . . ."[1]

Miró worked on this series as if possessed, ignoring outside events until
Varengeville was directly threatened by the
advancing German armies. Urged by
friends, he finally caught the last train to
Paris and then took a refugee train to
Spain. He finished the series on Majorca
and at Montroig, on the Spanish mainland,
in 1941.

All twenty-three paintings are the same
size and are on heavy paper that has been
saturated with thin washes of oil paint
over which Miró developed a linear composition, painting in certain flat shapes
with gouache. Breton remarked about
these paintings: "At a time of extreme per-
turbation . . . by a reflex striving for the
purest, the least changeable, Miró let go
with the full range of his powers, showing
us what he could really do all the time."[2]

*Woman with Blond Armpit Combing Her
Hair by the Light of Stars* is one of the first
ten of the series that Miró completed at
Varengeville. The oil ground was laid on in
a succession of thin layers, which were
matted, blotted, rubbed, and caressed into
a velvety, sooty ground. On this soft,
warm surface Miró developed a pattern of
dots, circles, and irregular shapes that he
wove into a linear design indicating a
female figure, a moon, stars, and a horizon. The skillfully articulated images and
the tightly integrated, formal order attest
to the artist's conscious control of his
material even if his early moves were spontaneous.

Twenty-two of these works were exhibited at the Pierre Matisse Gallery in
New York in 1945; they were the first
works created in Europe during World War
II to be shown in the United States after
the War ended. The exhibition was seen
by some of the young American painters
who had just begun to form a coherent
movement called Abstract Expressionism.

Indebted to the Surrealist artists who had
sought refuge in the United States during
the War, the Abstract Expressionists were
also influenced by the creative methods of
Picasso, Paul Klee, and Miró, all of whom
remained in Europe. EBH

1. James Johnson Sweeney, "Joan Miró:
Comment and Review," *Partisan Review*,
no. 2 (February 1948): 10-11.

2. Quoted in Jacques Dupin, *Miró* (New
York: Harry N. Abrams, 1962), p. 360.

Paul Klee
German (b. Switzerland), 1879-1940
39. Karneval im Schnee (Carnival in the Snow)

Watercolor on paper, 1923, 26.7 x 30.5 cm.
Contemporary Collection of The Cleveland Museum of Art 69.46

Collection: (Eugene V. Thaw, New York).

Carnival in the Snow fits into a long-standing Klee theme—the puppet, marionette, acrobat, dancer, and clown. Three figures dominate the composition (a fourth is half-visible on the right): a female juggler, a male juggler aloft, and his support, a somewhat portly man who is evidently the leader of the group. They are artificially jointed at elbows and knees, have mittenlike hands, and are constructed in part from pure geometric shapes and abstract signs. Essentially puppets without strings, they are denizens of both a semi-animal, primitive world and a world of grace.

Klee's earlier automatons are fierce and satirical. Anti-bourgeois, thus parallel in concept to the marionettes and stiff, tubular costumes that the Zurich Dadaists made, they brutally satirize the moral and psychological inflexibility of a society caught in the midst of tumultuous change. In *Acrobats* (1918) or *Acrobats and Jugglers* (1916), for example:

The figures are themselves their apparatus; they are transparent mannikins sharing body-lines which also map out their descent. The fall is ungraceful, for the jointed mannikin limbs are capable of only two-way action. The acrobat reverses the normal positions of the body, he stands on his hands, he demonstrates his flexibility and his sense of balance. He has been called "a living symbol of inversion or reversal," an upsetter and a reverser of the established order.[1]

Although Klee's unstable acrobats survived the First World War, after 1920, that is, at the same time he was invited to teach at the recently formed Bauhaus in Weimar, they tended both to increase in grace and to become more metaphorical.

Carnival in the Snow, although composed in terms of color blocks rather than line, shares verve, buoyancy, and resiliency with linearly conceived works such as *Twittering Machine* (1922), *Tightrope Walker* (1923), and *A Young Lady's Adventure* (1922). Undoubtedly the optimistic and organic Bauhaus credo, which promised human betterment through humanistically conceived and artfully executed structures, had something to do with the change. Likewise did Klee's own "creative credo," which stressed a rigorous use and exploitation of a limited number of forms and movement (Klee's famous taking a line for walk). "Klee wanted each picture to be seen as 'genesis'; ideally the viewer should take a chair, sit down, and identify with the construction in time of the art work."[2]

Edward B. Henning has emphasized the metamorphic, metaphorical, and musical machine that *Carnival in the Snow* is.[3] Not only do points lengthen to line, and lines become planes, but circles metamorphose to balls, genitals, heads, eyes, mouths, stomachs, a dot over a lower-case "j," and pompoms on shoes. And, depending upon how one looks at it, the chief acrobat is at the same time man, man with inscribed little man, arm-biting bird or beast. Klee had explored a half-animal, half-human, and patently sexual world since the early years of the century, when he did a series of "sour" prints such as *Woman and Beast*

and *Virgin in a Tree* (both 1903). In his early Bauhaus years, however, he conjoined erotic fantasy with form-giving fantasy, such that *Carnival* celebrates acrobatic feats possible with basic building blocks of design, as well as a joyful and slightly macabre orgy. Indeed, "the most primitive abstract forms are at once made analogies of actions and processes in the larger physical and mental world . . . . Klee's line is figuratively endowed with legs."[4]

Nineteen twenty-three was an important year for Klee. He began to create Constructivist works in free space and explored the concept of force lines. He had thoroughly absorbed, and for the most part exhausted, Picasso's fracturing and planar blending (*passage*), and Delaunay's luminous color glazing.

Considered in this sense, *Carnival* is not a radical work. Its two-dimensionality and vestigial "magic square" gridding relate it to Klee's post-Tunisian works of the mid-teens. Neither is its sly yet formally effervescent earthiness radical. Eros governs this work, as it also underlies Dada and Surrealism. Although Klee was neither a member of the Surrealist circle nor an advocate of creation from the unconscious, the Surrealists considered him a pioneer for their explorations of the mid-1920s and 1930s. "As a child plays at being grown-up," Klee wrote, "so the painter imitates the play of those forces which create and are still creating the world."[5] GWK

1. Margaret Plant, *Paul Klee, Figures and Faces* (London: Thames and Hudson, 1978), p. 58.

2. Ibid., p. 52.

3. Edward B. Henning, "Paul Klee, *Carnival in the Snow*," *Bulletin of The Cleveland Museum of Art* 57 (April 1970): 112-17.

4. Marcel Franciscono, "Paul Klee in the Bauhaus: The Artist as Lawgiver," *Arts* 52 (September 1977): 125.

5. Henning, "Paul Klee," p. 115.

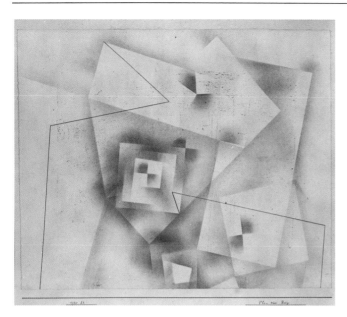

Watercolor on paper, 1930, 38.1 x 48.2 cm.
Private Collection

Collection: Phillip Johnson, New York.

Jim Jordan has specified that Klee's Constructivism consists of closed, regular shapes, a linear geometric system, and the absence of Cubist *passage*.[1] *Plan for a Castle* incorporates transparency—a meandering angular line moves upward and outward from the pictorial center to a point near the lower right corner, then emerges and rises from the lower left to suggest an outwardly angled quadrilateral. It also incorporates *passage*. Nonetheless, the Constructivist elements dominate. In fact, Klee's stacked squares and rectangles imply, as his title suggests, a plan for a castle (or perhaps a fortress), or an aerial view of the realized structure. From 1924 to 1928 the Russian Suprematist painter Kasimir Malevich, who had a great influence on László Moholy-Nagy, El Lissitzky, Alexander Rodchenko, and the entire European Constructivist group, constructed a group of models that he called *Arkhitektonics*. Since El Lissitzky proselytized Malevich's ideas in Germany from the early 1920s, and Malevich's theories were available in a Bauhaus book in 1927, it is possible that Klee may have seen either the models or photographs of them.

That Klee might have developed other affinities with Malevich is also a distinct possibility. In connection with some spatial studies of 1930 that he called *Studies in Three Dimensions*, Klee distinguished between "rational" and "irrational" connections. Rational connections joined parallelograms to form cubes; irrational ones formed open parallelogram constructions wherein

"the eye wanders from one rectangle to another without being able to perceive the logic of the spatial connections."[2] *Plan for a Castle* is replete with such irrational connections. The two small parallelograms that angle out from the void to meet at a common point operate according to Suprematist principles.

For Malevich, the cosmic flame "wavers in the inner man without purpose, sense, or logic."[3] For Klee, "Abstract formal elements are put together like numbers and letters to make concrete beings or abstract things; in the end a formal cosmos is achieved, so much like the creation that a mere breath suffices to transform religion into art."[4]

As Malevich considered his quadrilateral the icon of a new language, Klee posited the crystal as his foundation, even his alter-ego. For Klee, himself a child of the German post-Romantic philosophy of empathy codified by Wilhelm Worringer, the crystal was born of a regular, inorganic law. Both Worringer and Klee believed that "geometric-crystalline regularity" could "win from the unclear factors of perception, which is what really imparts to the external thing its relativity, an abstract of the object capable of forming a whole for the imagination."[5]

There is a centripetal, almost vortical force in *Plan for a Castle*. All energies converge in the bright checkered square. Beginning with works such as this, Klee in the thirties and forties explored the ramifications of another Romantic concept, the mystic center. As in the 1930 painting, these later paintings and drawings excavate and interpenetrate with space in a Constructivist manner. They ultimately reveal, however, that Klee's constructions

were romantically based. Perhaps with *Plan for a Castle* in his mind's eye, Klee began his *Creative Credo* thus: "Let us take a little trip into the land of deeper insight following a topographical plan. The dead center being the point."[6] GWK

1. Jim M. Jordan, *Paul Klee and the Bauhaus* (Princeton, New Jersey: Princeton University Press, 1984), p. 23.

2. Christian Geelhaar, *Paul Klee and the Bauhaus* (Greenwich: New York Graphic Society, 1973), p. 158.

3. Jean-Claude Marcade, "K. S. Malevich: From *Black Quadrilateral* (1913) to *White on White* (1917); From the Eclipse of Objects to the Liberation of Space," in *The Avant-Garde in Russia, 1910-1930: New Perspectives* (Los Angeles: Los Angeles County Museum of Art, 1980), p. 23.

4. Geelhaar, *Paul Klee*, p. 31.

5. Ibid., p. 44.

6. Robert Knott, "Paul Klee and the Mystic Center," *Art Journal* 38 (Winter 1978-79): 116.

Hans Hofmann
American (b. Germany), 1880-1966
**41. Smaragd, Red, and
Germinating Yellow**

Jackson Pollock
American, 1912-1956
42. Number 5, 1950

Oil on canvas, 1959, 134.7 x 101.6 cm.
Contemporary Collection of The Cleveland
Museum of Art 60.57

Collection: (Samuel M. Kootz Gallery, New
York).

Born in Germany, Hans Hofmann directed
his own school in Munich from 1915 to
1932. When he arrived in the United
States to stay in 1932, he was thoroughly
imbued with Expressionism, Fauvism,
Cubism, and Vasily Kandinsky's and Robert
Delaunay's colorful brands of abstraction.
Hofmann did not paint in a fully abstract
style, however, until 1939.

Smaragd, Red, and Germinating Yellow
demonstrates his concern with the illusion
of compensating movements in and out of
space—what he referred to as "push and
pull." While traditional perspective moves
the viewer's eye back into space without
an answering movement back out to the
surface, the space created by Hofmann in
his paintings is a "breathing," pictorial
space.

The flat, yellow-green rectangle in the
lower left corner of this work establishes a
plane parallel to the picture surface. The
loosely painted patches of red and red
violet to the right and above establish a
response to the yellow-green rectangle.
The oranges, blue greens, and browns
modulate between the two clashing areas,
while the greens and blues on the canvas's
edges move in and out of space depending on contiguous colors.

Color played a central role in Hofmann's
carefully integrated formal compositions
and indicates certain feelings and emotions. *Smaragd, Red, and Germinating
Yellow*, for example, is composed of compensating energies. The energy suggested
by each area of color reciprocates the
energy of other color areas. Transitional
areas modulate the intervals between major fields of color until the whole is
brought into balance, thus providing a picture of Hofmann's experience of the
world.

Hofmann did not rely on any one style:
each work was created through a unique
effort to forge the means for solving particular formal problems and achieving expression of inner experience. He conceived
of the creative act as spontaneous and intuitive, creating its own rationale as it
goes. This was a lesson well learned by
Jackson Pollock and many other young
American painters. EBH

Oil on canvas, 1950, 136.5 x 99.1 cm.
The Cleveland Museum of Art, Leonard C.
Hanna, Jr., Fund 80.180

Collections: Mr. and Mrs. Walter Bareiss,
New York; Museum of Modern Art, New
York.

By the time that Jackson Pollock painted
Number 5, 1950, he had reached the peak
of his powers as an artist. The mythological images that peopled his earlier canvases were replaced by the single image of
the entire painting.

With the fully mature paintings of the
late 1940s, Pollock joined Surrealist
automatism with a fully abstract style and
a suggested space reminiscent of Picasso's
and Braque's Cubist compositions of
1911-12. Going beyond the two inventors
of Cubism, however, Pollock allowed pure
form to articulate the painting's content.

It is impossible to put the content of a
painting such as *Number 5, 1950* into
precise verbal terms. It can, however, be
inferred from the dynamic, free-swinging
lines and areas of color. The over-all
character of this energetic, completely integrated composition recalls Monet's late
paintings of his lily pond, although it is
unlikely that Pollock saw these pictures.

Insofar as it can be argued that Pollock's
paintings imply a world view, *Number 5,
1950* indicates a poetic vision of a reality
in which all elements are related. There are
no discrete forms in space, only implications of energy responding to energy. Dis-
ruptive elements have been subordinated
or eliminated. Dynamic equilibrium, as
assured as that in Mondrian's abstractions,
has been arrived at intuitively. EBH

Robert Motherwell
American, b. 1915
43. Mallarmé's Swan

Mark Rothko
American (b. Russia), 1903-1970
44. Red Maroons

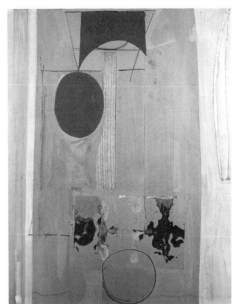

Motherwell gave up the representation of figures and objects to imaginatively project subjective experiences of things such as love, the death of the Spanish Republic, and Mallarmé's poem. References are indicated by means of common associations connected with formal elements such as color and shape. In line with the tenets of Symbolism, Motherwell said: "The 'pure' red of which certain abstractionists speak, does not exist, no matter how one shifts its physical context. Any red is rooted in blood, glass, wine, hunting caps, and a thousand other concrete phenomena. Otherwise we should have no feelings toward red or its relations, and it would be useless as an artistic element."[1] EBH

1. Quoted in Sam Hunter, *Art Since 1945* (New York: Harry N. Abrams, 1961), p. 15.

Oil on canvas, 1962, 200.7 x 205.7 cm. Contemporary Collection of The Cleveland Museum of Art 62.239

Collection: (Sidney Janis Gallery, New York).

Red Maroons is typical of Rothko's mature canvases in that it is composed of several blurred-edge rectangular shapes on a colored ground. Drawing, modeling, chiaroscuro, rectilinear perspective, and most other devices of traditional painting have been abolished. The large canvas has just three rectangles—dark brown, black, and red—of different sizes placed one above the other on a deep plum ground. Pigment was applied in thin, translucent glazes one over the other, thus creating multiple veils of color. Hues are intense but subdued, and values are close, producing subtle variations within each area.

Gouache, crayon, and paper on cardboard, 1944, 110.5 x 90.2 cm.
Contemporary Collection of The Cleveland Museum of Art 61.229

Collections: Mrs. Robert Motherwell; (Robert Elkon Gallery, New York).

Although Robert Motherwell is American, French culture has always played a role in his art. The title of *Mallarmé's Swan*, for example, refers to a poem by the French Symbolist poet Stephane Mallarmé, and the collage technique is derived from Cubism.

Mallarmé's poem begins: "*Le vierge, le vivace et le bel aujourd'hui.*" The crystalline "music" of the poem is echoed by the precision and grace of the collage. The imagery of the poem refers to a magnificent swan hopelessly trapped in the ice of a forgotten lake. He is horrified by the "soil" that catches his plumage, for he has never sung the "region of life." His own pure light and his cold contempt condemns him to useless exile.

Motherwell's collage in no way illustrates Mallarmé's poem; rather, it is itself a kind of visual poem, the spirit of which parallels that of the written text. It was created because Motherwell knew the poem and sought to express in visual form his experience of it.

In the same spirit as Mallarmé's pure poetry, Motherwell created a purely abstract painting-collage. Restrained, precise, clear, and elegant, it reflects the dominant French artistic tradition and contrasts with the headlong impetuosity of paintings by other American artists such as Pollock and Franz Kline.

If we venture beyond empirical evidence to obvious implications, we find that the translucent layers of color and soft-edged shapes connote a hazy atmosphere and ambiguous space. Though the blurred rectangular shapes have depth, they lack solidity, weight, and defined form. The deep, intense red of the topmost rectangle draws the observer's eye upward and seems to hold the larger black and brown shapes in place. The close values and lack of strong contrasts serve to avoid any suggestion of clashes, but imply instead a deep sonority—or even silence. The intense hues lacking definite boundaries suggest light emanating from within the painting and seeming to pulsate and expand into the space surrounding the canvas. The psychological atmosphere, however, is brooding and ominous.

Rothko reduced painting to a few essential elements in an effort to gain clarity, which he defined as "the elimination of all obstacles between the painter and the idea, and between the idea and the observer." He declared that his paintings are "nothing but content,"[1] and he rejected the suggestion that they are spiritual or mystical. Nevertheless, perhaps they do provide insight into the kind of intense and exalted state that is usually associated with a spiritual or mystical experience. EBH

1. Elaine de Kooning, *Art News Journal* 27 (1958): 3.

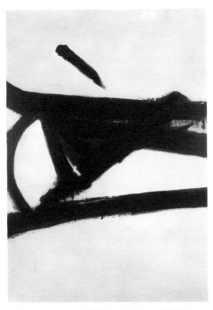

Oil on canvas, 1955, 191.1 x 131.5 cm. The Cleveland Museum of Art, Anonymous Gift 67.3

Collection: Mrs. John D. Rockefeller III, New York.

This is one of a series of stark, dynamic, black-and-white compositions done in the early and mid-1950s by Franz Kline. The black struts slash across the canvas, entering and leaving it at the edges, dividing the surface into irregular white areas. The artist worked back and forth from the black bars to the white shapes until they were brought to a state of precarious visual balance.

Each black strut in Kline's painting appears to have been brushed in with a single, sweeping stroke, but careful examination reveals a number of overlapping strokes. This contrasts with paintings such as Motherwell's black-and-white *Elegies*; the broad, flat, black bars and lozenge shapes of *Elegy to the Spanish Republic No. LV*, for example, were first roughly sketched in and the areas between the contours then painted. Kline's bars, on the other hand, provide an actual record of the artist's arm gestures.

A series of triangular shapes—black and white—make up a rhythmical theme in the composition. The diagonal black slash above the uppermost black bar creates a vigorous thrust into the white field at the top of the picture, visually exciting that area. The movement is echoed below by a smaller white slash within the central black area. These two sharp strokes—especially the black one—undoubtedly inspired the title of the painting.

Kline's unequivocal composition establishes an over-all dynamic equilibrium. This kind of panting does not belong to any painting tradition, for it is artless. Kline, along with other Abstract Expressionists, attempted to reinvent the art of painting by creating abstract forms that provide insight into the artist's subjective experiences of the world. Paintings such as *Accent Grave* are bold, dynamic, terse, open, and balanced. They reveal the generosity and integrity of Kline's spirit. EBH

David Smith
American, 1906-1965
46. Pilgrim

Steel, 1957, h. 207 cm.
Contemporary Collection of The Cleveland Museum of Art 66.385

Collection: (Marlborough-Gerson Gallery, New York).

One of the most important American sculptors of the twentieth century, David Smith was originally trained as a painter. He also was the first American to consistently employ the technique of direct-welding. Smith enrolled in the Art Student's League in 1926, but did not begin making sculptures until 1932. He created his first welded sculpture in 1933. For the remainder of that decade, Smith experimented widely, assimilating elements of Cubism, Constructivism, Surrealism, and ideas from the sculpture of Picasso, Julio Gonzalez, and Alberto Giacometti.

In the 1950s Smith created a series of large totemic figures, including *Pilgrim*. Lacking a central spine or core, *Pilgrim* can be described as a series of "gestures" freely drawn in space, whose open linear construction looks back to the "space drawing" sculptures of Picasso and thus defies the traditional syntax of sculpture, which is concerned with volume and mass. In effect, the linear construction of *Pilgrim* is a pictorial element borrowed from the aesthetics of painting. "I do not recognize," Smith once said, "the boundaries between painting and sculpture aesthetically." Indeed, crossing the boundaries between painting and sculpture is one method by which Smith explored new avenues of creativity.

The composition of *Pilgrim* consists of a series of interlocking curved and straight shapes, arranged in eccentric asymmetrical patterns, so that no single view completely describes the object. Instead, as one walks around this sculpture, a series of constantly changing silhouettes and disjunctive views unfold. From certain angles, the top of sculpture even suggests a monstrous laughing head.

Pilgrim was constructed of prefabricated steel bars and found objects, such as discarded tractor parts, I-beams, and boiler-tank tops. "The material called iron or steel," Smith observed, "possesses little art history. What associations it possesses are those of this century: power, structure, movement, progress, suspension, destruction, brutality."[1] Yet, Smith combined and manipulated these materials in ways that evoke personal and metaphoric associations, referred to by the artist as "after-images." The following statement by Smith sheds considerable light on his creative process:

I cannot conceive a work and buy material for it. I can find or discover a part. To buy a new material—I need a truckload before I can work on one. I look at it every day—to let it soften—to let it break up in segments, planes, lines, etc.—wrap itself in hazy shapes. Nothing is so impersonal, hard and cold as straight rolling-mill stock. If it is standing or kicking around, it becomes personal and fits into visionary use.[2]

At his studio/farm at Bolton Landing in upstate New York called the Terminal Iron Works, *Pilgrim* sat outdoors adjacent to a group of sculptures called "Sentinels" (1956-61). All of these works have distinctly vertical orientations, implying anthropomorphic associations similar to Surrealist personages. In *Pilgrim*, the abstract torso is divided into bodylike segments, with a head at the top, a circular abdomen in the middle, and two "legs" at the bottom; the one curving leg introduces an element of humor that mediates against the impersonality of the geometric shapes and steel surfaces. In fact, various parts of *Pilgrim* can be read in several different ways, similar to the double images in Picasso's paintings, so that the sculpture appears to be in a constant state of dreamlike metamorphosis.

Abandoning traditional carving and modeling techniques, Smith used the modern industrial process of welding to combine found objects into abstract compositions of interlocking curved and straight shapes, whose splayed and open forms interact with the surrounding environment. Smith also took the radical step of eliminating the traditional pedestal, so that the sculpture becomes continuous with the viewer's space. The curved leg also introduces a feeling of kinesthesis.

Working largely by intuition and impulse, Smith discovered that the welding torch was an ideal instrument for his improvisatory technique. Rather than attempting to conceal the welds, he exploited the harsh surfaces resulting from the direct-weld technique in order to emphasis the physical nature of his materials and the creative process. WHR

1. Quoted in Fairfield Porter, "David Smith," *ArtNews* 56 (September 1957): 41.

2. Fogg Art Museum (Cambridge, Massachusetts), *David Smith: A Retrospective Exhibition* (1966), p. 102.

Isamu Noguchi
American, b. 1904
47. Woman with Child

Pentelic marble, 1958, h. 111.8 cm.
Contemporary Collection of The Cleveland
Museum of Art 66.48

Collection: (Cordier and Ekstrom, New
York).

In 1957 Noguchi began making regular
visits to Greece, where he purchased the
Pentelic marble used to create this sculpture. In the late 1950s, after a period of
working in metal, Noguchi returned to the
direct-carve technique he had learned from
Brancusi, perhaps paying homage to his
former teacher, who had died in 1957.
Brancusi taught Noguchi to seek essential
forms in nature, to distill abstract shapes
to their simplest and purest state, and to
bring out the inherent beauty of natural
materials. Along with Brancusi, Noguchi
was one of the few modern sculptors to
carry forward the tradition of direct stone
carving.

The highly polished, sleek, vertical shaft,
tapering slightly at the top in *Woman with
Child*—so startling in its sheer beauty and
simplicity—is reminiscent of Brancusi's *Bird
in Space* (Figure 16). Yet, Noguchi balanced
the spirituality of this ascending element
with a more earthbound form in the rough-
hewn rectangular block in the center of
the composition. Formally, this block functions to bind the vertical elements together. But the juxtaposition of horizontal to
the vertical elements may be metaphorically interpreted to symbolize states of harmony between opposite and complementary forces, such as organic and inorganic,
spiritual and earthly, intellectual and
physical.

The sensuous Pentelic marble that
Noguchi selected for this sculpture reflects
his deep affection for the art and humanis-
tic culture of ancient Greece. The subject
also brings to mind the recurring "mother
and child" theme in Western art. If the title of this work is taken literally, then the
horizontal block can be interpreted to
represent a Japanese obi (sash), traditionally used to bind a woman to her child. At
the same time, the entire sculpture suggests a visual metaphor for the spiritual
bonds that unite a mother and child.

The delicate play of light and shadow
over the varied textural surfaces gives
Woman with Child both a human warmth
appropriate to the theme and a sensuality
corresponding to the erotic implications of
the vertical phallic shape. While Noguchi
first employed the mother and child theme
during the 1930s, he reinterpreted and
presented it here in an entirely new and
original way that weds the purity of ancient Japanese Haniwa sculpture to the
sensuality of Classical Greek art. Through
the greatest economy of means, the artist
has created a visual sign with universal and
timeless implications—a pure balance of inner spiritual harmony within an integrated,
abstract composition of both pristine
shapes and tactile surfaces. WHR

Bibliography

Alexander, S. *Beauty and Other Forms of Value*. New York: Thomas Y. Crowell, 1968.

Antal, Frederick. *Florentine Painting and Its Social Background*. London: Routledge and Kegan Paul, 1947.

Ashton, Dore. *A Reading of Modern Art*. Cleveland: Press of Case Western Reserve University, 1969.

_____. *The Unknown Shore: A View of Contemporary Art*. Boston and Toronto: Little, Brown and Company, 1962.

Austin, James H. *Chase, Chance, and Creativity: The Lucky Art of Novelty*. New York: Columbia University Press, 1978.

Baljeu, Joost. "The Problem of Reality with Suprematism, Constructivism, Proun, Neoplasticism, and Elementarism," *The Lugano Review* 1 (1965): 105-23.

Barnett, Lincoln. *The Universe and Dr. Einstein*. New York: William Sloane Associates, 1948.

Bergson, Henri. *The Creative Mind*. New York: Philosophical Library, 1946.

Boas, George. *The Heaven of Invention*. Baltimore: Johns Hopkins University Press, 1962.

_____. *The History of Ideas*. New York: Charles Scribner's Sons, 1969.

_____. *The Inquiring Mind*. LaSalle, Illinois: Open Court Publishing Company, 1959.

Breton, André. *Manifestoes of Surrealism*. Translated from the French by Richard Seaver and Helen R. Lane. Ann Arbor: University of Michigan Press, 1969.

_____. *Surrealism and Painting*. Translated from the French by Simon Watson Taylor. New York: Harper and Row, 1973.

_____. *What Is Surrealism? Selected Writings*. Edited by Franklin Rosemont. New York: Monad Press, 1978.

Bronowski, Jacob. *Magic, Science, and Civilization*. New York: Columbia University Press, 1978.

_____. *Science and Human Values*. New York: Julian Messner, 1956.

Burnham, Jack. *The Structure of Art*. New York: George Braziller, 1973.

Calder, Nigel. *Einstein's Universe*. New York: Viking Press, 1979.

Capra, Fritjof. *The Tao of Physics*. Berkeley, California: Shambhala Publications, 1975.

Carmean, E. A., Jr., and Eliza E. Rathbone with Thomas B. Hess. *American Art at Mid-Century: The Subjects of the Artists*. Washington, D.C.: National Gallery of Art, 1976.

Chevreul, M.-E. *The Principles of Harmony and Contrast of Colours, and Their Applications to the Arts*. Translated by Charles Martel. London: George Bell and Sons, 1890.

Chomsky, Noam. *Language and Responsibility*. New York: Pantheon Books, 1979.

_____. *Problems of Knowledge and Freedom*. New York: Vintage Books, 1971.

Crease, Robert P., and Charles C. Mann. *The Second Creation: Makers of the Revolution in 20th-Century Physics*. New York: Macmillan Co., 1986.

Curtin, Deane W., ed. *The Aesthetic Dimension of Science*. New York: Philosophical Library, 1980.

Dabrowski, Magdalena. *Contrasts of Form, Geometric Abstract Art 1910-1980*. New York: Museum of Modern Art, 1985.

Dampier, William C. *A History of Science*. Cambridge: Cambridge University Press, 1968.

Davies, Paul. *Superforce*. New York: Simon and Schuster, 1984.

Dewey, John. *Art as Experience*. New York: Capricorn Books, G. P. Putnam's Sons, 1958.

_____. *Experience and Nature*. New York: Dover Publications, 1958.

Dobzhansky, Theodosius, and Ernest Boesiger. *Human Culture: A Moment in Evolution*. Edited and completed by Bruce Wallace. New York: Columbia University Press, 1983.

Dyson, Freeman. *Disturbing the Universe*. New York: Harper and Row, Colophon Books, 1979.

Ehrmann, Jacques, ed. *Structuralism*. Garden City, New York: Doubleday, Anchor Books, 1970.

Einstein, Albert. *Relativity: The Special and General Theory*. Translated by Robert W. Lawson. New York: Bonanza Books, 1961.

_____. *Sidelights on Relativity*. New York: Dover Publications, 1983.

Fallico, Arturo B. *Art and Existentialism*. Englewood Cliffs, New Jersey: Prentice-Hall, 1962.

Fowlie, Wallace. *Age of Surrealism*. Bloomington: Indiana University Press, 1960.

Fraasen, Bas C. van. *An Introduction to the Philosophy of Time and Space*. New York: Columbia University Press, 1985.

Freud, Sigmund. *Creativity and the Unconscious: Papers on the Psychology of Art, Literature, Love, Religion*. New York: Harper and Row, 1958.

Fry, Edward. *Cubism*. New York: Oxford University Press, 1966.

Gamow, George. *One, Two, Three . . . Infinity*. New York: Viking Press, 1947.

_____. *Thirty Years That Shook Physics: The Story of Quantum Theory*. New York: Dover Publications, 1966.

Gardner, Howard. *The Quest for Mind: Piaget, Lévi-Strauss, and the Structuralist Movement*. New York: Alfred A. Knopf, 1974.

Gauss, C.E. *The Aesthetic Theories of French Artists*. Baltimore: Johns Hopkins University Press, 1966.

Ghiselin, Brewster, ed. *The Creative Process*. Berkeley: University of California Press, 1985.

Gillispie, Charles C. *The Edge of Objectivity: An Essay in the History of Scientific Ideas*. Princeton, New Jersey: Princeton University Press, 1960.

Gilson, Etienne. *Painting and Reality*. New York: Meridian Books, 1959.

_____. *The Unity of Philosophical Experience*. New York: Charles Scribner's Sons, 1937.

Golding, John. *Cubism: A History and an Analysis, 1907-1914*. New York: George Wittenborn, 1959.

Goldwater, Robert. *Primitivism in Modern Art*. Enlarged edition. Cambridge, Massachusetts: Harvard University Press, 1986.

Gombrich, E.H. *Art and Illusion*. New York: Pantheon Books, 1960.

Goodman, Nelson. *Languages of Art*. Indianapolis: Hackett Publishing Co., 1976.

_____. *Ways of Worldmaking*. Indianapolis: Hackett Publishing Co., 1978.

Gottshalk, D.W. *Art and the Social Order*. New York: Dover Publications, 1962.

Gray, Christopher. *Cubist Aesthetic Theories*. Baltimore: Johns Hopkins University Press, 1953.

Greenberg, Clement. *Art and Culture*. Boston: Beacon Press, 1961.

Gribbin, John. *In Search of Schrödinger's Cat: Quantum Physics and Reality*. New York: Bantam Books, 1984.

Hall, Everett W. *Modern Science and Human Values*. New York: Dell, 1956.

Hauser, Arnold. *The Social History of Art*. New York: Alfred A. Knopf, 1951.

Heelan, Patrick A. *Space-Perception and The Philosophy of Science*. Berkeley: University of California Press, 1983.

Heil, John. *Perception and Cognition*. Berkeley: University of California Press, 1983.

Heisenberg, Werner. *Physics and Philosophy: The Revolution in Modern Science*. New York: Harper and Row, 1958.

Henning, Edward B. *The Spirit of Surrealism*. Cleveland: Cleveland Museum of Art, 1979.

Holton, Gerald. *The Advancement of Science and Its Burdens*. Cambridge: Cambridge University Press, 1986.

Hunt, Morton. *The Universe Within: A New Science Explores the Human Mind*. New York: Simon and Schuster, 1982.

Huyghe, René. *Art and the Spirit of Man*. New York: Harry N. Abrams, 1962.

Jaffe, Hans L. C. *De Stijl, 1917-1931*. Amsterdam: J. M. Meulenhoff, 1956.

Jameson, Frederic. *The Prison-House of Language*. Princeton, New Jersey: Princeton University Press, 1972.

Jung, C. G. *Psyche and Symbol*. Garden City, New York: Doubleday, Anchor Books, 1958.

Kaelin, Eugene F. *An Existentialist Aesthetic: The Theories of Sartre and Merleau-Ponty*. Madison: University of Wisconsin Press, 1962.

Kern, Stephen. *The Culture of Time and Space, 1880 to 1918*. Cambridge, Massachusetts: Harvard University Press, 1983.

Kline, Morris. *Mathematics and the Search for Knowledge*. New York: Oxford University Press, 1985.

_____. *Mathematics in Western Culture*. New York: Oxford University Press, 1953.

Koestler, Arthur. *The Act of Creation*. New York: Macmillan Co., 1964.

Kuhn, Thomas S. *The Essential Tension*. Chicago: University of Chicago Press, 1977.

_____. *The Structure of Scientific Revolutions*. Chicago: University of Chicago Press, 1979.

Lacan, Jacques. *The Language of the Self*. Edited and translated by Anthony Wilden. Baltimore: Johns Hopkins University Press, 1968.

Lane, Michael, ed. *Introduction to Structuralism*. New York: Basic Books, 1970.

Langer, Susanne K. *Feeling and Form*. New York: Charles Scribner's Sons, 1953.

_____. *Problems of Art*. New York: Charles Scribner's Sons, 1957.

Lanham, Url. *Origins of Modern Biology*. New York: Columbia University Press, 1968.

Laporte, Paul M. "The Space-Time Concept in the Work of Picasso," *Magazine of Art* 41 (January 1948): 26-32.

Lovell, Bernard. *Emerging Cosmology*. New York: Columbia University Press, 1981.

Malraux, André. *The Voices of Silence*. Garden City, New York: Doubleday, 1953.

Maritaine, Jacques. *Creative Intuition in Art and Poetry*. Cleveland: World Publishing, 1968.

Mason, Stephen, F. *A History of the Sciences*. New York: Macmillan Co., 1962.

McConnell, R. B., ed. *Art, Science and Human Progress*. New York: Universe Books, 1983.

Mesarović, Mihaljo D., ed. *Views on General Systems Theory*. New York: John Wiley and Sons, 1964.

Métraux, Guy S. and François Crouzet, eds. *The Evolution of Science*. New York: UNESCO, Mentor Books, 1963.

Miller, David, ed. *Popper Selections*. Princeton, New Jersey: Princeton University Press, 1985.

Morris, Richard. *Dismantling the Universe*. New York: Simon and Schuster, 1983.

Munro, Thomas. *Evolution in the Arts*. Cleveland: Cleveland Museum of Art, 1963.

_____. *Toward Science in Aesthetics*. New York: Liberal Arts Press, 1956.

Nagel, Ernest, and James R. Newman. *Gödel's Proof*. New York: New York University Press, 1958.

Nye, Mary Jo. *Molecular Reality*. London: MacDonald, 1972.

Ortega Y Gasset, José. *The Dehumanization of Art*. Garden City, New York: Doubleday, Anchor Books, 1956.

Pagels, Heinz R. *Perfect Symmetry*. New York: Simon and Schuster, 1985.

Perry, Ralph Barton. *Realms of Value*. Cambridge, Massachusetts: Harvard University Press, 1954.

Piaget, Jean. *Structuralism*. Edited and translated by Chaninah Maschler. New York: Harper and Row, Colophon Books, 1970.

Prall, D.W. *Aesthetic Judgment*. New York: Thomas Y. Crowell, 1967.

Reese, Lawrence L. Ruiz. "Scientific Analogies in Cubism." 2 vols. Ph.D. dissertation, University of California, Los Angeles, 1981.

Reichenbach, Hans. *The Rise of Scientific Philosophy*. Berkeley: University of California Press, 1951.

Rewald, John. *The History of Impressionism*. New York: Museum of Modern Art, 1980.

_____. *Post-Impressionism: From Van Gogh to Gauguin*. New York: Museum of Modern Art, 1977.

Richardson, John Adkins. *Modern Art and Scientific Thought*. Urbana: University of Illinois Press, 1971.

Richter, Hans. *Dada: Art and Anti-Art*. London: Thames and Hudson, 1965.

Ritterbush, Philip C. *The Art of Organic Forms*. Washington, D.C.: Smithsonian Institution Press, 1968.

Rosenberg, Harold. *The De-definition of Art*. New York: Horizon Press, 1972.

_____. *The Tradition of the New*. New York: Horizon Press, 1959.

Rosenblum, Robert. *Cubism and Twentieth-Century Art*. New York: Harry N. Abrams, 1961.

Rosenthal-Schneider, Ilse. *Reality and Scientific Truth: Discussions with Einstein, von Laue, and Planck*. Edited by Thomas Braun. Detroit: Wayne State University Press, 1980.

Roskill, Mark. *The Interpretation of Cubism*. Philadelphia: Art Alliance Press, 1985.

Rubin, William S. *Dada and Surrealist Art*. New York: Harry N. Abrams, 1968.

Sacks, Sheldon, ed. *On Metaphor*. Chicago: University of Chicago Press, 1981.

Sandler, Irving. *The Triumph of American Painting: A History of Abstract Expressionism*. New York: Praeger, 1970.

Schapiro, Meyer. *Modern Art: 19th and 20th Centuries*. New York: George Braziller, 1978.

Sherman, Paul D. *Colour Vision in the Nineteenth Century*. Bristol: Adam Hilger, 1981.

Smith, Cyril Stanley. *A Search for Structure*. Cambridge, Massachusetts: M.I.T. Press, 1981.

Streller, Justus. *Jean-Paul Sartre: To Freedom Condemned*. Translated by Wade Baskin. New York: Philosophical Library, 1960.

Valéry, Paul. *Aesthetics*. Translated by Ralph Manheim. New York: Pantheon Books, 1964.

Waddington, C. H. *Behind Appearance*. Cambridge, Massachusetts: M.I.T. Press, 1970.

Walker Art Center, Minneapolis. 1982. *De Stijl 1917-1931, Visions of Utopia.*

Wechsler, Judith, ed. *On Aesthetics in Science*. Cambridge, Massachusetts: M.I.T. Press, 1979.

Whitehead, Alfred North. *Process and Reality: An Essay in Cosmology*. New York: Harper and Row, Torchbooks, 1957.

Wolf, Fred Alan. *Taking the Quantum Leap*. San Francisco: Harper and Row, 1981.

Zee, Anthony. *Fearful Symmetry: The Search for Beauty in Modern Physics*. New York: Macmillan Co., 1986.

Comparative Illustrations

Figure 1. Edgar Degas, *Little Dancer of Fourteen Years*. Bronze, ca. 1880-81 (cast ca. 1922), h. 99 cm. The Metropolitan Museum of Art, New York, Bequest of Mrs. H. O. Havemeyer, 1922.

Figure 2. James Abbott McNeill Whistler, *Nocturne in Black and Gold: The Falling Rocket*. Oil on oak panel, ca. 1874, 60.3 x 46.7 cm. Copyright 1987 The Detroit Institute of Arts, Gift of Dexter M. Ferry, Jr.

Figure 3. Auguste Rodin, *The Thinker*. Bronze, h. 72.3 cm. The Cleveland Museum of Art, Gift of Alexandre P. Rosenberg, 79.138.

Figure 4. Georges Seurat, *Sunday Afternoon on the Island of La Grande Jatte*. Oil on canvas, 1884-86, 207.6 x 308 cm. Helen Birch Bartlett Memorial Collection, 1926.224, Copyright 1987 The Art Institute of Chicago. All rights reserved.

Figure 5. Georges Seurat, *Le Chahut*. Oil on canvas, 1889-90, 169 x 139 cm. Copyright 1987 Rijksmuseum Kröller-Müller, Otterlo, Netherlands.

Figure 6. Vincent van Gogh, *The Potato Eaters*. Oil on canvas, signed, 1885, 82 x 114 cm. Vincent van Gogh Foundation, Rijksmuseum Vincent van Gogh, Amsterdam.

Figure 7. Henri Rousseau, *The Dream*. Oil on canvas, 1910, 204.5 x 299 cm. Collection, The Museum of Modern Art, New York, Gift of Nelson A. Rockefeller.

Figure 8. Pablo Picasso, *Les Demoiselles d'Avignon*. Oil on canvas, 1907, 243.8 x 233.7 cm. Collection, The Museum of Modern Art, New York, Acquired through the Lillie P. Bliss Bequest.

Figure 9. Henri Matisse, French, 1869-1954, *Joie de Vivre*. Oil on canvas, 1905-6, 174 x 238.1 cm. Copyright The Barnes Foundation, Merion, Pennsylvania.

Figure 10. Georges Braque, *Le Portugais*. Oil on canvas, 1911, 117 x 81.5 cm. Kunstmuseum Basel, Öffentliche Kunstsammlung.

Figure 11. Pablo Picasso, *Three Musicians*. Oil on canvas, 1921, 200.7 x 222.9 cm. Collection, The Museum of Modern Art, New York, Mrs. Simon Guggenheim Fund.

Figure 12. Pablo Picasso, *Three Musicians*. Oil on canvas, 1921, 203 x 188 cm. Philadelphia Museum of Art, A. E. Gallatin Collection. Photograph by A. J. Wyatt.

Figure 13. Pablo Picasso, *Three Dancers*. Oil on canvas, 215 x 142 cm. The Tate Gallery, London.

Figure 14. Pablo Picasso, *Glass of Absinthe*. Bronze and plaster, 1914, h. 22.6 cm. Philadelphia Museum of Art, A. E. Gallatin Collection.

Figure 15. Frantisek Kupka, *The First Step*. Oil on canvas, 1910-13(?) (dated on painting 1909), 83.2 x 129.5 cm. Collection, The Museum of Modern Art, New York, Hillman Periodicals Fund.

Figure 16. Constantin Brancusi, *Bird in Space*. Bronze, unique cast, 1928(?), h. 137.2 cm. Collection, The Museum of Modern Art, New York, given anonymously.

Figure 17. Marcel Duchamp, *The Large Glass*, or *The Bride Stripped Bare by Her Bachelors, Even*. Oil and lead wire on glass, 1915-23, 278.2 x 175.6 cm. Philadelphia Museum of Art, Bequest of Katherine S. Dreier.

Figure 18. Joan Miró, *Carnival of Harlequin*. Oil on canvas, 1924-25, 66 x 93 cm. Albright-Knox Art Gallery, Buffalo, New York, Room of Contemporary Art Fund, 1940.

Figure 19. Jackson Pollock, *Full Fathom Five*. Oil on canvas with nails, tacks, buttons, key, coins, cigarettes, and matches, 1947, 129.3 x 76.5 cm. Collection, The Museum of Modern Art, New York, Gift of Peggy Guggenheim.

Figure 20. Franz Kline, *New York*. Oil on canvas, signed, 1953, 200.6 x 128.3 cm. Albright-Knox Art Gallery, Buffalo, New York, Gift of Seymour H. Knox, 1956.

Library of Congress Cataloging-in-Publication Data

Henning, Edward B.
  Creativity in art and science, 1860-1960.

  Bibliography: p. 138.
  1. Art, Modern—19th century—Exhibitions.
2. Art, Modern—20th century—Exhibitions. 3. Art and
science—Exhibitions. 4. Creation (Literary, artistic,
etc.)—Exhibitions. I. Cleveland Museum of Art.
II. Title.
N6447.H46 1987   759.06′074′017132   87-23881
ISBN 0-910386-90-0
ISBN 0-910386-91-9 (pbk.)